Study Guide to accompany
Macroeconomics
Eighth Edition

By Dornbusch, Fischer, and Startz

Study Guide

to accompany

Macroeconomics

Eighth Edition

Rudiger Dornbusch
Massachusetts Institute of Technology

Stanley Fischer
International Monetary Fund
On leave from
Massachusetts Institute of Technology

Richard Startz
University of Washington

Prepared by
Jes Rutledge
University of Washington

Boston   Burr Ridge, IL   Dubuque, IA   Madison, WI   New York   San Francisco   St. Louis
Bangkok   Bogotá   Caracas   Kuala Lumpur   Lisbon   London   Madrid   Mexico City
Milan   Montreal   New Delhi   Santiago   Seoul   Singapore   Sydney   Taipei   Toronto

McGraw-Hill Higher Education
*A Division of The **McGraw-Hill** Companies*

Study Guide to accompany
MACROECONOMICS, EIGHTH EDITIOIN
Rudiger Dornbusch, Stanley Fischer, and Richard Startz

Published by McGraw-Hill/Irwin, an imprint of the McGraw-Hill Companies, Inc., 1221 Avenue of the Americas, New York, NY 10020. Copyright © 2000, 1998, 1994, 1990, 1987 by the McGraw-Hill Companies, Inc. All rights reserved.
No part of this publication may be reproduced or distributed in any form or by any means, or stored in a database or retrieval system, without the prior written consent of The McGraw-Hill Companies, Inc., including, but not limited to, in any network or other electronic storage or transmission, or broadcast for distance learning.

1 2 3 4 5 6 7 8 9 0 QPD/QPD 0 9 8 7 6 5 4 3 2 1 0

ISBN 0-07-239111-1

www.mhhe.com

CONTENTS

To the Student *ix*

Part One   **Introduction and National Income Accounting**

1. **Introduction**   1
   Language: "Models"   6
   Technique: "Active Learning"   6

2. **National Income Accounting**   9
   Language: "Exogenous, Endogenous, and Policy Variables"   14
   Technique: "Moving from Levels to Rates of Change"   15

Part Two   **Growth and Aggregate Supply and Demand**

3. **Growth and Accumulation**   23
   Language: "Stocks and Flows, or 'About Your Bathtub'"   31
   Technique: "Balancing Flows Into and Out of the Tub: Finding a Steady-State"   31

4. **Growth and Policy**   37
   Language: "What is Endogenous About Endogenous Growth?"   41
   Technique: "Returns to Scale"   42

5. **Aggregate Supply and Demand**   47
   Language: "Expansionary/Contractionary Policies"   51
   Technique: "Working With Graphs"   53

6. **Aggregate Supply: Wages, Prices, and Unemployment**   59
   Language: "Rational Expectations"   66
   Technique: "Reading Equations"   67

7 The Anatomy of Inflation and Unemployment 73
Language: "The Definition of Unemployment" 78
Technique: "Weighting" 78

8 Policy 83
Language: "Bear Markets and Bull Markets" 88
Technique: "Associating Money Growth With Output Growth" 88

Part Three First Models

9 Income and Spending 97
Language: "Autonomous Spending" 101
Technique: "Infinite Geometric Series" 102

10 Money Interest and Income 107
Language: "Endogenous Variables Revisited" 113
Technique: "Solving a Two Equation System Graphically and Algebraically" 115

11 Monetary and Fiscal Policy 121
Language: "Stabilization" 126
Technique: "Working with Multipliers" 126

12 International Linkages 131
Language: "Accommodation" 140
Technique: "Interpreting Changes in Real and Nominal Exchange Rates" 140

Part Four Behavioral Foundations

13 Consumption and Saving 149
Language: "Theories and Hypotheses" 153
Technique: "Errors in Variables" 153

14 Investment Spending 159
Language: "Investment" 163
Technique: "Working with Lagged Variables" 164

15 The Demand for Money 169
Language: "Liquidity" 173
Technique: "Working with Natural Logarithms" 174

16 The Fed, Money, and Credit 179
Language: "The Fed" 185
Technique: "Reading a Balance Sheet" 185

17 **Financial Markets** 191
Language: "Arbitrage" 193
Technique: "Compound Interest" 194

Part Five Big Events, International Adjustments, and Advanced Topics

18 **The Economics of Depression, Hyperinflation, and Deficits** 201
Language: "Debt and Deficits" 206
Technique: "Dynamic Expectations" 207

19 **International Adjustment and Interdependence** 213
Language: "Sterilization" 218
Technique: "Units of Measurement" 219

20 **Advanced Topics** 223
Language: "New Keynesians and New Classicists" 227
Technique: "Taking a Random Walk" 229

Answers to Questions and Problems 236
Glossary 293
Data Tables 308

TO THE STUDENT

This study guide is designed for use with Dornbusch, Fischer, and Startz's *Macroeconomics*, seventh edition. The only reason for its existence is to *make your life easier*.

FORMAT

Each of the twenty–one chapters in this study guide is comprised of the following sections:

Focus of the Chapter: A quick overview of the chapter's main conclusions.

Section Summaries: These briefly summarize each section of the text.

Key Terms: A list of new or important terms used in the chapter

Graph It: Exercises that ask you to plot data, complete a graph, or sometimes fill in a chart. Most are quite simple, and are an easy way to start playing with data. Taking a pencil in your hand is a way to loosen up your brain, and helps you focus on the subject at hand.

The Language of Economics: Presents a brief definition and sometimes discussion of a piece of economic jargon.

Review of Technique: Presents a brief introduction to or review of a useful mathematical tool.

Crossword Puzzle: Helps you review some of the terminology introduced in the chapter. Besides, they're fun.

Fill–in Questions: Like the crossword puzzle, helps you review some of the terminology introduced in the chapter. Reviews important concepts.

True–False Questions: Encourage you to develop your intuition; reviews some of the chapters basic conclusions.

Multiple–Choice Questions: Provide yet another way to review terminology and work out simple problems.

Conceptual Problems: The seventh edition of Macroeconomics separates conceptual and technical problems. We do the same here. Conceptual problems give you an opportunity to work through problems and ideas qualitatively rather than quantitatively, giving your intuition a bit more exercise.

Technical Problems: Allow you to work through numerical examples and mathematical problems.

At the back of the book you will find answers to the questions and problems in each chapter, a glossary with definitions of many key terms, and a set of data tables.

HOW TO STUDY MACROECONOMICS

Do not! It wastes too much time. Instead, try the following:

Practice Macroeconomics

You can underline all of the points you want and spend hours upon hours trying to memorize facts and theories, but none of those will get you half so far as *practice*. Instead of looking at the graphs in the textbook, try to work through them. Instead of wasting valuable hours trying to memorize the material, spend a small amount of time trying to focus on its structure. Always ask, "why am I learning this?" "What question am I trying to answer?" Look for real–world applications of the material you're learning; they're out there.

The questions in this study guide are not meant to serve as lists of points to remember. They are intended to illustrate basic principles, refine concepts, and give you a chance to develop your economic intuition. Try to answer the questions without consulting the answers at the back of the book; often struggling through a problem helps you to catch a glitch in your understanding. Many of the problems are quite easy. Some are more time consuming. If it becomes necessary for you to choose whether to reread the text or work through some problems, *do the problems*.

The Language of Economics

Economics, like many disciplines, is filled with jargon. Many words, when we use them, do not mean the same thing they do on the street. The language reviews nested in each chapter highlight the way a particular word or phrase is used in the discipline of macroeconomics. You may find that you know many of them, but they're worth reading through anyway. Understanding the language through which a model is presented can often be the key to unlocking its secrets.

Review of Technique

The Review of Technique found in each chapter is a special feature of this study guide. Each one presents a quick introduction to or review of a mathematical tool. Many are simply "tricks," facts that help you to simplify problems. You will probably find that you are already familiar with many of the techniques presented; some you may not have seen in quite some time. Most of the reviews are at least somewhat connected to the material covered by the chapters in which they appear; a few are not, but seemed nonetheless worthy of inclusion. When you have time, browse through the reviews to find those most useful to you.

Acknowledgments

My thanks, first and foremost, must go to Richard Startz, both for having taught me a great deal and for having given me the chance to put together this study guide. Much of the material in this guide has been borrowed from previous editions that he put together; much of the material that is new was inspired by discussions with him. Thanks must also go to Lucille Sutton and Tom Thompson at McGraw Hill, who put up with all of my late submissions of this manuscript. All mistakes, of course, remain mine.

JES RUTLEDGE

Part 1

Introduction and National Income Accounting

1 INTRODUCTION

FOCUS OF THE CHAPTER

- We begin our study of macroeconomics with an introduction to the three models around which it is organized and the time horizons to which they apply. We also take a preliminary look at economic growth, inflation, unemployment, and the business cycle, and provide an overview of the textbook.

SECTION SUMMARIES

1. Macroeconomics Encapsulated in Three Models

Almost everything you will learn about macroeconomics can be understood in the context of three models: *growth theory*, which describes the behavior of the economy in the *very long run* when capital, labor, and technology can all vary, and the *aggregate supply–aggregate demand (AS–AD) model*, which describes the behavior of the economy at all shorter horizons. This is really a combination of two different models: one of aggregate supply, another of aggregate demand. Different assumptions about *aggregate supply* determine the time horizon over which the model applies.

It is useful to have some working definitions of the time frames we're talking about. The "very long run," the domain of growth theory, refers to periods of decades or more, during which all of the inputs to production—capital, labor, the level of technology and size of the population—can change. We look at the behavior of *potential* rather than *actual output* over this period; we watch the amount of output that *would* be produced, if all inputs to production were fully employed.

The terms "long", "medium" and "short" run refer to periods of time during which the supplies of capital, labor, etc are fixed, or during which the level of *potential output* is constant. The main difference between these time periods is whether we assume these inputs are fully employed: in the long run we assume that they have to be, so that output equals potential output; at shorter horizons, we let them be either over- or underemployed and look at the *output gap* that results.

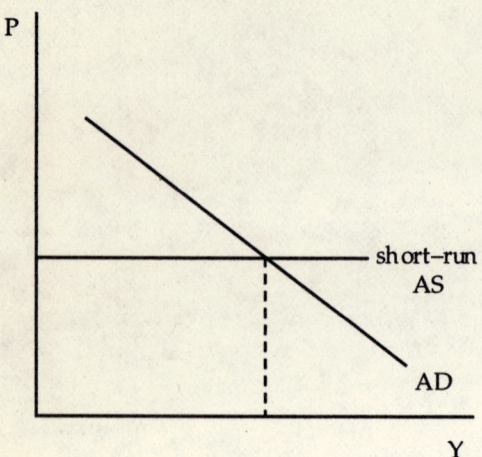

Figure 1 - 1

AS –AD IN THE SHORT RUN

Aggregate Supply is <u>horizontal</u> in the short run, when prices are fixed.

The AS–AD model looks at the way that the demand for all of a country's products (described by the AD curve) interacts with the supply of those products (described by the AS curve) to determine its price level and level of output. Potential output in this model is always fixed; only actual output can change.

We determine the time horizon over which the AS–AD model applies by changing our assumptions about the aggregate supply curve:

- In the *long run*, when all inputs are fully employed, the AS curve is vertical at the level of potential output, and output is determined by aggregate supply alone.

- In the *short run*, a period of time so brief that the price level does not have time to change, the AS curve is flat, and that output is determined by aggregate demand alone.

- In the medium run, somewhere between these extremes, inputs do not have to be fully employed, the price level is not frozen, and the AS curve slopes upward.

We will return to this topic in Chapter 5.

2. To Reiterate…

The *growth rate* of the economy is the rate at which output is increasing. The *trend path of GDP* is the rate at which output would grow, were all inputs to production fully employed.

How are these different? The first is the amount by which *actual output* grows. The second is the amount by which *potential output* grows.

The *business cycle* is the cycle of expansion and contraction around the trend path of output.

The *output gap* measures the difference between potential and actual output. It moves with the business cycle—increasing during recessions, and decreasing during recovery, sometimes decreasing so far that it becomes negative (it does this when inputs are over-employed).

Inflation is inversely related to the output gap—prices and output rise together when they are caused by changes in AD, and increases in output, when potential output is fixed, cause the output gap to fall.

When inputs are underemployed, output is below its potential. When inputs are overemployed (think of everyone in the economy working overtime and missing dinner), output is above potential output. We will find later that this second situation is inflationary.

And what is inflation? *The rate of inflation* is the percentage change in the price level. That price level is often measured with the *consumer price index (CPI)*—a series that keeps track of the cost of a "typical" urban consumer's basket of goods. The percentage change in the CPI over one year would be a measure of that year's consumer inflation.

3. Outline and Preview of the Text

Chapter 2, which covers national income accounting, introduces a number of identities that are used throughout the text. Chapters 3 and 4 cover growth theory, the behavior of potential output over the very long run. Chapters 5 and 6 introduce the AS–AD model, our framework for thinking about output at business-cycle frequencies. Chapter 7 looks at inflation and unemployment over this same horizon. Chapter 8 examines some policy issues and points out the difficulties of moving from theory to application. Chapters 9 – 12 delve deeper into aggregate demand; 12 broadens our perspective to include international trade. Chapters 13 – 17 take a closer look at the individual pieces of the domestic economy: consumption, investment, etc. Chapter 18 highlights the issues surrounding high inflation and large government deficits, and chapter 19 serves as an introduction to the basics of international macroeconomics. Chapter 20 introduces several concepts from the frontiers of economic research.

Aggregate Supply is <u>vertical</u> in the long run, when output must equal potential output.

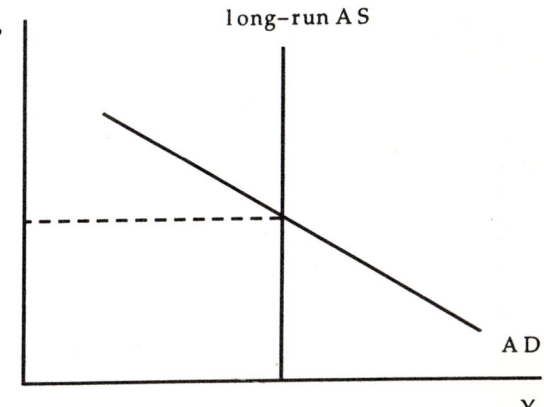

Figure 1 - 2

AS –AD IN THE LONG RUN

4. Prerequisites and Recipes

It is always best to read economics with a pencil in your hand. You will periodically need to stop and scribble a graph, highlight a problem area, or make note of an important definition. Do not be afraid to do this; textbooks aren't supposed to read like novels. In some of the more difficult chapters you should be stopping quite often.

You might also want to get into the habit of following current events, if you don't already. It will remind you that you're learning all this theory only in order to understand the world more fully.

KEY TERMS

very long run
long run
short run
growth theory
aggregate supply/demand (AS–AD) model
aggregate supply (AS) curve
aggregate demand (AD) curve
Phillips curve

growth rate
business cycle
trend path of output
output gap
potential output
inflation
consumer price index (CPI)

GRAPH IT 1

The easiest way to check an economy's health is to chart its real GDP. When real GDP is increasing by more than usual, the economy is doing well—and vice versa. This Graph It asks you to plot the annual rate of change in US real GDP for the years 1980 through 1999, and to compare it to the trend rate of growth. We assume the trend rate of growth to be 3%—a rough estimate of the economy's average growth rate since 1960. Can you identify the up–swings and down–swings of the business cycle?

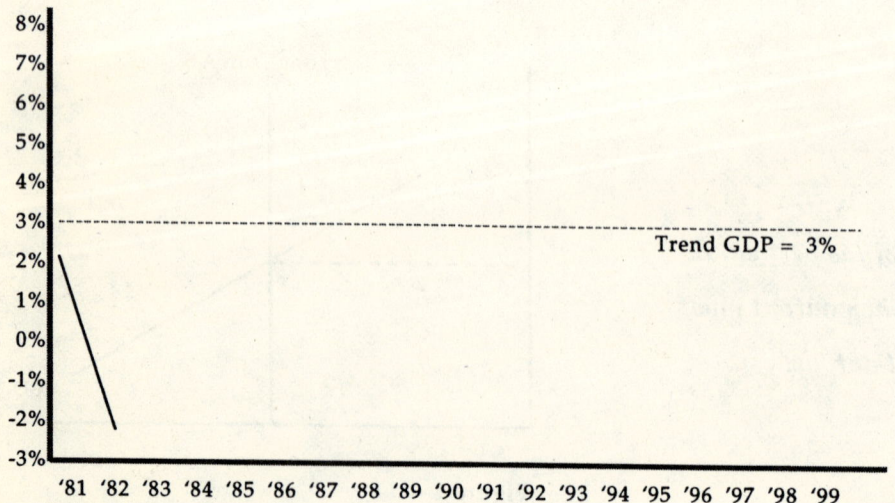

TABLE 1-1

Year	GDP	Percent change from previous year
1980	4,900.9	—
1981	5,021.0	2.5
1982	4,919.3	-2.0
1983	5,132.3	4.3
1984	5,505.2	7.3
1985	5,717.1	3.8
1986	5,912.4	3.4
1987	6,113.3	3.4
1988	6,368.4	4.2
1989	6,591.8	
1990	6,707.9	
1991	6,676.4	
1992	6,880.0	
1993	7,062.6	
1994	7,347.7	
1995	7,543.8	
1996	7,813.2	
1997	8,159.5	
1998	8,515.7	
1999	8,875.8	

Source: See Table B, Economic Data Tables

In order to fill out the chart, you must first calculate the rates of change of GDP and then plot them. For example, real GDP was $4,900.9 billion in 1980 and $5,021.0 billion in 1981. The annual growth rate, therefore, was 100 x {(5,021.0 - 4,900.9)/ 4,900.9}, or roughly 2.5%. We've filled in the first few years for you on the chart, and on Table 1–1. You do the rest!

THE LANGUAGE OF ECONOMICS 1

Models

An economic model consists of a set of assumptions and of one or more equations. The equations describe how the model's variables—inputs or outputs whose value is not necessarily constant—relate to one another.

Assumptions are very, very important. As we have seen in the case of the aggregate supply–aggregate demand model, an assumption (like a vertical AS curve) may be valid in some cases (when markets fully clear, for example) but not others. We would never assume the aggregate supply curve to be vertical. And we would never use growth theory to describe business cycle fluctuations (it just can't do it). The validity of a model's assumptions is a key consideration when we decide whether to use it to answer a question.

We must always exercise judgment when applying models. A good model *simplifies* the real world by choosing not to worry about the aspects that aren't relevant to whatever problem it is meant to explain. Because it does this, there will be problems to which a model should not be applied—problems for which some omitted relationship is relevant. Modeling requires more than just math; it requires *judgment*.

REVIEW OF TECHNIQUE 1

Active Learning

There are two components of active learning: *active reading* and *active review*. Active reading is a particularly good skill to develop, as you can use it while reading your textbooks, reading the newspaper, or reading the reports of your many advisors once you become president. The key to reading actively is *reading with a pencil*. That way, as you read, you can underline key ideas, write down the assumptions that lie behind argumentative statements (a weather person, for example, might say "tomorrow will be sunny" and mean "tomorrow will be sunny *if there is no change in the prevailing winds*, which should blow Hurricane Hubert directly to the north, right past us"), and translate statements into graphs (the statement "this year the price of corn has increased, and the quantity sold has decreased," for example, could be illustrated as a shift in the supply curve on a basic, microeconomic supply/demand graph).

To review actively, look back through everything you've underlined. Work through as many problems as possible. Make flash cards for key terms, to make sure you are able to define them. If you have trouble defining key terms, consult the glossary at the back of this study guide. Make a list of key assumptions for each model, and think about when these assumptions are and are not valid. This will help you to decide when and when not to apply a particular model to a problem. Keep a "big picture" map, where you can mark the connections between the various models that you learn. Then, when you get lost, you can simply refer to your map.

CROSSWORD

ACROSS

2 Measure of the price level
6 Slope of this curve determines time horizon of AS-AD model
8 Type of theory used for very long run
9 What you're studying
11 Growth theory and the AS/AD model are applicable over different lengths of _____

DOWN

1 Output produced when all inputs are fully employed
3 Rate of change of the price level
4 Type of cycle, fluctuates around trend path of output
5 ___ run, vertical AS
7 We simply the real world using
8 Type of gap, measures difference between potential and actual output

FILL-IN QUESTIONS

1. The very long-run behavior of the economy is the domain of __GROWTH__.

2. The economy's behavior over the short, medium, and long run, however, is best described by the __AS-AD__ model.

3. The __SUPPLY__ curve describes the quantity of output that firms are willing to supply at each price level.

4. The __DEMAND__ curve describes the total demand for goods at each price level.

5. The __SUPPLY__ curve is vertical in the long run, when all inputs are fully employed.

6. In the long run, the output gap is _____.

7. The __CPI__ measures the cost of a typical urban consumer's purchases.

TRUE–FALSE QUESTIONS

(T) F 1. In the short run, the aggregate supply curve is horizontal.

T (F) 2. In the long run, the aggregate supply curve is vertical. *only when all inputs are fully employed.*

(T) F 3. It turns out that prices adjust pretty slowly, so that over a one–year horizon, the aggregate supply curve is relatively flat.

T (F) 4. Very little you will learn about macroeconomics can be fit into a growth theory/aggregate supply/ aggregate demand framework.

2 NATIONAL INCOME ACCOUNTING

FOCUS OF THE CHAPTER

- Under the heading "national income accounting," we consider the different ways in which the national economic pie can be sliced into its component parts.

- This is more than just simple accounting. While we dissect GDP, we are actually learning how the many sources of aggregate demand can be added together to determine total national income, and just why a nation's income and output must necessarily be the same.

SECTION SUMMARIES

1. The Production of Output and Payments to Factors of Production

Production transforms inputs (factors of production), such as capital and labor, into output. This output is then used to make *factor payments*—to pay labor (N) its wage (w) and capital (K) its rate of interest (i). Total payments to labor equal the amount of labor hired multiplied by the wage paid to each worker, and turn out to be about ¾ of all factor payments. Total payments to capital equal the amount of capital hired multiplied by the interest rate. Anything left over (typically not very much) is kept as profit. These simple facts let us write an identity equating output with the sum of its factor payments and of profit:

$$Y = (w \times N) + (i \times K) + profit$$

Output = (Wage × Labour) + (Interest Rate × Capital) + PROFIT.

Of course, not all of the factors of production that we use today come from our own country, and not all domestically owned factors of production are employed in our own country. This problem has led economists to develop two different measures of output: *gross national product (GNP)*, and *gross domestic product (GDP)*.

GNP includes payments made to factors that are owned domestically but employed outside the country, and excludes payments made to factors that are owned by foreigners, but domestically employed. GDP does just the opposite—it counts any output produced within the borders of a country, regardless of who owns the factors of production, and does not count any output

9

produced outside of the country, even if it uses domestically owned factors of production. In practice the difference between these two measures is negligible.

We might also want to take *depreciation* into account when we measure output. It is a sad fact that capital wears out (depreciates) over time, and must be replaced. *Net domestic product (NDP)* subtracts from total GDP the amount of output used to replace worn out capital. We could then subtract taxes to get *national income*.

2. Outlays and Components of Demand

We could break up output another way, by looking at who buys it and what it is used for. Output can be (1) consumed by individuals, (2) used for investment, (3) consumed by the government, and (4) exported, on net. This last term deserves a bit of discussion—as we both export and import, part of our domestic income will be spent on foreign goods, and part of our domestic output will be sent to foreign countries. The difference between exports and imports (called *net exports*) is the net amount of domestic output purchased by foreigners. It can be negative when we are purchasing more output from foreigners than we are selling to them.

3. Some Important Identities

The most important identity of all to remember is that *income ≡ output*. Some other important ones are written below, and are absolutely worth memorizing. A warning, however: be sure that you understand these identities in terms of the economic relationships they describe. Do *not* just memorize the symbols!

$$Y \equiv C + I + G + NX \qquad \textit{fundamental national income accounting identity}$$

$$YD \equiv C + S \qquad \textit{uses of disposable income}$$

$$YD \equiv Y + TR - TA \qquad \textit{sources of disposable income}$$

$$BD \equiv G + TR - TA \qquad \textit{definition of the budget deficit}$$

Where Y = income (or output); C = consumption; I = investment; G = government purchases; NX = net exports; YD = disposable income; TR = transfers; TA = taxes; S = savings; and BD = the budget deficit. The symbol "$\equiv$" means *"identically, or always, equal to"*.

All of these are summarized by the basic identity:

$$C + I + G + NX \equiv Y \equiv YD + (TA - TR) \equiv C + S + (TA - TR)$$

Which reduces to the following identity equating excess savings with the sum of the budget deficit and net exports:

$$S - I \equiv (G + TR - TA) + NX$$

4. Measuring Gross Domestic Product

To avoid double-counting, we measure GDP as the value of all *final* goods and services *currently produced*. If a good has been previously produced and is merely sold from one person to another, it is not counted. If one good is used as an input in the production of another (if it is an *intermediate good*), it is not counted. We could also measure GDP by adding up the *value added* to the inputs at each stage of the production process.

There is one serious problem associated with the measurement of GDP: some types of output—cooking, cleaning and child care in the home, for example—are not traded on the open market, and therefore do not contribute to measured GDP. This can have serious consequences when these products move into the commercial sector.

There are serious problems with using GDP as a measure of welfare, as well: (1) some types of output, such as the maintenance of a police force, are intended only to contain "bads," like crime; (2) natural resources are valued at zero, so that nothing is added for environmental reclamation or subtracted for environmental degradation; and (3) it is hard to account for quality improvements.

5. Inflation and Price Indices

Because prices change from year to year, we distinguish real GDP from nominal GDP. Real GDP is a measure of physical production. Nominal GDP is the value of that output in *current dollars* (i.e., at prevailing prices).

Inflation (π) is measured as the change in the price level, or as:

$$\pi \equiv \frac{P_t - P_{t-1}}{P_{t-1}}.$$

It is worth noting that you must multiply the number that you get from this equation by 100 to express it properly in percentage terms. An answer $\pi = 0.12$, for example, would give you an inflation rate of 12%.

The price level can be measured by the *consumer price index (CPI)*, the *producer price index (PPI)*, or the *GDP deflator*. The CPI measures the cost of living for a "typical" urban family. The PPI tracks the prices of a range of goods used in production. Both measure the cost of the a particular, unchanging basket of goods from year to year. The GDP deflator is defined as the ratio of nominal GDP to real GDP. Its basket of goods changes every year to reflect the actual composition of output. It does *not* consider the effect of import prices on the domestic price level, however.

6. Interest Rates and Real Interest Rates

An interest rate, as you undoubtedly know, is the percentage return on an investment. For example, if you left $100 in an account that paid 6% annual interest, at the end of the year you'd have $106. That same $100 in an account that paid 10% interest would leave you with $110.

This, of course, tells you nothing about the value of those dollars at the time you get them back... with six or ten percent inflation, your real return is going to be zero. That's why we make a distinction between *real* and *nominal interest rates*: a real interest rate tells you the *real* return on your investment, rather than just the apparent one, by *correcting for the effects of inflation*.

Let's look at an example. If that same $100 earned a 6% nominal rate of interest, at the end of the year you'd have $106. With no inflation, your 6% nominal return would also be a 6% real return, and the real interest rate would be 6% as well. But with 5% inflation your money will be worth less when you get it back. The real return will be lower... approximately 5% lower! The real interest rate would be roughly 1%.

Where To Grab A Look At The Data

There are some great data archives that are accessible through the internet. The book provides several suggestions; for a comprehensive list, check out Bill Geoffe's "Resources for Economists on the Internet" at http://rfe.wustl.edu.

Just for kicks, though, try the following page: http://wuecon.wustl.edu/~bob/econwalknet.html. It will take you through a random sampling of economics pages on the web.

KEY TERMS

gross domestic product (GDP)
factors of production
factor payments
production function
gross national product (GNP)
net domestic product (NDP)
depreciation
national income accounting identity
consumer spending
government purchases
transfer payments
government expenditure
gross private domestic investment
durable goods
gross/net investment
net exports

national income
investment
saving
government budget deficit
final/intermediate goods
value added
adjusted GNP
real/nominal GDP
inflation
deflation
GDP deflator
consumer price index (CPI)
producer price index (PPI)
nominal interest rate
real interest rate

GRAPH IT 2

CPI– and PPI–based measures of inflation are not always the same. This Graph It asks you to calculate and plot CPI–based inflation between the years 1980 and 1999, and to compare it to PPI–based inflation. We have already graphed PPI–based inflation for you, so your job won't be difficult.

TABLE 2–1

Year	CPI	Percent change from previous year
1980	82.4	—
1981	90.9	10.3
1982	96.5	6.2
1983	99.6	
1984	103.9	
1985	107.6	
1986	109.6	
1987	113.6	
1988	118.3	
1989	124.0	
1990	130.7	
1991	136.2	
1992	140.3	
1993	144.5	
1994	148.2	
1995	152.4	
1996	156.9	
1997	160.5	
1998	163.0	
1999	166.6	

Source: See Table F, Economic Data Tables

14   CHAPTER 2

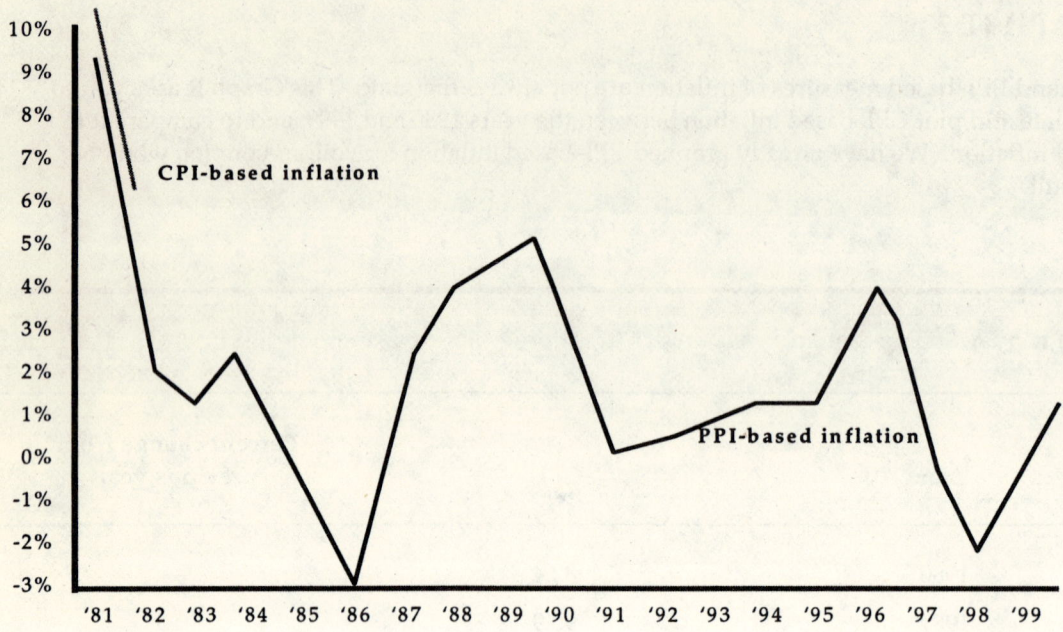

Chart 2 - 1

CPI- AND PPI-BASED INFLATION

Your first task is to convert consumer price indices (you'll find them in Economic Data Table F, at the back of this text) into rates of inflation. We ask you to do this in Table 2–1. After you've done this, all you need to do is plot each year's rate of inflation and connect the dots. We've filled in the first few years for you on both the table and the chart. You do the rest.

THE LANGUAGE OF ECONOMICS 2

Exogenous, Endogenous, and Policy Variables

Some variables are taken as inputs to a model. These are called *exogenous variables*. There are three general types of exogenous variables: those that are given by nature (the weather, for example) or taken to be outside the scope of a particular model (perhaps investor psychology); those, like taxes and government spending, that can be set by policymakers (these are also called *policy variables*); and variables that may affect the reactions of economic agents, but are not of direct interest themselves (these are *parameters*). The marginal propensity to consume is an important parameter in many macroeconomic models. It is also exogenous—determined outside of these models.

Other variables are determined within a model. These are, basically, the model's output. We call them *endogenous variables*. Endogenous variables are determined by exogenous variables, just as the equilibrium price and quantity exchanged of an item are determined by consumers' preferences, mood, and income, by the prices of its substitutes and complements, and by the technologies and resources available to its producers. A variable may be *endogenous* in one model and *exogenous* in another. Be sure you always know whether each variable is endogenous or exogenous in the model you're working with.

Two points are useful in thinking about economics models. The first is of fundamental importance; the second is a useful trick.

The relationship between exogenous and endogenous variables is one of cause and effect. A useful question to ask is "when an exogenous variable changes by 1 unit, how much does the endogenous variable change in response?" It is not sensible to ask about the effect of a change in an endogenous variable. A change in an endogenous variable is always the result of some more fundamental change in one or more exogenous variables.

You should have at least as many equations as endogenous variables in your model. If you have more, some of your equations must be combinations of the others; this isn't a problem. If you have less, however, **something fundamental has been omitted**. Look for another equation.

REVIEW OF TECHNIQUE 2

Moving from Levels to Rates of Change

We measure the *rate of change* (or *percentage change*) of a variable by looking at the difference in its level between two consecutive periods, and then dividing that difference by its level in the first of these periods. For ease of expression, we generally multiply this number by 100.

The rate of change of some variable x, then, would be equal to

$$\left(\frac{x_t - x_{t-1}}{x_{t-1}} \right) \times 100$$

where x_{t-1} represents the level of this variable x in the initial period, and x_t represents the level of x in the subsequent period. An increase in x from 100 to 120, then, will produce a rate of change equal to 100 times [(120 – 100)/100], or 20%. Notice that if x *decreased* from 120 to 100, its percentage change would be 100 times [(100 – 120)/120], or approximately -17%. Can a 20% increase and a 17% decrease return our variable x to its initial level? The answer, of course, is an emphatic *yes*. The base used in these calculations makes a difference. For small changes in x, however, it makes *less* of a difference: a jump in x from 99 to 100 is a 1.01% increase, and a drop in x from 100 to 99 is a 1% decrease. The difference is negligible.

FILL-IN QUESTIONS

1. _____ is the value of all final goods and services produced within the country.

2. To calculate net domestic product, it is necessary to adjust GDP for _____.

CHAPTER 2

CROSSWORD

ACROSS

2 Money that we do not spend we
6 A type of investment, does not subtract depreciation
7 Type of variable, input to model
9 A variable whose value is determined *within* a model
13 Measures an urban consumers' cost of living
14 A good that lasts a long time is
15 A measure of output, subtracts depreciation
17 Output equals

DOWN

1 Type of GDP, measures physical output
3 Type of GDP, tries to measure welfare
4 Increases the capital stock
5 People who buy things
6 Includes output produced abroad using domestically owned factors
8 This chapter covers national income _____.
10 When the price level falls there is
11 Output bought by people in other countries
12 Measure of output produced within a country
16 Type of goods and services measured by GDP

3. Inputs such as capital and labor are called _____; the payments made to them are called _____.

4. To avoid double–counting, _____ like welfare payments and social security benefits are not counted as part of GDP.

5. _____ is a measure of the increase in the domestic business sector's stock of capital, not accounting for depreciation.

6. Net exports are defined as _____ minus _____.

7. The difference between government expenditures and taxes is called the _____.

8. The increase in the value of the output produced at a given stage in production is called the _____.

9. _____ is a series which attempts to correct for the presence of economic "bads," like pollution, in standard measures of output, and for the absence of other, difficult to measure economic goods.

10. The ratio of nominal to real GDP is a useful price index, called the _____.

TRUE–FALSE QUESTIONS

T F 1. Roughly ¾ of all factor payments are payments to capital.

T F 2. The accumulation of inventories is a kind of investment.

T F 3. In a model with no government and no foreign trade, private saving must equal investment.

T F 4. In a model with both government and foreign trade, *when saving is equal to investment*, it must be the case that the government's budget deficit (TA – G – TR) is equal to its trade deficit (NX).

T F 5. GDP includes the transfers of existing commodities, like old houses.

T F 6. The sum of the value added to each good, at each stage of processing in an economy is equal to that economy's GDP.

T F 7. GDP is a nearly perfect measure of output.

T F 8. The CPI, PPI, and the GDP deflator all include the prices of imports.

T F 9. The GDP deflator measures the price of a much wider basket of goods than either the CPI or PPI.

T F 10. The PPI, because it measures the prices of goods at an early stage of production, is a good business cycle indicator.

MULTIPLE–CHOICE QUESTIONS

1. Which of the following is not a component of aggregate demand?
   a. government spending
   b. investment spending
   c. tax payments
   d. foreign demand (NX)

18 CHAPTER 2

2. Social security payments are counted as part of

   a. government purchases
   b. transfers
   c. net exports
   d. consumption

3. Which of the following is not considered a part of national income?

   a. factor payments
   b. welfare payments
   c. salaries
   d. net interest

4. Which of the following is *not* a measure of total output?

   a. all factor payments + profit
   b. the sum of all values added
   c. C + I + G + NX
   d. adjusted GNP

5. All of the following are considered physical investment *except*

   a. inventory accumulation
   b. housing construction
   c. building a new machine
   d. purchasing a government bond

6. Suppose that investment and output are fixed. Which of the following four items is able to change without affecting any of the others?

   a. government budget surplus
   b. net exports
   c. saving
   d. taxes

7. In an economy with both foreign trade and a government sector, the excess of private saving over investment (S - I) is equal to

   a. net exports
   b. the trade surplus
   c. the budget deficit
   d. (b) + (c)

8. Which of the following measures of output is likely to be most directly useful for measuring the change in physical output from year to year?

   a. real GDP
   b. nominal GDP
   c. adjusted GNP
   d. the GDP deflator

9. Which of the following price indices are based on a fixed basket of goods (one which remains constant from year to year)?

   a. CPI
   b. PPI
   c. GDP deflator
   d. (a) & (b)

10. Which of the following is most likely to overstate the inflation which might result from an increase in the world price of grain?

    a. CPI
    b. PPI
    c. GDP deflator
    d. (a) & (b)

CONCEPTUAL PROBLEMS

1. What would happen to GDP if a large number of women entered the workplace, and hired others to cook, clean, and care for their children? Is this change reflective of an actual change in the physical output of the economy?

2. Find an example of a product whose quality has changed over time, but whose price (in real terms) has not.

3. If savings = investment in the private sector, what must be true of the budget and trade deficits? *(Note: we have a trade deficit when imports exceed exports, or NX is negative.)*

4. Now suppose that we want to decrease the government's budget deficit. How could we accomplish this?

TECHNICAL PROBLEMS

1. This is a national income accounting problem. You are given the following facts about the economy: Consumption = $1,000; saving = $100; and government expenditures = $300. Net exports are zero. The government's budget is balanced. What is the value of GDP?

2. Suppose that saving = $200, the budget deficit = $50, and the trade deficit (the difference between imports and exports, or –NX) = $10. What must be the level of investment?

3. If GDP = $1,000, government expenditure = $250, consumption = $500, net exports = $100, and the budget deficit = $40, what is disposable income?

4. If GDP = $500, consumption = $350, transfers – taxes = $20, investment = $150, and the budget deficit = $120, what are net exports?

5. Calculate the rate of inflation that would result from an increase in the CPI from 1.75 to 2. The numbers are not intended to be realistic—don't worry if the rate of inflation seems too low or too high.

6. If the nominal interest rate on an asset is 6% and inflation is also 6%, what is the real interest rate of that asset? What if inflation is 8%?

Part 2

Growth and Aggregate Supply and Demand

3 GROWTH AND ACCUMULATION

FOCUS OF THE CHAPTER

- In this chapter we study how *potential output*—the output that *would* be produced if all factors were fully employed—grows over time.

- To better accomplish this, we learn growth accounting and the fundamentals of neoclassical growth theory. Together, they tell us that output growth results both from improvements in technology and from increases in one or more of the inputs to the production process—capital, labor, and natural resources. Neoclassical growth theory also tells us that in the long run, growth in potential output results entirely from technological improvement.

- *Note: The authors in this chapter and the next use the term "long run" in a way that is inconsistent with the rest of the textbook. They should be saying "very long run".*

SECTION SUMMARIES

1. Growth Accounting

Output grows because of increases in *factors of production* like capital and labor, and because of improvements in technology. The *production function* provides a link between the level of technology (A), the amount of capital (K), labor (N), and other inputs used, and the amount of output (Y) created. The generic formula for the production function is:

$$Y = AF(K,N)$$

The *Cobb–Douglas production function*, a more specific formula, is frequently used as well, as it provides a good approximation of production in the actual economy. The formula for the Cobb–Douglas production function is:

$$Y = AK^\theta N^{1-\theta}$$

θ, pronounced "theta", represents *capital's share of income*—total payments to capital, as a fraction of output, or *(iK)/Y*. *(1-θ)* is *labor's share of income*, given by *(wN)/Y*. To derive these results algebraically, you need one more fact: When the markets for capital and labor are in equilibrium (i.e., when the supply of capital equals the demand for capital, and the supply of labor equals the demand for labor), capital and labor are each paid their *marginal product*. For the Cobb–Douglas function, the *marginal product of capital (MPK)* is $\theta A K^{\theta} N^{\theta}$. The *marginal product of labor (MPL)* is $(1-\theta)AK^{\theta}N^{-\theta}$.

We can express our production function in terms of growth rates rather than levels:

$$\Delta Y/Y = [(1-\theta) \times \Delta N/N] + [\theta \times \Delta K/K] + \Delta A/A$$

The symbol Δ, pronounced "delta" means "change in". The term $\Delta Y/Y$, then, should be interpreted as the growth rate of output. The terms $\Delta N/N$ and $\Delta K/K$ should be interpreted as the growth rates of labor and capital, respectively. The last term, $\Delta A/A$ is the rate of improvement of technology, often called the growth rate of *total factor productivity* **(TFP)**. It is the amount that output increases as a result of technological progress alone (plug in $\Delta N/N = \Delta K/K = 0$, and you'll see why).

Because growth in *GDP per capita* (output per person) tells us more about increases in the standard of living, it is useful to subtract the rate of population growth ($\Delta N/N$) from both sides, and write the above equation in per capita terms:

$$\Delta y/y = (\theta \times \Delta k/k) + \Delta A/A$$

The terms y and k represent output and capital per person: $y = Y/N$, $k = K/N$. (There is an implicit assumption here that the fraction of the population in the labor force is constant. This is why we can get away with using the terms "population" and "labor supply" interchangeably.) The terms ($\Delta y/y$) and ($\Delta k/k$) are the growth rates of output and capital per person: $\Delta y/y = \Delta Y/Y - \Delta N/N$, and $\Delta k/k = \Delta K/K - \Delta N/N$. The term K/N is often called the *capital–labor ratio*.

2. Empirical Estimates of Growth

Since 1929, US economic growth has averaged about 2.9% a year. Of this, estimates suggest that about 1.09% has been due to increases in the labor supply, 0.32% has been due to capital accumulation, and 1.49% has been the result of technological progress.

Labor and physical capital are not the only inputs to production. Two other important factors of production are *natural resources* and *human capital*—the skills and talents of workers. The shares of income (also called *factor shares*) of physical capital, human capital, and raw labor are estimated to be roughly 1/3 each.

3. Growth Theory: The Neoclassical Model

Neoclassical growth theory studies the way that growth in the capital stock per worker affects the long run level of *per-capita potential output*. A key result is that, while the rate of saving has a significant impact on the *level* of per capita potential output in the long run, the rate of improvement in technology entirely determines its growth rate.

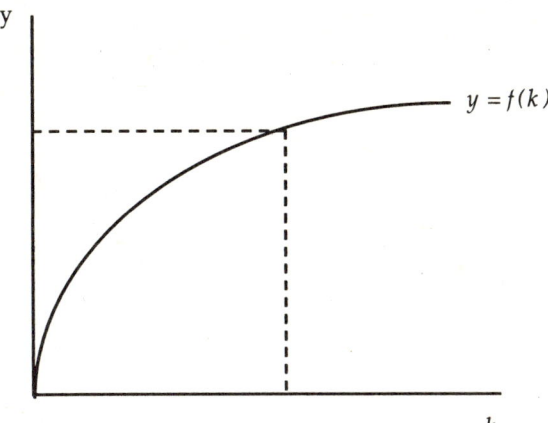

Figure 3 - 1

THE PER-CAPITA PRODUCTION FUNCTION

In the constant returns to scale production function, capital & labor have <u>diminishing</u> <u>marginal</u> <u>returns</u>.

To build our model, we begin with a few *simplifying assumptions*: (1) the level of technology is fixed, so that there is no growth in total factor productivity; (2) the production function has *constant returns to scale* (see Review of Technique 4), so that increasing the amount every input used in production will increase output by the same amount.

A consequence of this second assumption is that all factors of production must have *diminishing marginal products*—as more of one input is added, and the others are held constant, each unit contributes less to output than did the previous one. (Buying more tractors for your construction company without hiring any more workers to drive them will not help increase your output much.)

We also need to write our variables in *per capita* form; as before, $y = Y/N$ and $k = K/N$. We write the per capita production function:

$$y = f(k)$$

We then consider the flows into and out k—the stock of capital per worker.

Investment increases the total stock of capital (K), which increases k. It can be thought of as a flow *into* each worker's pool of capital.

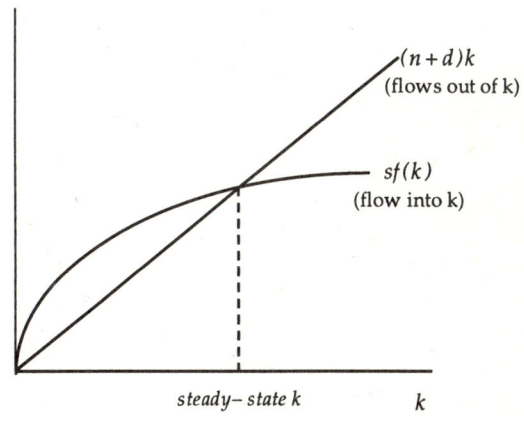

Figure 3 - 2

STEADY–STATE IN THE NEOCLASSICAL MODEL

Both depreciation and population growth decrease *k*—depreciation because it decreases the stock of functional capital, and population growth because it increases the number of workers sharing this capital. Both depreciation and population growth can be visualized as flows *out of* each worker's pool of capital. When the flow into this pool is greater than the flows out, *k* grows. When the flows out of this pool are greater than the flow in, *k* shrinks. And when the flows in and out exactly balance, the level of capital per worker will remain fixed.

We call this last case the ***steady state***, because it is the point at which the level of capital in each worker's pool remains steady, or stable. It is the point of *equilibrium* in our model; we will find that the capital stock per worker grows or shrinks toward this point, and that once it get there it stays. At least until some shock forces it to move.

It is not difficult to express the dynamics described above as an equation. We know that saving must equal investment. If we assume that people save a constant fraction (*s*) of their incomes, we can write the flow into *k* as (*s x y*), or, using our per capita production function, as (*s x f(k)*). The standard assumption about depreciation is that a constant fraction (*d*) of the capital stock becomes obsolete each period. Using this assumption, we can express the flow out of each worker's pool of capital which result from depreciation as (*d x k*). Similarly, when population grows at a constant rate (*n*), we can express the flow out of this pool resulting from population growth as (*n x k*). Putting all of these terms together, we get the following equation:

$$\Delta k = sf(k) - (n + d)k$$

We find an expression for the *steady–state* by simply plugging in the requirement $\Delta k = 0$:

$$sf(k^*) = (n + d)k^*$$

k* represents the steady–state value of *k*. The steady–state value of *y* is $y^* = f(k^*)$.

The growth process can be studied graphically as well. Figure 3 - 2 graphs the flows into and out of *k* against the *level* of *k*. The outflows are graphed as a straight line, with slope (*n + d*). This is often called the *investment requirement line*, as it shows the amount that must be invested, if the capital stock is to remain constant. The slope of the line that represents the flow into *k* shrinks as *k* increases, because we have assumed it to have ***diminishing marginal returns***. Where these two lines intersect, the flows into and out of *k* balance, and *k* is at its steady–state. Whether the savings line lies above the investment requirement line, so that *k* is increasing, or the investment requirement line lies above the savings line, so that *k* is decreasing, ***k always moves toward the steady–state***.

Using this graph, is particularly easy to see the consequences of changes in *s*, *n*, or *d*. An increase in the savings rate (*s*) will shift the savings line, *sf(k)*, upward, increasing the steady–state capital–labor ratio, and hence the steady–state level of per capita potential output. It will also, temporarily, increase the *growth rate* of both *y* and *k* (remember, the growth rate of *k* is zero at the steady–state, and without improvements in technology per capita output has no other reason to grow). An increase in either the rate of depreciation or the rate of population growth will increase the slope of the investment requirement line, *decreasing* the steady–state levels of *k* and *y*, and causing both to "grow", temporarily, at negative rate.

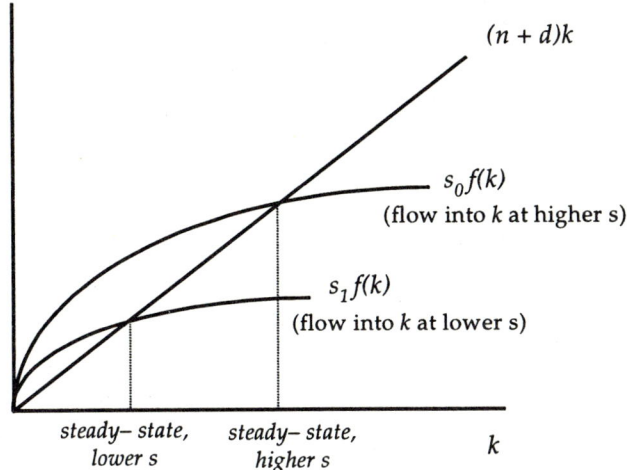

Figure 3 - 3

A DECREASE IN THE SAVINGS RATE REDUCES THE STEADY–STATE CAPITAL–LABOR RATIO

A reduction in the savings rate will decrease steady–state levels of capital and output.

When the level of technology is permitted to change, we add in another term: "g", or the growth rate of technology. Technological improvement is represented on our graph as an upward shift in the savings line, now written $s \times Af(k)$. Notice that it causes the steady–state levels of *k* and *y* to rise.

Notice also, though, that with the addition of technological growth our production function no longer has constant returns to scale—doubling capital and labor will more than double output. In order to fix this problem, growth theorists often assume that technology has a very particular characteristic: it is assumed to be *labor augmenting*, so that technological improvements increase the productivity *specifically of labor*.

The production function, under this assumption, is written as follows:

$$Y = F(K, AN)$$

or, in its Cobb–Douglas form,

$$Y = K^{\theta}(AN)^{1-\theta}$$

Now when we divide through by N we get something a little different:

$$y = f(k, A)$$

(*trust me on this one*), or

$$y = k^{\theta} A^{1-\theta}$$

Now, when technology increases at a constant rate (the savings line shifts continually upward), the steady-state levels of *k* and *y* will grow at that same rate:

$$\%\Delta k^* = \%\Delta y^* = \%\Delta A$$

This is not true when technology is takes a more general form (the one where it affects the productivity of both capital and labor identically, for example).

Appendix

The appendix discusses, in some detail, the how to derive the fundamental growth equation $\Delta Y/Y = [(1-\theta) \times \Delta N/N] + [\theta \times \Delta K/K] + \Delta A/A$. There is one assumption needed to do this: that markets are perfectly competitive, so that capital and labor are each paid their marginal products.

Note: The fundamental growth equation takes a slightly different form when labor-augmenting technology is assumed,

$$\Delta Y/Y = [(1-\theta) \times \Delta N/N] + [\theta \times \Delta K/K] + [(1-\theta) \times \Delta A/A]$$

or, in per-capita terms,

$$\Delta y/y = [\theta \times \Delta k/k] + [(1-\theta) \times \Delta A/A].$$

Just in case you were curious.

A technological improvement will increase steady-state levels of capital and output.

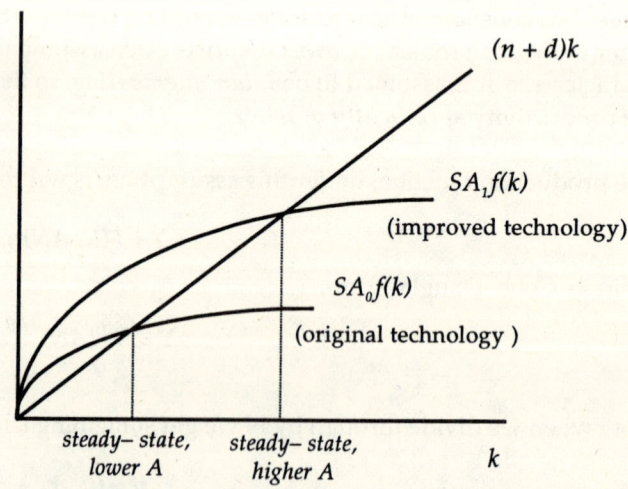

Figure 3 - 4

A TECHNOLOGICAL IMPROVEMENT INCREASES THE STEADY-STATE CAPITAL-LABOR RATIO

GROWTH AND ACCUMULATION

KEY TERMS

growth accounting
growth theory
production function
Cobb-Douglas production function
marginal product of labor (MPN)
marginal product of capital (MPK)
total factor productivity
GDP per capita

capital-labor ratio
diminishing marginal returns
convergence
Solow residual
human capital
neoclassical growth theory
steady-state equilibrium

GRAPH IT 3

When two economies *converge*, their growth rates, and, in some cases, the levels of their output eventually become equal. This Graph It asks you to plot some historical growth rates for the US and Japan between 1950 and 1970, to see if convergence was occurring. Table 3–1 provides these growth rates. All that you need to do is plot each country's growth rate every year, and connect the dots. You will get two lines.

You will notice that the rate of growth in per capita output is noticeably higher for Japan than for the US during much of this period. It is this high rate of growth that has brought the Japanese standard of living into line with the standards of living enjoyed by others in the industrialized world. Convergence, however, cannot be said to have occur unless Japan's growth eventually slows, approaching the average growth of other nations. Can you see this happening in Chart 3 - 1? Can this data help you to argue that Japan's high growth during this period was a transitory phenomenon?

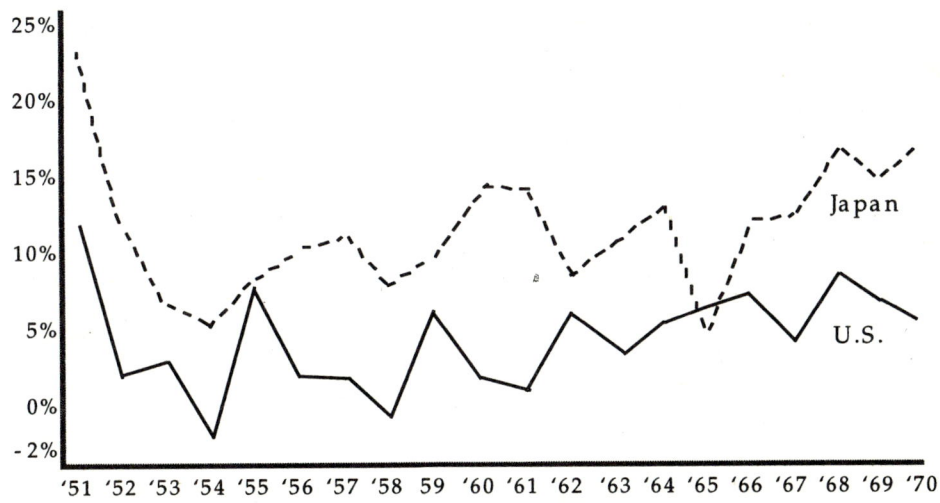

Chart 3 - 1

PERCENTAGE CHANGE IN GDP FOR JAPAN AND THE U.S.: 1951–1970

TABLE 3-1

Year	Percentage growth in GDP (Japan)	Percentage growth in GDP (US)
1951	23.6	13.3
1952	11.8	3.2
1953	6.8	3.6
1954	5.5	-1.7
1955	7.9	7.6
1956	10.4	3.5
1957	11.0	3.4
1958	7.5	-0.2
1959	9.8	6.3
1960	14.5	2.4
1961	14.3	1.6
1962	7.7	6.1
1963	10.9	3.9
1964	13.4	5.3
1965	5.1	6.9
1966	13.2	8.2
1967	14.0	4.5
1968	16.8	7.9
1969	15.1	6.7
1970	16.8	5.7

Source: Penn World Tables

THE LANGUAGE OF ECONOMICS 3

Stocks and Flows, or "About Your Bathtub"

It is always important to know whether a given variable is a *stock* or a *flow*. It is easiest to understand the difference between stocks and flows in the context of your bathtub. The *level* of the water in your bathtub is a *stock variable*—it rises and falls depending on the amount of water entering through the faucet, and, if the drain is unplugged, leaving through the drain. The amounts of water *flowing* into and out of the tub are, not surprisingly, *flow variables.*

Let's think through some examples of stock and flow variables. We already know that *capital* is a stock variable. We also know that *investment* is a flow into the capital stock, and that *depreciation* is a flow out of it. *Population* is a stock variable. Its level is affected by *the birth rate* (births are a flow into the pool of living, breathing people) and *the death rate* (deaths are a flow out of that pool). The *unemployment rate*, despite its name, is yet another stock variable. In chapter 7 we will see that those losing their jobs and those entering the labor force are a flow *into* this pool, and that those who find jobs or leave the labor force are a flow out of it.

REVIEW OF TECHNIQUE 3

Balancing Flows Into and Out of the Tub: Finding a Steady–State

When more water flows into a bathtub than flows out of it, the level of water in the bathtub will rise. When more water flows out than in, that level will fall. Most importantly, when the flow of water into and out of this bathtub are exactly the same, the *level* of water will remain constant. This is all that a steady–state is—a point at which the flows into and out of some "pool" balance.

In the neoclassical growth model, each worker has an identical pool of capital. Investment is a flow into these pools. Depreciation is a flow out. Population growth, as it increases the number of pools without adding any more "water", decreases amount available to each individual and can also be viewed as a flow out. Thus, at the steady–state, per capita savings = the flow out of each worker's pool of capital caused by depreciation + the flow out of that pool caused by population growth.

If we wanted to find the steady–state level of a population, we would find the point where the number of people being born was exactly equal to the number of people dying. There can, in some cases, be more than 1 steady–state, but that's an issue for another day.

CROSSWORD

ACROSS

1. MPK assumed in neoclassical model
6. Type of variable, the growth rate of technology in this chapter is an example
9. Kind growth theory studied in this chapter
10. Growth rate of steady-state, per–capita output when TFP is fixed
11. Type of output, its growth is modeled in this chapter
13. Type of function, provides link between inputs and outputs
14. Type of growth, reduces the steady-state capital labor ratio

DOWN

2. Type of capital, includes knowledge
3. _____ returns to scale
4. If the growth rates of two countries become equal over time, they
5. Type of variable, capital is an example
7. Affects the steady–state level of output, but not its growth rate
8. Type of variable, investment is an example
12. At the steady-state, flows into and out of the capital stock are

FILL-IN QUESTIONS

1. _____ helps us to determine how much of the growth in total output is the result of growth in different factors of production.

2. The _____ provides a quantitative link between the inputs to production, and the output produced.

3. We call the amount by which output increases when 1 more unit of labor is used the _____. It _____ as more labor is used in production.

4. When more output can be generated without using more inputs, it must be the case that _____ has increased.

5. Output per person (total output divided by population) is called _____.

6. We call the stock of machines and buildings used in production _____ capital.

7. The stock of knowledge and skills is called _____ capital.

8. The capital/labor ratio and output per person are constant at the _____.

9. If two countries have the same rate of population growth, and access to the same technologies, the rate at which their potential output grows will _____ over time, and be identical at the steady state.

10. When they also have the same rate of savings, the _____ of their potential output will be identical at this steady state as well.

TRUE–FALSE QUESTIONS

T F 1. An increase in the rate of population growth will change the rate at which per capita potential output grows in the steady state.

T F 2. An increase in the rate of population growth will change the *level* of per capita potential output at the steady state.

T F 3. An increase in the rate of population growth will change the rate at which *total* potential output grows in the steady state.

T F 4. An increase in the savings rate will change the rate at which *total* potential output grows in the steady state.

T F 5. An increase in the savings rate will *immediately* change the growth rate of total potential output.

T F 6. After this, the growth rate will remain constant.

T F 7. An increase in the rate of depreciation will change the *levels* of the capital/labor ratio and of per capita potential output at the steady state.

T F 8. When we allow productivity to grow over time, the rate at which per capita potential output grows in the steady state is both positive and exogenous.

T F 9. Two countries with the same rate of population growth, and with access to the same technologies will have the same level of output (and therefore income) at the steady state.

T F 10. The growth rate of their potential output, at the steady state, will (also) be the same.

MULTIPLE–CHOICE QUESTIONS

1. The rate of growth of potential output is the same as the
   a. business cycle
   b. growth rate of the economy
   c. trend path of GDP
   d. output gap

2. Which of the following *can* affect the growth rate of per capita potential output in the steady-state?
   a. savings rate
   b. rate of population growth
   c. rate of depreciation
   d. rate of productivity growth

3. Which of the following *cannot* affect the growth rate of total potential output in the steady-state?
   a. savings rate
   b. rate of population growth
   c. rate of depreciation
   d. (a) & (c)

4. Which of the following need to be equal, if two countries are to achieve the same growth rate of per–capita potential output at the steady state?
   a. savings rate
   b. rate of population growth
   c. rate of depreciation
   d. access to technology

5. Which of the following is a realistic estimate of capital's share of income (the fraction of total output that is used to pay capital's "wage") in the US?
   a. 0.25
   b. 0.5
   c. 0.75
   d. 1

6. Which of the following *would not* increase labor's productivity (measured as Y/N)?
   a. technological progress
   b. an increase in the capital/labor ratio
   c. more natural resources
   d. an increase in the population growth rate

7. Which of the following *would not* increase capital's productivity (measured as Y/K)?
   a. technological progress
   b. an increase in the capital/labor ratio
   c. more natural resources
   d. an increase in the population growth rate

8. With the production function $y = k^{1/4}$, a 1% increase in the capital/labor ratio should increase per capita potential output by

   a. 0.25 %
   b. 0.5 %
   c. 0.75 %
   d. 1 %

9. Which of the following would *not* increase the stock of human capital?

   a. education
   b. on the job training
   c. more natural resources
   d. vaccinations

10. Human capital's share of income in industrialized countries is roughly

    a. 1/10
    b. 1/3
    c. 1/2
    d. 3/4

CONCEPTUAL PROBLEMS

1. Can human capital depreciate?
   Does it have diminishing marginal returns?

2. Do natural resources depreciate?
   Do they have diminishing marginal returns?

3. Name two important assumptions at the foundation of the neoclassical model of growth.

4. Which of the following are stock variables? flow variables?

   a) capital, b) per–capita GDP, c) depreciation, d) investment

TECHNICAL PROBLEMS

1. Consider the following production function: $Y = K^{1/4}N^{3/4}$

   a) What is capital's share of income?

   b) Find an equation for the productivity of capital (Y/K).

   c) What is labor's share of income?

   d) Find an equation for the productivity of labor (Y/N).

   e) Does this production function have constant returns to scale?
      (Translation: Do the exponents add to 1?)

   f) Write this production function in per capita terms.
      (Translation: Divide both sides by N.)

2. If in a fixed population the number of people in the labor force doubles, what will happen to:

   a) the steady–state level of per capita potential output

   b) the steady–state growth rate of per capita potential output

   c) labor's share of income

   d) labor productivity

3. If, instead, the number of people in the population doubles (you may assume that the number of people in the labor force doubles as well) what will happen to:

   a) the steady–state level of per capita potential output

   b) the steady–state growth rate of per capita potential output

   c) labor's share of income

   d) labor productivity

4. Now suppose that, in an economy initially at steady–state, there is an exogenous increase in the savings rate. Show how per capita output changes over time.

5. Use the growth accounting equation to answer the following question:

   If capital's share of income is 25% and labor's share of income is 75%, the stocks of both capital and labor increase by 50% ($\Delta K/K = \Delta N/N = 0.5$), and there is no technology growth, at what rate will potential output grow? Will the capital–labor ratio increase at all?

4 GROWTH AND POLICY

FOCUS OF THE CHAPTER

- In the last chapter, we learned that the rate of growth of potential output is determined by the rate of population growth, by changes in the level of natural resources, and by improvements in technology. In this chapter, we recognize that society's choices affect these parameters.

- The first part of this chapter investigates the forces that bring about technological change, focusing in particular on the new ideas generated by the process of capital investment, and the fact that it is difficult, if not impossible, for any individual firm to capture all the benefits of these ideas. It also looks more carefully at convergence—the question of whether economies with different levels of income will eventually achieve the same standard of living.

- The second part of this chapter looks at problems of population growth and development, and at the unique setbacks and challenges to economic growth experienced by countries which have made or are making the transition from centrally planned (in which production and pricing decisions are made by the government) communist to free market capitalist economies.

SECTION SUMMARIES

1. Growth Theory: Endogenous Growth

Endogenous growth theory does something fairly radical—it uses a production function which has *increasing returns to scale*. It is able to do this by assuming that there are *external benefits* associated with private investment, so that an individual firm does not reap all of the benefits from its own investment. New knowledge, inventions, and discoveries are a by–product of some kinds of investment, and all of these benefit society as well. Thus it turns out that capital can have a *diminishing marginal product* in the eyes of individual producers, but, because of these external benefits, a *constant marginal product* in the eyes of society.

This tiny modification makes a world of difference. It was capital's diminishing marginal product that gave us a savings curve with a declining slope, and it was this savings curve with the

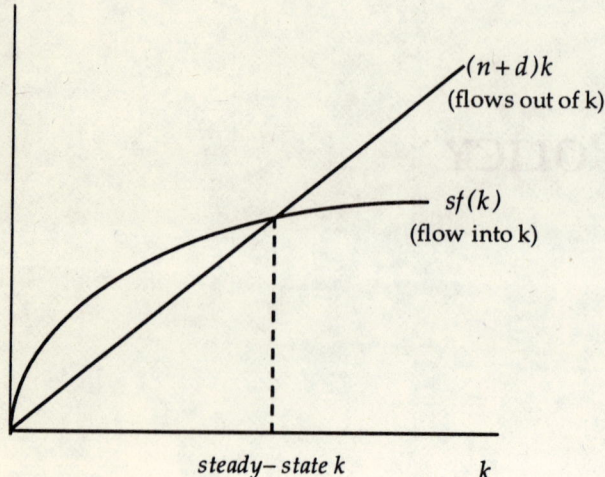

Figure 4 - 1

THE NEOCLASSICAL GROWTH MODEL

declining slope that guaranteed that the investment requirement line and the savings line would eventually intersect, so that there would be a steady–state.

When we allow capital to have a constant marginal product, the savings curve becomes a straight line. There is no steady–state.

When the savings curve is everywhere above the investment requirement line, as in figure 4–2, we get ongoing growth. When it is everywhere below the investment requirement line (not shown), output and the capital stock eventually fall to zero, as depreciation and population growth erode each worker's stock of capital more quickly than it can be replaced.

Interestingly, if the savings and investment requirement lines happen to coincide (of one is right on top of the other), whatever level of capital per worker and, thus, of per capita output exists will be in a steady–state. The growth rate of per capita output will be zero.

The simplest production function that will produce endogenous growth is:

$$Y = aK$$

Dividing both sides by N, we can express it in per capita terms:

$$y = ak$$

The marginal product of capital in this function is constant and equal to a. (A 1 unit increase in the capital stock will increase output by an amount a.) Per capita savings curve is just equal to sak, giving the savings line a constant slope equal to sa. The growth rate of per capita output, $\Delta k/k$, is determined by the following equation:

$$\Delta k = sf(k) - (n + d)k = sak - (n + d)k,$$

so that

$$\Delta k /k = sa - (n + d).$$

The difference between the flows into and the flows out of the capital stock determine its growth rate, and, as a result, the growth rates of technology and of per–capita output.

> *In endogenous growth theory, there is no steady-state.*
>
> *The growth rate of per capita potential output depends on the rate of saving.*

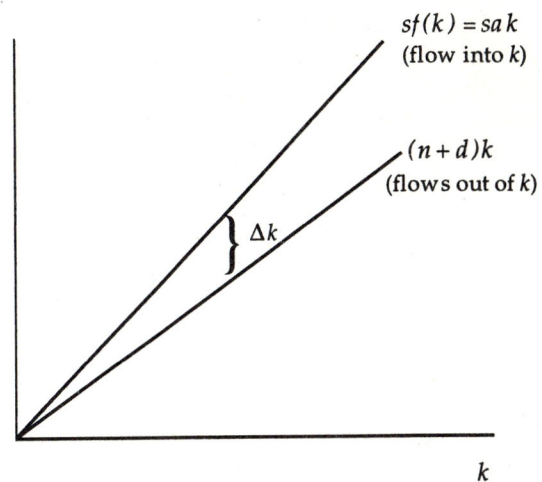

Figure 4 - 2

THE ENDOGENOUS GROWTH MODEL

Neoclassical and endogenous growth theories have different predictions regarding *convergence*—the theory that growth rates and, under certain conditions, standards of living (measured as levels of per capita output) should become equal across countries.

Neoclassical theory predicts that countries will *absolutely converge*—will reach the same level of steady-state income, and that their steady-state income will grow at the same rate—when they have the same rate of saving, the same rate of population growth, and have access to the same technologies. When population growth or savings rates differ, it predicts that they will *conditionally converge*, or that, while their steady-state incomes will differ, the growth rate of these incomes will be the same. Endogenous growth theory does not predict any kind of convergence.

NOTE: One optional component of this section has not been covered. It combines elements of neoclassical and endogenous growth models to produce a model with two equilibria—one with low income and no growth, and another with high income and positive growth.

2. Growth Policy

The first part of this section recognizes that the rate of population growth may itself depend on income. An optional section develops a model with endogenous population growth, assuming this to be true. The second part looks at the "miracle" of East Asian growth, and finds that it is due to high rates of saving, stable governments, and outward-looking economic policies. It does not discuss the currency crises that hit many of these economies in late 1997, or ask why none of these factors helped to prevent it. If you have to write a paper for your class, you might research this question further. It is interesting to wonder why the "tigers" of the 1980's became the "dominos" of the late 1990's, and at this point many economists consider it an open question.

This section also takes a look at some problems associated with reform in the formerly communist countries of Eastern Europe, many associated with their lack of a market infrastructure (much of the legal framework required to run an organized market was simply absent at the beginning of reform in many places, as were institutions such as banks). It observes that substantial declines in output—some of them more severe than the decline that occurred during the Great Depression in the US—have occurred during the early stages of reform.

KEY TERMS

endogenous growth
increasing returns to scale
absolute convergence
conditional convergence

stable equilibrium
unstable equilibrium
golden-rule capital stock

GRAPH IT 4

Many of the inhabitants of former communist countries in Eastern Europe have found, and are finding the transition from a planned to a free market economy a painful one. In this exercise, you track the per capita GDP of a particular transition economy—the economy of Bulgaria. Chart 4 - 1 provides the per capita GDP of Bulgaria between 1980 and 1992. Your job is to transform this data into rates of change, and to graph these rates of change during the sample period.

Can you guess, based on the information provided here, when Bulgaria began to make the transition to a market economy?

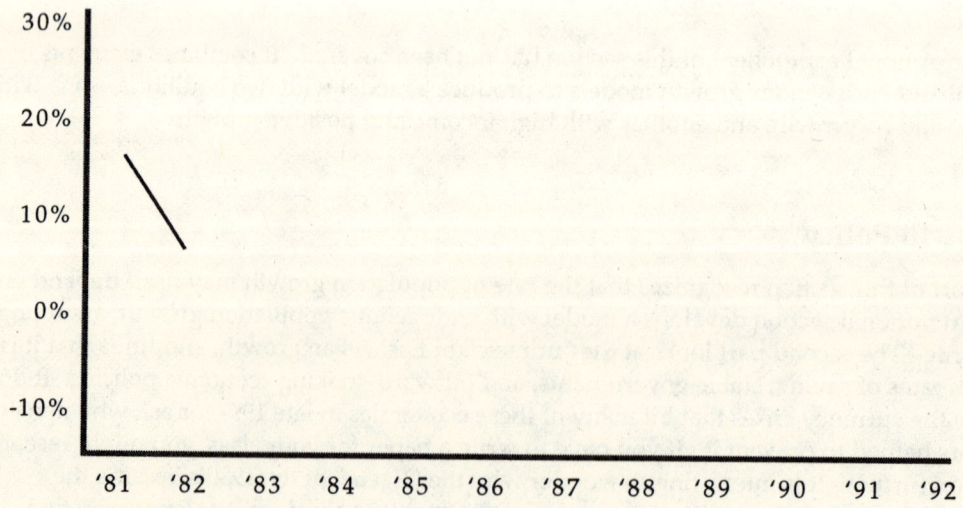

Figure 4 - 3

GROWTH RATE OF PER CAPITA GDP, BULGARIA

TABLE 4-1

Year	per capita GDP	Percent change from previous year
1980	3139	—
1981	3623	15.4
1982	3888	7.3
1983	4221	
1984	4366	
1985	4773	
1986	6284	
1987	6918	
1988	8030	
1989	8135	
1990	7529	
1991	6715	
1992	6774	

Source: Penn World Tables

THE LANGUAGE OF ECONOMICS 4

What is Endogenous About Endogenous Growth?

Endogenous growth theory gets its name from the fact that the growth rate of output is a function of the rate of saving. As the rate of saving is a variable we can affect (after all, we *could* save more), we can essentially choose how fast we want output to grow, weighing the costs of saving more against the benefits of faster growth. The rate of output growth is determined within our model—it is *endogenous*.

REVIEW OF TECHNIQUE 4

Returns to Scale

A production function is said to exhibit *constant returns to scale (CRTS)* if whenever we double every input, output doubles. All inputs must be increased in a balanced way for this to be the case—when we increase capital, labor must be increased by the same amount. The Cobb–Douglas production function has constant returns to scale—we can tell because its exponents add up to 1 (this is always a good, quick way to check).

We double K and L below to show, rigorously, that they cause output to double as well.

$$A(2K)^{\theta}(2L)^{1-\theta} = A(2)^{\theta}(2)^{1-\theta}(K)^{\theta}(L)^{1-\theta} = A(2)^{[\theta + (1-\theta)]}(K)^{\theta}(L)^{1-\theta}$$

$$= A(2)^{1}(K)^{\theta}(L)^{1-\theta} = (2)(AK^{\theta}L^{1-\theta}) = 2Y$$

A mathematical note may help you through the algebra above:

$$(x)^{a}(x)^{b} \text{ can also be written as } (x)^{a+b}$$

A production function has *increasing returns to scale* if doubling all inputs more than doubles output; if it is in a form similar to that of the Cobb–Douglas function (factors of production raised to some power and then multiplied together), its exponents will add up to a number greater than one.

CROSSWORD

ACROSS

1 Has a constant marginal product for society but a diminishing marginal product for individuals
3 A rate, drives endogenous output growth
5 When countries "catch up" with others
6 In a CRTS production function, whenever we double inputs, this doubles
9 MPK in the eyes of individual firms
10 Technology growth in the neoclassical model is determined

DOWN

2 Type of convergence, requires same rate of saving
4 Returns to scale, produce continuing growth
7 When countries move from being centrally planned to free market they are in
8 There need not be a steady state when the MPK is

FILL-IN QUESTIONS

1. When an individual firm captures all the benefits of its investment, as is assumed in the neoclassical model of growth, capital will have a _____ marginal product.

2. When it does not capture all these benefits, so that some of the ideas generated as a by-product of their capital accumulation are beneficial to *other* firms, capital can have a _____ marginal product.

3. A major difference between the neoclassical model of growth and endogenous models of growth is whether the production function has constant or increasing _____.

4. Another difference is that endogenous growth models have no (non-zero) _____.

5. In both neoclassical and endogenous growth models, long–term growth in per capita output results only from growth in _____.

6. The rate of technology growth, in the neoclassical model, is an _____ variable.

7. The rate of technology growth in endogenous growth models depends on the rate of capital accumulation, and therefore on the rate of _____.

8. This is why, in the neoclassical model, _____ cannot affect the long–term growth rate of per capita output, while in endogenous growth models it can.

9. Neoclassical growth theory predicts _____ convergence for countries with equal rates of saving, equal rates of population growth, and equal access to technology; it predicts _____ convergence for those with different rates of saving or population growth.

10. Empirical evidence suggests that, over long periods of time, countries converge _____.

TRUE–FALSE QUESTIONS

T F 1. The presence of increasing returns to scale in the production function will create a tendency toward monopolization (will make 1 large firm more efficient than many smaller ones).

T F 2. There is no steady–state in endogenous growth models.

T F 3. There can be no long–term growth in per capita output in the neoclassical growth model.

T F 4. There *is* long–term growth in per capita output in the neoclassical growth model, but it is independent of the rate of saving.

T F 5. There is no steady–state in the neoclassical growth model.

T F 6. There *is* a steady–state in the neoclassical model, but it is unaffected by changes in the rate of saving.

T F 7. Models of endogenous growth suggest that when countries have the same rates of depreciation and population growth, their potential output will grow at the same rate.

T F 8. The impact of higher saving on growth is transitory in the neoclassical model.

T F 9. The impact of higher saving on growth is transitory in models of endogenous growth.

T F 10. The low and negative rates of growth experienced by the formerly communist economies of Eastern Europe, during the early stages of reform, are a result of low and negative rates of saving.

MULTIPLE–CHOICE QUESTIONS

1. An increase in the rate of saving in neoclassical growth theory increases the steady–state
   a. level of per capita output
   b. growth rate of technology
   c. growth rate of per capita output
   d. rate of capital accumulation

2. An increase in the rate of saving in models of endogenous growth increases *everything except* the

   a. rate of population growth
   b. growth rate of per capita output
   c. growth rate of technology
   d. rate of capital accumulation

3. The assumption that there are substantial external returns to capital is most reasonable when capital is in the form of

   a. machinery
   b. tools
   c. ideas
   d. all of the above

4. In endogenous growth theory, the marginal product of capital is

   a. constant
   b. increasing in k
   c. decreasing in k
   d. variable

5. In neoclassical growth theory, the marginal product of capital is

   a. constant
   b. increasing in k
   c. decreasing in k
   d. variable

6. The production function used in endogenous growth theory has _____ returns to scale (for society).

   a. constant
   b. increasing
   c. decreasing
   d. variable

7. Some of these returns, however, are not captured by individual firms. We call these benefits "_____".

   a. internal
   b. external
   c. sideways
   d. fractured

8. As a result, the production function used in endogenous growth theory has _____ *private* returns to scale.

   a. constant
   b. increasing
   c. decreasing
   d. variable

9. When two countries move toward steady–states which have the same level *and* growth rate of potential output, they are said to converge

   a. absolutely
   b. partially
   c. relatively
   d. conditionally

10. When two countries move toward steady–states with the same growth rate, but a different level of potential output, they are said to converge only

    a. absolutely
    b. partially
    c. relatively
    d. conditionally

CONCEPTUAL PROBLEMS

1. What assumption changes when we move from neoclassical to endogenous growth theory?

2. Does this production function have constant returns to scale? $Y = K^\theta N^{1-\theta}$
   Does this one? $Y = K^\theta N^{2-\theta}$

3. How will an increase in the savings rate affect the growth rate of per capita output in an endogenous growth model?

4. How will an increase in the savings rate affect the growth rate of per capita output in the neoclassical growth model?

5. What can endogenous growth theory explain that neoclassical growth theory cannot? What *can't* endogenous growth theory explain?

TECHNICAL PROBLEMS *(all from optional sections)*

1. Consider the following neoclassical production function: $Y = K^{1/2} N^{1/2}$

   a) Write this production function in per capita form

   b) Find the golden rule level of the (steady–state) capital–labor ratio, when the rate of depreciation is 0.05, and the (exogenous) rate of population growth is 0.20.

   (Translation: find the point at which the marginal product of capital $\left(\frac{1}{2\sqrt{k}}\right) = n + d$.

2. Find the rate of growth of the capital–labor ratio ($\Delta k/k$) for the endogenous growth production function: $f(k) = k$. Assume that the rate of saving is 0.3, that the rate of depreciation is 0.05 and that the rate of population growth is 0.20.

3. How does the neoclassical model of growth change when we endogenize the rate of population growth (make n a function of y)? Are there any assumptions about the function $n(y)$ that are necessary to get the textbook's result?

4. How can we generate a model in which some countries have low growth and low income and others have high growth, high income (a model with a growth trap)?

5 AGGREGATE SUPPLY AND DEMAND

FOCUS OF THE CHAPTER

- In this chapter we begin to study how output varies over the short and long run, when *potential output* is fixed.

- We develop the aggregate supply/demand model to show how the supply and demand sides of the economy interact to uniquely determine output and the price level.

SECTION SUMMARIES

1. The Aggregate Supply Curve

The *aggregate supply (AS) curve* describes the amount of output that firms are willing to supply at different price levels. The fact that there *is* a relationship between output and the price level should be somewhat disturbing—*if everyone is perfectly informed and all markets clear (so that supply equals demand in each of them), output should be fixed at the level of potential output whatever the price level*.

In the *long run*, when markets clear and all inputs are fully employed, output is fixed at the level of potential output, and the AS curve is vertical. We call this the *classical case*.

If we characterize the short run as a period over which prices cannot adjust, the short–run AS curve must be horizontal. (We call this a *Keynesian aggregate supply curve*.)

The assumption that prices are fixed (and therefore that the AS curve is horizontal) in the short run works well when output is below potential output. It does not work, however, when output is *above* potential output. In this case resources are over employed. Workers must be paid a higher wage to entice them to work more; the owners capital must similarly be paid a higher rate of interest. These higher wages drive up the price level, making the short–run AS curve slope sharply upwards at the point where output equals potential output.

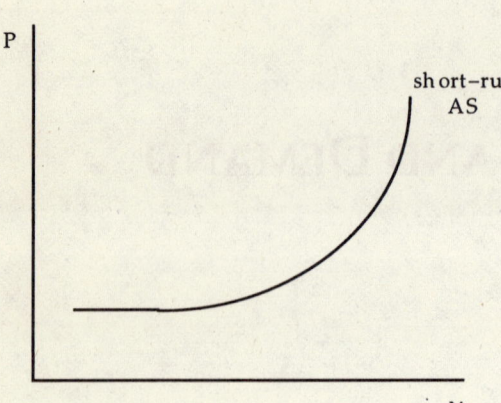

Figure 5 - 1

A MORE ACCURATE PICTURE OF AGGREGATE SUPPLY IN THE SHORT RUN

The AS curve, even in the short run, is really a curve and not a straight line.

The fact that resources *can* be over-employed suggests that the natural rate of unemployment is not zero. This is true. Some *frictional unemployment* exists even when resources are "fully employed," as there are always people switching jobs and looking for new ones.

2. The Aggregate Demand Curve

The *aggregate demand curve* describes all of the combinations of output and the price level for which the goods and assets markets are *simultaneously* in equilibrium. It slopes downward because of the interaction between these markets: a decrease in the price level, because it increases the *real money supply*, causes the real interest rate to fall. Lower interest rates make investment less costly, so that more occurs. Aggregate demand increases.

Most of us have great intuition about goods markets. We know that a tax cut will leave us with more money to spend. We are also willing to believe that an increase in consumer confidence causes people to spend more of the money that they already have, as they do not need to save as much in anticipation of trouble. It isn't terribly difficult to convince us that aggregate demand increases in either of these cases.

Few of us have as strong an intuitive understanding of the way that asset markets work. For this reason, we provide a brief introduction to them here.

The key to understanding asset markets is to think in terms of interest rates. The real interest rate is the equilibrium "price" of money, and, like all prices, is determined by the intersection of supply and demand. It is also a variable that firms care a lot about: the real interest rate is the cost, for firms, of investing. (Think of these firms as having to borrow money in order to invest.) So the first step is to ask how a particular change in some asset market affects the real interest rate. The second is to ask how the change in the real interest rate affects investment demand. By looking at the effect of the real interest rate on investment, we connect assets and goods markets, and are able to translate changes in assets markets into shifts in AD.

It is necessary to distinguish between *nominal* and *real money balances* when looking at the market for money. Nominal balances are just the number of bills and coins floating around (M); real balances are the *value* of these bills and coins (M/P). *The real interest rate is determined by the supply of and demand for <u>real</u> <u>money</u> <u>balances</u>.*

Although the central bank only has direct control over <u>nominal</u> money balances, it *is* able to affect real money balances in the short run, when the price level is fixed. A decrease in nominal balances lowers real balances for any given price level, and therefore shifts out the AD curve.

Always think in terms of interest rates when analyzing monetary policy: How does the real interest rate change, and how does that change affect investment demand? An increase in investment demand will increase AD; a decrease will cause it to fall.

The *quantity theory of money* provides more good intuition. It tells us that the total value of output must equal the number of dollars circulating in the economy multiplied by the number of times the average dollar changes hands:

$$M \times V = P \times Y$$

"M" here represents the money supply; "V" is a term representing the *velocity of money*, or the number of times one dollar changes hands in the course of a year. "P" is the price level, and "Y" output—together, they represent either nominal GDP or nominal GNP. Notice that when both velocity and the money supply are assumed to be constant, there is an inverse relationship between P and Y; when one rises, the other must fall. This is consistent with our downward-sloping aggregate demand curve. Likewise, an increase in the money supply will increase output for any given price level (or increase the price level for a given level of output); it will cause the aggregate demand curve to shift outwards.

An increase in the money supply will raise output for any given price level, shifting the AD curve outward.

Still, we can't say what will happen to output and the price level until we introduce an AS curve...

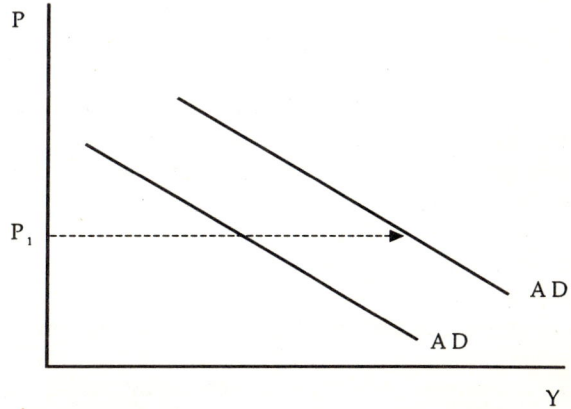

Figure 5 - 2

AN INCREASE IN THE MONEY SUPPLY SHIFTS THE AGGREGATE DEMAND CURVE OUTWARD

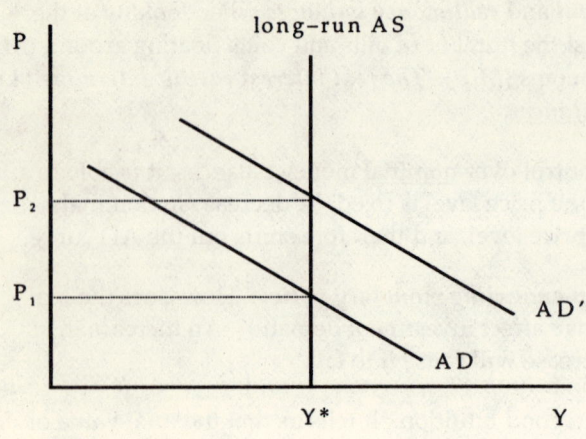

Figure 5-3

THE LONG–RUN EFFECT OF A SHIFT IN AD

> *Demand management policies (policies that shift only the AD curve) cannot affect output in the long run.*

3. Aggregate Demand Policy Under Alternative Supply Assumptions

Changes in aggregate demand only affect output in the short and medium run, when the AS curve is not vertical.

When the AS curve *is* vertical (in the long run, or classical case), neither fiscal nor monetary policy can affect output. Shifts in the AD curve only change the price level. Output is fixed at potential output (Y^*).

4. Supply–Side Economics

Because the AS curve is vertical in the long run, only supply–side policies (policies which shift the aggregate supply curve) can produce long–run growth. Deregulating industries, making laws and regulations easier to comply with, and changing or removing unnecessary laws all have the capacity to do this.

You might wonder how the long–run AS curve can shift at all, as all factors of production are *fixed* in the long run by definition. The answer, of course, is that this shift does not occur because more inputs are being used. It occurs because these inputs are being used more effectively. It is similar, in this way, to technological improvement.

The political meaning of the term "supply–side economics" is slightly different than the more general economic one. This term has been used, in recent years, to refer to the idea that tax cuts will increase output by so much that tax receipts will rise or remain constant, rather than fall.

The assumption that tax cuts increase aggregate supply as well as aggregate demand results from an *incentive effect*: Tax cuts, because they allow people to keep more of the money they earn, significantly increase the incentive to work, and therefore lower the natural rate of unemployment (raise potential output).

Economists don't argue about whether this incentive effect exists, or about whether a shift in long-run AS is likely to occur. What they *do* argue about is the magnitude of this shift—specifically, about whether the AS curve shifts far enough to the right to compensate for the effect of the lower tax rate on total tax receipts.

What do *you* think? Can you support your position?

KEY TERMS

aggregate supply (AS) curve
aggregate demand (AD) curve
classical aggregate supply curve
Keynesian aggregate supply curve
frictional unemployment

natural rate of unemployment
real money supply
nominal money supply
full crowding out
neutrality of money

GRAPH IT 5

This Graph It asks you to work through the effect of an increase in the money supply on the real interest rate, on investment, and on aggregate demand in the short run. To help you accomplish this, we have provided three charts: Chart 5–1 shows the supply and demand for real money balances as a function of the interest rate; Chart 5–2 is an investment demand function; and Chart 5–3 sets up an AS–AD diagram for you.

You should work through these diagrams sequentially, first finding the short–run effect of a monetary expansion on the real interest rate, then figuring out how this change affects investment demand and, through its effect on investment demand, aggregate demand.

THE LANGUAGE OF ECONOMICS 5

Expansionary/Contractionary Policies

Monetary and fiscal policy can be either *expansionary* or *contractionary*—can either increase or decrease aggregate demand. The central bank (the Federal Reserve, in the US) runs expansionary monetary policy when it increases the money stock. This drives down real interest rates, increases investment demand, and shifts AD to the right. It runs contractionary monetary policy when it reduces the real money supply, driving up interest rates and shifting AD to the left. This is pretty easy to remember, as contractionary monetary policy is nothing more than a *contraction* in the real money supply (it shrinks), and expansionary monetary policy nothing more than an *expansion* of the money stock (it grows).

Tax cuts and spending increases are both examples of expansionary fiscal policy, as they increase people's demand for consumption goods, and thus shift AD outward. Tax increases and spending cuts are both types of contractionary fiscal policy.

Note: Both monetary and fiscal policies are types of "aggregate demand policy".

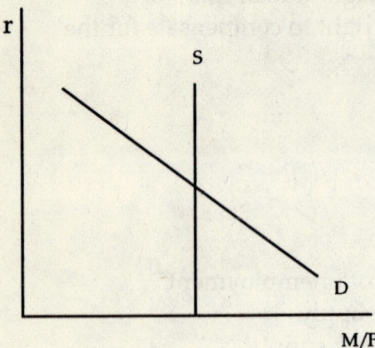

Chart 5–1

SUPPLY & DEMAND FOR REAL MONEY BALANCES

1. Show how an increase in the money supply affects the real interest rate.

2. Show how the change in the real interest rate that you found in the first step affects the quantity of investment demanded.

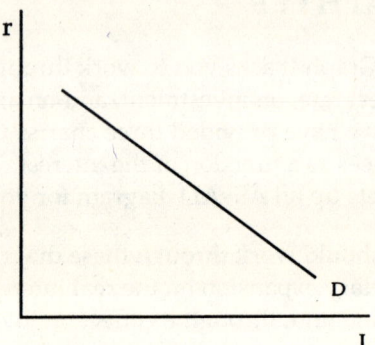

Chart 5–2

INVESTMENT DEMAND

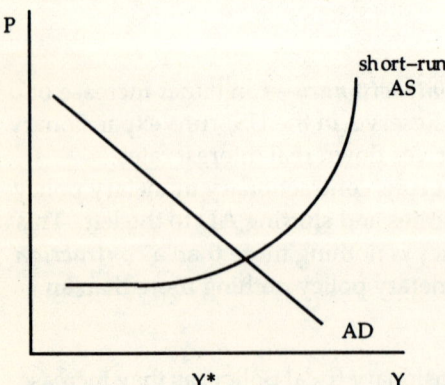

Chart 5–3

AS–AD IN THE SHORT RUN

3. How does the change in investment demand (above), affect aggregate demand?

What will happen to prices and output in the short run?

What will happen to prices and output in the long run?

REVIEW OF TECHNIQUE 5

Working With Graphs

It is often easier to work with graphs instead of equations—especially, as will often be the case in this text, when a qualitative answer is all that is needed. (Take, for example, the question: Do interest rates rise or fall in response to a monetary expansion? As we only need to know the direction of change in this case, a graph is all that is needed to provide a complete answer.) To make sure you are comfortable working with graphs, we provide a brief review of some techniques here.

Suppose you have an equation of the form:

$$Z = aX + bY,$$

where X, Y, and Z are three (unspecified) economic variables, and a and b are arbitrary constants, assumed to be greater than zero. First, a brief interpretation of this equation: the variable Z is a function of both X and Y. Because a and b are both assumed to be positive, Z will increase when either of these other variables increases, and will decrease when either falls.

Now, suppose we choose to graph this equation in Z and X. It is a convention that the dependent (endogenous) variable be on the vertical axis.* For this reason, we place Z on the vertical axis, and X on the horizontal axis. We then find the *slope* of this equation—the amount that Z changes in response to a 1 unit change in X.

In this case, our slope is the constant a (increase X by 1, holding Y constant, and see for yourself), so we know that our line slopes upward and to the right.

It is important to remember that we are holding our "extra" variable, Y, constant throughout this entire process. Once Y changes, we have to pick up the line we've graphed and move it to a place that's consistent with the new value of Y. We do this in Figure 5–4.

Let's suppose, for example, that Y increases by 1 unit. What happens to our line? We know that for any given value of X, Z will increase by $(1 \times b)$ units. This tells us that our line must shift upward by an amount b.

We could also hold Z constant in order to see how X could have to change to compensate for Y's increase. This approach is a little more difficult—at least in this case. (As the vertical and horizontal shifts will produce the same final line, you should always just use whichever method is easiest, given the problem you're working on.) We work through an example below:

---

* It is often the case with economic models that both the vertical and horizontal axes are occupied by endogenous variables: supply–demand and AS–AD models are an example. When this is the case we place price on the vertical axis.

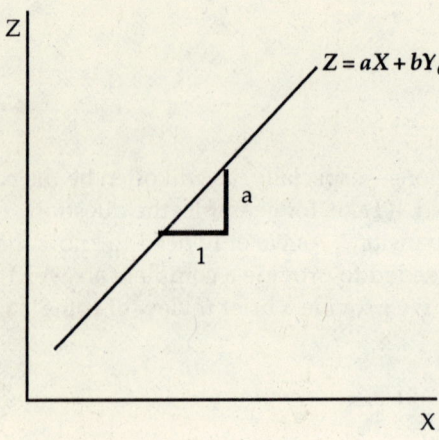

Figure 5-4

GRAPHING AN EQUATION

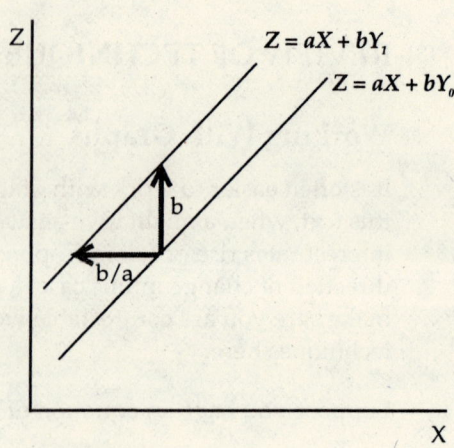

Figure 5-5

GRAPHING THE SHIFT OF A LINE

Suppose again that *Y* increases by 1 unit. To find how far (and in what direction) our line shifts *horizontally*, we hold *Z* constant and see how much *X* must change. We do this by first subtracting the quantity "*bY*" from both sides, so that

$$aX = \overline{Z} - bY.$$

We then divide each side by *a* to isolate the variable *X*. We end up with the equation

$$X = \frac{1}{a}\overline{Z} - \frac{b}{a}Y$$

which tells us that in order to maintain a constant value of Z when Y increases by 1 unit, X must fall (this is because there's a minus sign) by exactly (1 × *b/a*) units. We must shift our curve exactly this far to the left to accommodate.

An increase in X, of course, is nothing more than a shift along the line we've already drawn.

CROSSWORD

ACROSS

1. M/P represents the _____ money supply
3. both monetary and fiscal policy affect the aggregate _____ curve
6. type of output affected by supply side policies
8. rate of unemployment, labor market in equilibrium
9. type of monetary policy, decrease in M is an example
10. horizontal AS curve

DOWN

2. type of fiscal policy, tax cuts are an example
4. the central bank can only *directly* affect _____ money balances
5. vertical AS curve
7. theory of money, MV=PY

FILL-IN QUESTIONS

1. Output and the price level, in the aggregate supply/demand model, are _____ variables.

2. Taxes, transfers, government spending, and the money supply are all _____ variables.

3. The _____ curve describes how much output firms are willing to supply at different price levels.

4. The _____ curve describes the combinations of output and the price level at which the goods market and the financial market are simultaneously in equilibrium.

5. In the long run, when markets have time to fully clear, the aggregate supply curve is _____ , and output is equal to _____ .

6. In the short run, when prices do not have time to change at all, the aggregate supply curve is _____ .

7. When output is at its potential, there is only _____ unemployment, and unemployment is at its _____.

8. Under _____ supply assumptions, neither monetary nor fiscal policy can affect output. These assumptions are most appropriate in the _____.

9. Fiscal and monetary policy both affect the _____ curve.

10. Only changes in the _____ curve can affect output in the long run.

TRUE–FALSE QUESTIONS

T F 1. Keynesian supply assumptions are most appropriate in the long run, when output is at its potential.

T F 2. The Keynesian aggregate supply curve is flat.

T F 3. In the long run, output is fixed.

T F 4. Under Keynesian supply assumptions, price is fixed.

T F 5. Supply-side policies primarily change output in the short run.

T F 6. The AS/AD model explains how *potential output* changes in the short and medium run.

T F 7. The level of potential output is fixed in the short, medium and long run—and hence in the AS/AD model. It is the difference between output and its potential that varies.

T F 8. Monetary and fiscal policies primarily affect output in the long run.

T F 9. The assumption that the AS curve is flat in the short run is an over–simplification …it would be better modeled as being flat until output reaches its potential, but after that rises sharply, as not much more can be produced without driving up the price level.

T F 10. The natural rate of unemployment is zero.

MULTIPLE–CHOICE QUESTIONS

1. If government spending increases, the aggregate demand (AD) curve will
   a. shift in
   b. shift out
   c. remain constant
   d. change slope

2. If government spending increases, the aggregate supply (AS) curve will
   a. shift in
   b. shift out
   c. remain constant
   d. change slope

3. In the long run, when output is equal to potential output, an increase in government spending will raise
   a. output
   b. the price level
   c. taxes
   d. the money supply

4. In the long run, when output is equal to potential output, an increase in government spending will cause
   a. the price level to rise
   b. the price level to fall
   c. output to rise
   d. output to fall

5. Which of the following can shift the aggregate demand (AD) curve?
   a. only fiscal policy
   b. only monetary policy
   c. both fiscal & monetary policy
   d. none of the above

6. A "negative supply shock" is represented by _____ the aggregate supply (AS) curve.
   a. an inward (left) shift in
   b. an outward (right) shift in
   c. a movement along
   d. a change in the slope of

7. Over time, as prices adjust to bring markets into equilibrium, the slope of the aggregate supply (AS) curve will
   a. increase
   b. decrease
   c. remain constant
   d. fall to zero

8. Which of the following type of policy is most likely to increase output in the long run?
   a. supply side
   b. demand side
   c. neither
   d. both

9. An increase in the aggregate demand (AD) that exists at a given price level is represented, graphically, as _____ the AD curve.
   a. an inward (left) shift in
   b. an outward (right) shift in
   c. a movement along
   d. a change in the slope of

10. On the AD curve, which markets are in equilibrium?
    a. only the financial market
    b. only the goods market
    c. both goods & financial markets
    d. neither goods nor financial markets

CONCEPTUAL PROBLEMS

1. Why does the AD curve slope downward?

2. Why is short–run AS best represented by an upward–sloping curve, as opposed to a horizontal line (as in the Keynesian case)?

3. How can supply–side policies increase long–run AS when we've assumed potential output to be fixed at this horizon? (Recall that we've assumed potential output to be fixed in the AS–AD model because all factor inputs are assumed to be fixed. *This* assumption has not changed… what has?)

4. Which of the following constitute expansionary aggregate demand policy? Which constitute contractionary aggregate demand policy? *(For a review of expansionary and contractionary aggregate demand policy, see The Language of Economics, this chapter)*

   a) an increase in the benefits paid to welfare recipients

   b) a decrease in the capital gains tax

   c) an increase in the inheritance tax

   d) an increase in the number of available tax exemptions

   e) a decrease in social security benefits

   f) an increase in real money balances

   g) an increase in the velocity of money
   HINT: ask yourself what raising V will do to Y, holding P and M constant.

TECHNICAL PROBLEMS

1. When we graph AD, what variables do we hold constant?

2. Suppose that the government increases its spending.

   a) What will happen to price and output in the short–run?

   b) What will happen to price and output in the long–run?

   c) In what way do your answers in parts (a) and (b) make use of an *assumption*?

3. a) What is the immediate effect on real interest rates when the money supply is reduced?

   b) How does this affect individuals' investment decisions, and, as a result, AD?

6 AGGREGATE SUPPLY: WAGES, PRICES, AND UNEMPLOYMENT

FOCUS OF THE CHAPTER

- In this chapter we take a closer look at the aggregate supply curve, and notice that we can use it to examine the link between inflation and unemployment. We look at the process of adjustment from short–run to long–run equilibrium. We consider the effect of inflationary expectations.

- We also try to justify the positive relationship that the AS curve describes between the amount of output produced and the price level, and to explain why classical supply assumptions do not hold at all horizons *(this last part boils down to explaining why prices are "sticky," or slow to adjust)*.

SECTION SUMMARIES

1. The Aggregate Supply Curve and the Price Adjustment Mechanism

The aggregate supply curve describes the price adjustment mechanism of the economy. In the very short run, when prices are fixed, the AS curve is horizontal. In the medium run, because prices are able to partially adjust, it slopes upward. In the long run, when prices are able to fully adjust and all markets are in equilibrium, it is vertical.

The progression of time in the AS–AD model is represented by a gradual (counterclockwise) rotation of the AS curve. As time passes, prices are able to better adjust to old shocks, and output is less able to deviate from potential output. The rate at which the AS curve rotates reflects the rate at which prices in an economy are able to change—when prices adjust quickly to macroeconomic shocks, the AS rotates quickly, reaching its long–run equilibrium earlier than it would, were its prices less able to respond to changing market conditions.

We use the following equation to describe the adjustment of prices over time:

$$P_{t+1} = P_t \left[1 + \lambda(Y - Y^*)\right]$$

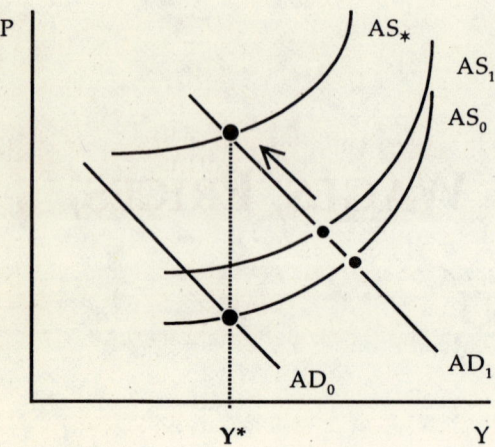

Figure 6-1

THE TRANSITION FROM THE SHORT RUN TO THE LONG RUN

> *We can visualize the transition form the short run to the long run as a series of inward shifts in the short-run AS curve.*

This simply says that the price level rises when output is above potential output, and fall when output is below potential output. λ describes the *speed of price adjustment*—high values of λ mean that prices adjust quickly to clear markets, so that output will return quickly to potential output. Low values mean that prices adjust slowly.

We also can visualize the transition from the short to the long run as a series of inward shifts in the short-run AS curve. Suppose, for example, that we had a monetary expansion at a time when output was already equal to potential output. The expansion would both increase both output and the price level in the short run, but over time prices would have to rise and output would have to return to its long-run equilibrium; the AS curve would have to shift gradually inward.

2. Inflation and Unemployment

The rate of unemployment fluctuates too much for unemployment to be at its natural rate all the time—the labor market must sometimes be out of equilibrium. There is also a systematic relationship between the rate of unemployment and the rate of *wage inflation*—the rate at which wages rise over time. The rate of wage inflation seems to rise as the unemployment rate falls.

This tradeoff between wage inflation and the rate of unemployment is captured by the *Phillips curve*. It is also described by the following equation:

$$g_w = -\varepsilon(u - u^*)$$

where g_w is the rate of wage inflation and u^* the natural rate of unemployment. ε is a measure of how responsive wages are to changes in the rate of unemployment.

While the original Phillips curve was intended only to capture the tradeoff between wage inflation and unemployment, over the years the Phillips curve has also been used to describe a similar relationship between the rates of inflation—the rate of increase in the price level—and unemployment.

3. Stagflation, Expected Inflation, and the Inflationary–Expectations Augmented Phillips Curve

The simple Phillips curve developed in section 6–2 is missing a very important element: it fails to consider the effect of people's *inflationary expectations*. People negotiate their nominal wage with a particular real wage in mind. If their expectations regarding the rate of inflation are wrong, this real wage will be higher or lower than they'd anticipated ...making them want to work more or less than they'd planned.

The *inflationary–expectations augmented Phillips curve*,

$$g_w - \pi^e = -\varepsilon(u - u^*),$$

and its more general form, in which the rate of price inflation (π) is substituted for the rate of wage inflation (g_w),

$$\pi - \pi^e = -\varepsilon(u - u^*),$$

take inflationary expectations into account by adding another factor which can affect the height of the Phillips curve. **The natural rate of unemployment is defined as the rate of unemployment at which actual inflation equals anticipated inflation** ...$u = u^*$ when $\pi = \pi^e$.

The equations above show that an increase in people's inflationary expectations will change the rate of wage or price inflation around which the inflation/unemployment trade–off occurs—the

The original Phillips curve was based on wage inflation rather than price inflation.

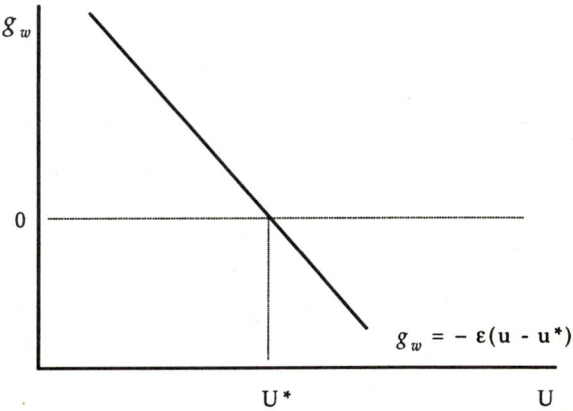

Figure 6 - 2

THE ORIGINAL PHILLIPS CURVE

(g_w = wage inflation)

The augmented Philips curve considers the effect of inflationary expectations.

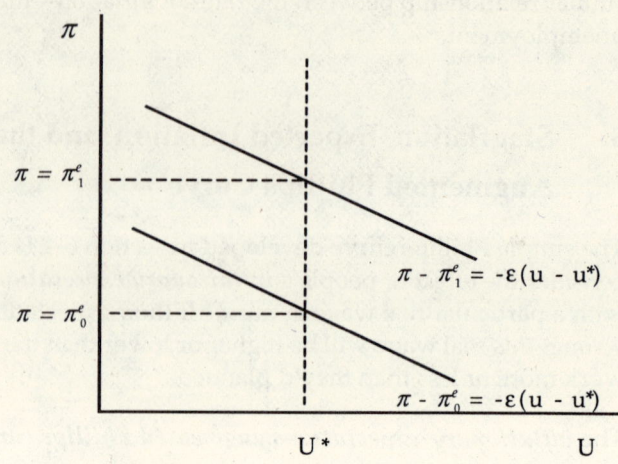

Figure 6 - 3

THE AUGMENTED PHILLIPS CURVE

point at which actual inflation equals anticipated inflation. The Phillips curve will shift upward.

Using the augmented Phillips curve, we can see how *stagflation*—a combination of high unemployment and high inflation—might occur. Once the economy is on a Phillips curve that includes a high expected rate of inflation, a negative shock can push the economy into recession, driving unemployment above its natural rate, and inflation below expected inflation. People's high inflationary expectations insure that, however far inflation falls below its expected level, it will still remain high.

Empirically, the short–run, inflationary–expectations augmented Phillips curve appears to be quite flat. The parameter ε in the above equation has been estimated to be roughly 0.5; it appears that 1/2 percentage point of inflation can be traded for 1 percentage point of unemployment in the short run.

4. The Rational Expectations Revolution

The theory of rational expectations states that nobody should make *predictable mistakes* when forming expectations. If I can form a better expectation than you, you're falling down and the job. Or at the least I ought to be able to sell you the right to use *my* expectation so you can make better decisions.

With rationally formed expectations, then, π^e on the Phillips curve should represent everyone's best guess about future inflation; unemployment should only deviate from its natural rate when something is happening that people don't know about. Is this a realistic assumption?

Economists today disagree about whether output and unemployment deviate from their long–term level entirely because of information problems (in which case people sure seem to be fooled for long periods of time), or whether there is some kind of wrench stuck in the wheels of the economy that prevents markets from adjusting as quickly to changes in expectations as they otherwise might. You will read more about this debate in the next section, and in chapter 20. Can you guess which explanation I lean towards?

5. The Wage–Unemployment Relationship: Why Are Wages Sticky?

When wages are unable to adjust instantaneously to insure that the labor market remains in equilibrium, we say they are *sticky*. There are a number of ways to explain why wages might take time to adjust, most of them falling into two categories: explanations in which markets clear but people lack the information they need to make good decisions (we call these *imperfect information* models), and explanations in which markets, for a variety of reasons, do not clear.

In the classic imperfect information model workers receive a raise but do not know whether it represents a cost of living increase, intended only to maintain their real wage in the face of rising prices, or a raise in real terms. Because they don't know what's happening, they decide to hedge their bets and act as if part, though not all, of their raise represents an increase in their real wage. This induces them to work more hours, increasing output and employment.

Because imperfect information models require that all markets be in equilibrium, they cannot explain the existence of involuntary unemployment—everyone who does not work in this model is unemployed by choice—the real wage that workers in their industry think they are receiving (remember, nobody actually knows their real wage here) is too low to make them want to work. For this reason, many economists favor models in which the labor market does not always clear.

There are several reasons that the labor market might not clear:

Firms negotiate wage agreements with those who have jobs (*insiders*), not with those who lack jobs (*outsiders*). Insiders like high wages, and do not care whether these wages leave others unemployed. Because it is costly for firms to hire and train new workers, these insiders are able to drive real wages above their market–clearing level, and create involuntary unemployment.

It may also be the case that some firms may pay *efficiency wages*—wages that exceed the market–clearing wage paid by other firms—to motivate their workers. At this higher wage, not everyone who wants a job can get one. Again, there is involuntary unemployment.

These two theories help to explain why involuntary unemployment exists, but do little to justify the existence of sticky *nominal* prices. To do this, either we need firms to find it costly to change their prices, in which case the price level and thus the nominal wage (the real wage times the price level) will be somewhat sticky, or we need nominal wages to be fixed for long periods of time.

Nominal wages may be fixed contractually for months or even years. The contract may be either formal or informal—a union labor contract or a verbal agreement kept by the firm and its workers in order to maintain a good long–term relationship. If contracts are not negotiated at the same time, wages will be even more sticky. Workers will be afraid to adjust their wages too much, as it will create too big a difference between their wages and the wages of others; nominal wages will therefore *not* be adjusted far enough to insure full–employment in any single negotiation. Output will be able to deviate from potential output for many rounds of negotiation.

If everyone could adjust their wages simultaneously and by the same amount, the economy would jump immediately to full–employment and output would be unable to deviate from potential output for any longer than the period of time between contract renegotiations. The difficulty associated with making sure that everyone does this is an example of a *coordination problem*.

6. From the Phillips Curve to the Aggregate Supply Curve

Okun's Law ties the level of employment to the level of output: unemployment in excess of the natural rate means output below potential output. Specifically, it states that a 1 percentage-point increase in the unemployment rate above its natural level will decrease output, relative to potential output, by 2%.

Wage increases can be translated into price increases if we assume that firms set their prices as a markup over labor costs. For example, suppose that the *unit labor cost*—the cost of paying someone to produce 1 unit of output—is $5. Firms might add $.50 to cover other costs, and set their price at $5 + $.50 = $5.50. Prices will rise with wages.

Using these two rules to transform unemployment and wage inflation along the Phillips curve, we find that output increases with the rate of inflation, or that higher prices are associated with higher levels of output—the aggregate supply relationship.

7. Supply Shocks

A *supply shock* is a disturbance which shifts the AS curve. Increases in the price of oil are a classic example of an *adverse supply shock*—a shock that shifts the short-run AS curve upward. Such increases raise production costs, drive up the price level and decrease output. They *may* decrease long-run aggregate supply as well.

Expansionary monetary and fiscal policy can alleviate the effects of adverse supply shock— when used in this way, they are considered *accommodating policies*. There is a cost associated with their use, however: an appropriately sized outward shift in the AD curve will return output to its previous value, but is likely also to cause considerable inflation.

Supply shocks can be favorable as well as adverse: an oil price decrease or a technological improvement will both shift the aggregate supply curve outward (increase potential output). This allows us greater freedom to increase aggregate demand without driving up inflation.

KEY TERMS

price adjustment mechanism
speed of price adjustment
Phillips curve
sticky wages
imperfect information
rational expectations
coordination approach
efficiency wage theory

staggered price adjustment
insider-outsider model
supply shock
adverse supply shock
monetary and fiscal accommodation
anticipated inflation
augmented Phillips curve
stagflation

GRAPH IT 6

After the OPEC oil shock of 1973 drove output down and the price level up in the US, people's inflationary expectations rose considerably. This increased the rate of inflation consistent with full–employment, shifting the augmented Phillips curve upward. This Graph It asks you to plot the rate of inflation against the rate of unemployment for the US both before and after the OPEC oil shock, and to identify the inflationary–expectations augmented Phillips curve belonging to each period.

Data is provided in Table 6–1 for the years 1961 through 1969 and 1976 through 1978. We suggest that you graph each combination of inflation and unemployment, noting the year that each point is associated with. When connected, they should form two downward–sloping (not necessarily straight) lines—the augmented Phillips curves for each of the periods we're considering. Use these curves to answer the two questions below. Assume that the natural rate of unemployment is 5.5%.

What must the expected rate of inflation have been during each period?

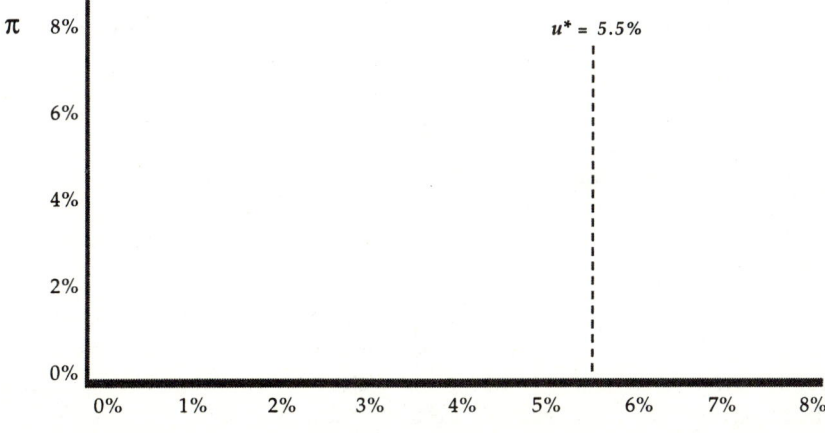

Chart 6 – 1

TABLE 6–1

Year	CPI	Rate of Inflation	Civilian Rate of Unemployment
1960	29.6	—	
1961	29.9	1.0%	6.7%
1962	30.2		5.5%
1963	30.6		5.7%
1964	31.0		5.2%
1965	31.5		4.5%
1966	32.4		3.8%
1967	33.4		3.8%
1968	34.8		3.6%
1969	36.7		3.5%
1975*	53.8	*(included for purposes of calculation only)*	
1976	56.9		7.7%
1977	60.6		7.1%
1978	65.2		6.1%

Source: See Tables C & F, Economic Data Tables

THE LANGUAGE OF ECONOMICS 6

Rational Expectations

Because none of us know what's going to happen in the future, we often have to base our decisions on what we *think* may happen; we form *expectations* about the future based on whatever information is currently available to us, and use those expectations to make decisions. (Should I go to the beach today? No. It's probably going to rain...)

People form expectations in any number of different ways. They might, perhaps, consult the stars. They might assume that whatever has happened in the recent past will continue happen.

They might try to adjust their previous expectations to correct what they now know was wrong with them.

A number of economists now believe, however, that it doesn't matter *how* people form their expectations as long as the errors that they make cannot be predicted. When this is the case, they say that expectations are *rational*—that all available information has been used to form them.

Imagine what it would mean if people made systematic, predictable errors when forecasting future events. Workers who systematically underestimated future inflation would consistently negotiate wages that were too low. Runners who made systematic errors about the weather would consistently dress too warmly, or fail to have their rain hats in predictable downpours. People able to forecast these errors—those able to form more accurate expectations—would be able to provide a valuable service to these folks. They could tell the workers what inflation is likely to be over the next three years, and the runners whether or not it is likely to rain on any given day. In fact, this service would be *so* valuable that they would probably be able to make a good bit of money. It is hard to imagine that such people would not exist…

When expectations are rational, it is assumed that systematic, predictable errors like the ones mentioned above do not occur. They should not be able to because, if they are predictable, someone is likely to come along and predict them. Once this happens, these errors will disappear.

REVIEW OF TECHNIQUE 6

Reading Equations

In Review of Technique 5, we discussed how to translate an equation into a graph. Graphing an equation is often the easiest and most useful way to make sense of it. It is also possible, however, to derive quite a bit of information from the visual inspection of an equation. As you begin read more articles and learn more advanced theory, this skill—you can think of it as the ability to "read" equations—will become increasingly more valuable to you. For that reason, and because there *are* a few equations in this text, we work through an example for you here.

Let's use a simple Phillips curve:

$$g_w = -\varepsilon(u - u^*)$$

What does this equation tell us?

It tells us in general that there is a relationship between wage inflation and the rate of unemployment. It tells us more precisely that the further the rate of unemployment rises above its full–employment level, the more quickly prices will fall ($g_w < 0$ when $u > u^*$), and the further the rate of unemployment falls below its full–employment level, the more quickly prices will rise ($g_w > 0$ when $u < u^*$).

This equation also tells us that there is no wage inflation when unemployment is at its natural rate ($g_w = 0$ when $u = u^*$). This is radically different than the result we find with the augmented

Phillips curve—that wage inflation equals expected wage inflation at the natural rate of unemployment.

To complete our interpretation of this equation, we must be careful to explain the purpose of the parameter ε (pronounced "epsilon"). What is it? How does it affect the relationship between π and u? To answer these questions, we must look again at our original equation, which tells that a one percentage point increase in the rate of unemployment will raise the rate of wage inflation by an amount ε, or that ε controls the degree to which output can be exchanged for wage inflation. When ε is high, a lot of inflation can be traded for a little unemployment. When ε is low, a little inflation must be traded for a lot of unemployment—an unattractive proposition if one is trying to reduce the rate of inflation. You can imagine why policy makers might want an estimate of this parameter.

Try interpreting other equations that you find in the text. In time, you'll be able to do this in your sleep.

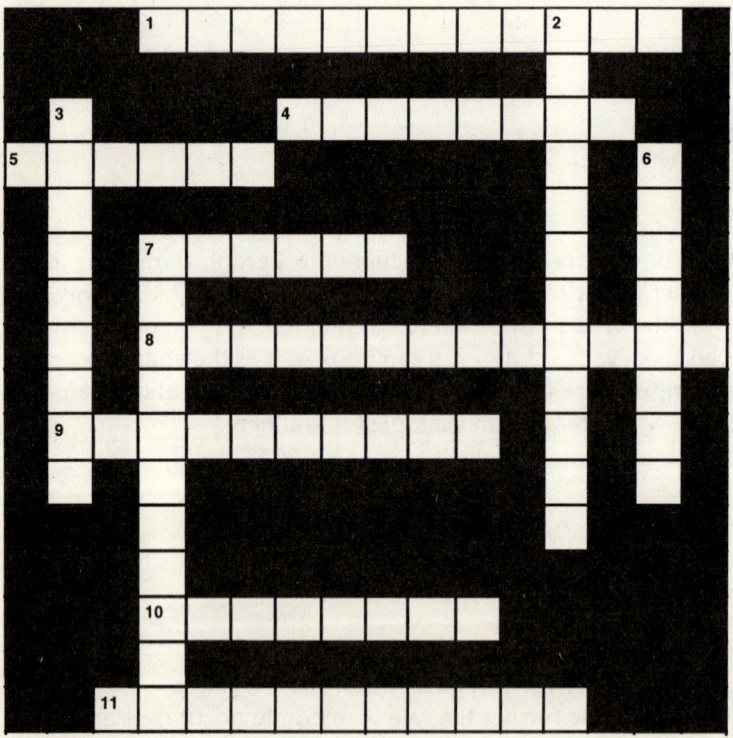

CROSSWORD

ACROSS

1 can be traded for inflation in the short run
4 curve, provides same information as AS
5 output can diverge from potential output in the short run because prices are
7 type of shock, shifts AS curve
8 using monetary/fiscal policy to counter real effects of a supply shock
9 type of wage, set high to motivate workers
10 sit at the bargaining table
11 important element in market–clearing explanations for short run AS curve

DOWN

2 missing from simple Phillips curve
3 prices set at different times are
6 type of expectation, no systematic errors made
7 high unemployment and high inflation

FILL-IN QUESTIONS

1. If output is above potential output, prices will eventually _____ the next period.

2. If unemployment is *below* its natural rate, wages will eventually _____ the next period.

3. When wages adjust slowly, over time, rather than being completely flexible, we say they are _____.

4. Sluggish wage adjustment can cause the _____ market to be out of equilibrium, and create _____.

5. Output and unemployment are related in the following way: when unemployment falls, output must _____.

6. The _____ curve illustrates the medium run tradeoff between inflation and unemployment.

7. The _____ curve illustrates the medium run tradeoff between output and the price level.

8. _____ suggests that wages might be set above the market clearing level in order to motivate workers.

9. The _____ model of price adjustment suggests that wages might be set above the market clearing level because those who are unemployed do not participate in wage bargaining.

10. A _____ is a disturbance whose immediate impact is to shift the AS curve.

TRUE–FALSE QUESTIONS

T F 1. The economy is always at full employment.

T F 2. The economy is never at full employment.

T F 3. There is a tradeoff, in the medium run, between inflation unemployment.

T F 4. There is a tradeoff, in the long run, between inflation unemployment.

T F 5. The tradeoff between inflation and unemployment can be easily exploited by politicians.

T F 6. In the augmented Phillips curve, inflation depends on people's *expectations* as well as on the level of unemployment.

T F 7. Unemployment is at its natural rate, on the augmented Phillips curve, when inflation is equal to expected inflation.

T F 8. When wages are sticky, money is neutral only in the long run.

T F 9. In the augmented Phillips curve, expected inflation is translated only partially into actual inflation.

T F 10. An adverse supply shock causes lower prices and lower output.

MULTIPLE–CHOICE QUESTIONS

1. Which of the following is *not* a necessary component of the price adjustment mechanism described by the aggregate supply curve?

   a. production function
   b. efficiency wage theory
   c. price–cost relation
   d. Phillips curve

2. Adverse supply shocks

   a. increase prices and decrease output
   b. decrease prices and increase output
   c. increase prices and increase output
   d. decrease prices and decrease output

3. According to Okun's Law, when unemployment rises from of 5.5% (its natural rate) to 6.5%, output will:

   a. rise by 1%
   b. fall by 1%
   c. rise by 2%
   d. fall by 2%

4. The position of the aggregate supply (AS) curve depends on

   a. potential output
   b. past prices
   c. both
   d. neither

5. Which of the following approaches explains the tradeoff between inflation and unemployment in a *market-clearing* context?

   a. imperfect information
   b. coordination problems
   c. efficiency–wage theory
   d. insider-outsider model

6. An increase in the price of oil is an adverse supply shock because it

   a. decreases interest rates
   b. increases labor costs
   c. decreases consumer confidence
   d. increases materials prices

7. Which of the following models is unable to explain the existence of involuntary unemployment?

   a. imperfect information
   b. long term wage contracts
   c. efficiency–wage theory
   d. insider-outsider model

8. Stagflation consists of

   a. high inflation & high unemployment
   b. high inflation & low unemployment
   c. low inflation & high unemployment
   d. low inflation & low unemployment

9. When stagflation occurs expected inflation

   a. exceeds actual inflation
   b. is equal to actual inflation
   c. is very high
   d. is very low

10. Monetary policy will be *accommodating* if, after an adverse supply shock, the real money supply

    a. is increased
    b. is decreased
    c. is kept constant
    d. is given away

CONCEPTUAL PROBLEMS

1. How are output and unemployment connected?

2. What information does the parameter λ in the equation below give you?

$$P_{t+1} = P_t \left[1 + \lambda \left(Y - Y^* \right) \right]$$

   What do you suppose would happen to the business cycle if λ increased? How would an increase in λ affect the government's decisions to use fiscal or monetary policy to stabilize the economy (keep output and employment close to their long–run values)?

3. Should accommodating monetary or fiscal policy always be used to bring output back to its full–employment level after a supply shock? Explain.

TECHNICAL PROBLEMS

1. Suppose that, in an economy initially at full–employment, the central bank increases the money supply.

   a) How will this affect output and unemployment in the short run?

   b) How will this affect output and unemployment in the long run?

   c) Use an AS–AD graph to show the transition from the short run to the long run.

2. Suppose that an economy initially at full–employment is hit by an adverse supply shock.

   a) What will happen to output and the price level in the short run?

   b) What will happen to output and the price level in the long run?

   c) If left to its own devices, the economy will follow an adjustment process very similar to the one you described in part (c) of the last question. Suppose, however, that the government intervenes. Show, using an AS–AD graph, how the government can use accommodating monetary or fiscal policy to return output and unemployment to their long run values.

7 THE ANATOMY OF INFLATION AND UNEMPLOYMENT

FOCUS OF THE CHAPTER

- In this chapter we examine the costs of both inflation and unemployment, and consider some of the policy questions that are raised by the tradeoff between them.

- We also look very carefully at the "anatomy" of unemployment—the different types of and reasons for unemployment; the difference between unemployment with high frequency and with high duration; and the effect of age distribution, and of other demographic and policy considerations on the natural rate.

SECTION SUMMARIES

1. The Anatomy of Unemployment

Unemployment in the US can be characterized by 5 "stylized facts":

   a) Different groups of people ("groups" in this case are defined by age, race, and experience) have very different unemployment rates.

   b) There are substantial flows into and out of the *unemployment pool*—the number of people who are unemployed at any given point in time. The number of people entering and leaving this pool is large relative to the number of people in and out of it; for this reason, we say there is high *labor market turnover*.

   c) The causes of the flows into this pool are somewhat cyclical in nature: layoffs tend to be high during recessions, while voluntary quits are high during booms.

   d) Most people who become unemployed remain so for only a short time.

   e) The unemployment pool is made up largely of people who are unemployed for long periods of time.

It is important to remember that that people can only be in the unemployment pool if they are also in the *labor force*—either working or actively seeking work. Individuals can thus enter and leave the unemployment pool by entering and leaving the labor force, as well as by losing and finding jobs. *Discouraged workers*—people who would like jobs but have given up looking for them—are not considered a part of the labor force, and thus, technically, are not unemployed.

It is also important to understand how the *aggregate*, or overall, rate of unemployment is formed. Because the labor force is made up of a number of different groups, many of which have radically different rates of unemployment, we must take a *weighted average* of them to find the overall rate:

$$u = w_1 u_1 + w_2 u_2 + \cdots + w_n u_n$$

The w_i, here, are "weights," equal to the fraction of the labor force represented by each group.

The u_i are the unemployment rates for each group. The aggregate rate can change either because the unemployment rate of one or more groups changes, or because the fraction of the labor force that they represent changes.

Finally, it is useful to distinguish between *cyclical* and *frictional* unemployment. Frictional unemployment, as we have already learned, is the unemployment that exists when the economy is at full employment, and results from job search. Cyclical unemployment is unemployment in excess of this amount. Because of the connection between output and unemployment, it tends to move with the business cycle.

2. Full Employment

The natural rate of unemployment is determined by a number of factors, some which affect the *duration of unemployment*—the average length of time person remains out of work—and others which affect the *frequency of unemployment*—the average number of times in a given period that workers become unemployed.

The duration of unemployment depends on the state of the economy (i.e., recession/boom). It is also affected by the organization of the labor market (e.g., the presence or absence of employment agencies), the demographic makeup of the labor force (i.e., the fraction of the labor force represented by different groups), and the amount of time people are willing or able to spend seeking new jobs. This last depends in part on the availability of unemployment benefits, which reduce the cost of joblessness as measured by the *replacement ratio*—the ratio of after–tax income while unemployed to after–tax income while employed.

The frequency of unemployment is determined by both the rate at which new workers enter the labor force, and the variability of labor demand across different firms in the economy (some firms will be shrinking, some growing; people will need move to those firms which are creating jobs for them).

The natural rate of unemployment varies over time, both because of changes in the composition of the labor force and because the natural rates of unemployment for the different groups that make up the labor force vary. The natural rate of unemployment is currently estimated to be between 5% and 6%.

Economists have tended to think of the natural rate of unemployment as a policy variable, affected by demographic factors, unemployment benefits and jobs programs, but unaffected by business cycle fluctuations. It is also possible, however, that extended periods of unemployment can raise the natural rate: workers may lose marketability or job skills while unemployed, or may learn to use the unemployment system more effectively. This is known as *unemployment hysteresis*.

3. The Costs of Unemployment

The largest single cost of unemployment is lost production. *Okun's Law*—an estimate of the relationship between output and unemployment—states that a one percentage point increase in the rate of unemployment will reduce output by 2%. There are also distributional costs—the poor, for example, tend to be more strongly affected by changes in the rate of unemployment than the rich.

4. The Costs of Inflation

Inflation is also costly …or can be. There is little cost associated with moderate levels of *perfectly anticipated inflation*—rates of inflation that are neither higher nor lower than anyone expects. The cost of holding currency does rise slightly, with higher inflation the value of any currency will erode more quickly. There is also a small cost associated with changing nominal prices—reprinting prices on signs and menus, for example. With low levels of inflation this cost is quite small.

Because contracts are negotiated with a level of anticipated inflation (π^e) in mind, there are much more substantial costs associated with *imperfectly anticipated inflation*. For example, a banker who makes a loan with a 5% nominal interest rate expects to receive a real return of $5\% - \pi^e$ (recall that the real interest rate is just the nominal interest rate – the rate of inflation). The student who receives this loan expects to pay a real interest rate of $5\% - \pi^e$. If the rate of inflation is higher than either of them expects, the bank receives a lower real interest rate than it had anticipated. The student pays a lower real interest rate than he or she had expected to. In short, the student wins, the bank loses. The opposite will be true if the rate of inflation is lower than expected; in this case, the real interest rate will be higher than anyone anticipates. Creditors will benefit; debtors will be hurt.

The effect of unanticipated inflation is mostly distributional.

5. Inflation and Indexation: Inflation–Proofing the Economy

The major ways that unanticipated inflation redistributes income are through loans and wage contracts. An alternative to negotiating contracts in nominal terms and worrying about the level of future inflation is to *index* them—tie their payoffs to the inflation rate. Wage contracts, for example, might include automatic cost of living adjustments, or COLA provisions, which tie nominal wages to the CPI. Interest rates might be adjusted for inflation as well.

Of course, the CPI is not a perfect measure of inflation, and by tying wages and interest rates to this measure we may just be trading one source of uncertainty for another. Indexation also makes it more difficult for the economy to adjust to supply shocks, as it prevents real wages from rising or falling without explicit negotiation. Indexation is used widely only in countries with extremely high rates of inflation.

6. Is a Little Inflation Good for the Economy?

Some economists argue that low rates of inflation can be beneficial, as they allow real wages to adjust when necessary, without explicit negotiation. This is controversial, however, and a significant departure from the traditional belief that zero inflation is always best.

7. The Political Economy of Inflation and Unemployment

Policymakers have the responsibility to choose the adjustment path that will return the economy to full–employment after it is hit by an adverse shock, choosing the combination of inflation and unemployment that will exist during the transition. They can increase aggregate demand rapidly, stabilizing output at the expense of high prices, or can fight inflation at the expense of a slow recovery. The *sacrifice ratio*—the percentage of output lost for each one percentage point reduction in the inflation rate—provides an estimate of how costly this last choice is likely to be.

In a perfect society, political leaders would weigh the costs and benefits involved, choosing the combination that would be best for their people. It has been suggested, however, that in our society, politicians manipulate the economy in order to aid their own reelection. The pattern of election year booms and mid–term recessions that this supposedly generates (empirical evidence is mixed) is called the *political business cycle*.

KEY TERMS

sacrifice ratio
Okun's law
labor force
unemployed person
unemployment pool
frictional unemployment
cyclical unemployment
spell of unemployment
search unemployment
frequency of unemployment
unemployment hysteresis

replacement ratio
reservation wage
insider-outsider theory
employment stability
experience rating
reporting effects
indexation
cost-of-living adjustment (COLA)
political business cycle theory
misery index

TABLE 7-1

Year	Civilian Rate of Unemployment
1981	7.6
1982	9.7
1983	9.6
1984	7.5
1985	7.2
1986	7.0
1987	6.2
1988	5.5
1989	5.3
1990	5.6
1991	6.8
1992	7.5
1993	6.9
1994	6.1
1995	5.6
1996	5.4
1997	4.9
1998	4.5
1999	4.2

Source: See Table C, Economic Data Tables

GRAPH IT 7

Although we generally use measures of output and output growth in order to determine whether the economy is doing well, we can also look at changes in the rate of unemployment. This Graph It asks you to chart the rate of unemployment in the US between the years 1981 and 1999, and to compare your graph to the one you created in chapter 1.

Can you see a connection between the rate of unemployment the growth rate of output?

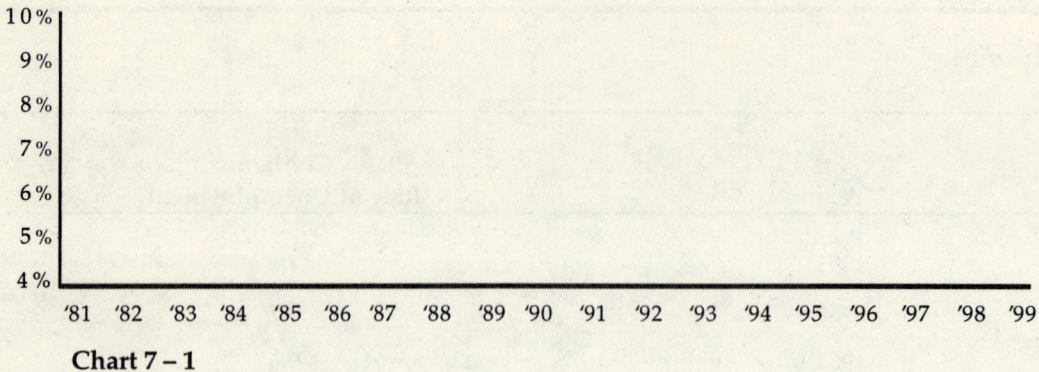

Chart 7 – 1

THE LANGUAGE OF ECONOMICS 7

The Definition of Unemployment

To be considered unemployed, in the economic sense, one must be more than simply jobless. It is also necessary to be *actively searching* for employment—i.e. you must (1) have actively looked for work during the last 4 weeks, (2) be waiting to be recalled to a job after having been laid off, or (3) be waiting to report to a new job that will begin within the next 4 weeks.

Those who do not have jobs and are not actively seeking them are not considered to be a part of the labor force; they are neither considered employed nor considered unemployed. This is an important point to remember, as it highlights the fact that there are people without jobs, people who may have given up looking because they believe themselves unemployable, who, because of the way that we measure unemployment, are not captured by unemployment statistics. These *discouraged workers* represent a very real social problem—one that is not measured at all by unemployment statistics.

REVIEW OF TECHNIQUE 7

Weighting

In order to construct a statistic that provides information about a diverse population, it is necessary to account for differences across groups within that population. As these groups are likely to be different sizes, a statistic will best represent the population if the characteristics of smaller groups affect it less than those of larger ones. Weighting—multiplying the statistic for each individual group by the fraction of the population that group represents—is an effective way to guarantee this.

Let's suppose, for example, that there are two groups of people in our society with very different sleeping habits. People in group A tend to sleep an average of 4 hours a night; people in group B tend to sleep an average of 10. If there are 10 people in group A and 40 in group B, the average number of hours that the 50 people in our society spend asleep will be equal to
((10/50) x 4) + ((40/50) x 10), or 8.8.

Multiplying each statistic by the fraction of the population it represents and then adding these statistics together is called taking a *weighted average*

CROSSWORD

ACROSS

4 came up with a "law" relating changes in output and unemployment
7 ratio, amount of after-tax income while unemployed to after tax income while employed
8 lose when inflation is higher than anticipated
9 percentage decline in GDP that results from a 1 percentage point increase in the rate of unemployment
11 says long periods of unemployment raise natural rate
12 type of worker, no longer actively seeking job
13 suspension of work without pay lasting at least 7 days

DOWN

1 rate of unemployment, synonymous with frictional
2 these guys benefit when inflation is higher than anticipated
3 ties nominal wages to price level & rate of inflation
5 method used to compose aggregate statistics from individual ones
6 age group with highest rate of frictional unemployment
10 index, attempts to measure political effect of inflation and unemployment

FILL-IN QUESTIONS

1. An unforeseen increase in the rate of inflation benefits _____, at the expense of _____.

2. An *expected* increase in the rate of inflation hurts people who hold _____.

3. The _____ is the amount of output (expressed in percentage terms) that is lost *for each one point reduction* in the inflation rate.

4. _____ is an empirical estimate of the amount of output (expressed, again, in percentage terms) which must be given up for each one percent decrease in the rate of unemployment.

5. To be considered unemployed, it is not enough to be without a job. An unemployed person must also count him/herself in the _____ (must be actively looking for work, or waiting to start a new job).

6. An increase in unemployment benefits will _____ the natural rate of unemployment.

7. The _____ of unemployment describes, on average, the flow into the unemployment pool.

8. The _____ of unemployment describes the amount of time the average person remains in that pool.

9. The _____ of unemployment is the level at which the flows into and out of the labor pool exactly balance.

10. If periods of high unemployment tended to raise the natural rate, there would be _____.

TRUE–FALSE QUESTIONS

T F 1. The rate of unemployment is a *flow variable*.
(See "The Language of Economics 3" for a review of stock and flow variables)

T F 2. A person is considered a part of the labor force as soon as they are old enough to work.

T F 3. People can move in and out of the labor force over their lifetimes.

T F 4. The effects of unemployment are mostly distributional.

T F 5. The effects of unanticipated inflation are mostly distributional.

T F 6. The costs of moderate (single digit) anticipated inflation are fairly trivial.

T F 7. The costs of *high* (triple & quadruple digit) anticipated inflation are quite serious.

T F 8. Optimally, the unemployment rate should be zero.

T F 9. An increase in unemployment benefits is likely to increase the duration of the average spell of unemployment.

T F 10. The natural rate of unemployment cannot be changed by government policies.

MULTIPLE–CHOICE QUESTIONS

1. Which of the following is present when the economy is at full–employment?
   a. cyclical unemployment
   b. frictional unemployment
   c. both
   d. neither

2. Unemployment benefits allow/create
    a. longer job search
    b. greater employment stability
    c. both
    d. neither

3. An unemployed person is likely to turn down a job offer if the wage they are offered is below their
    a. replacement ratio
    b. reservation wage
    c. experience rating
    d. COLA

4. *Anticipated* inflation transfers wealth from
    a. creditors to debtors
    b. debtors to creditors
    c. poor to rich
    d. none of the above

5. *Unanticipated* inflation transfers wealth from
    a. creditors to debtors
    b. debtors to creditors
    c. poor to rich
    d. none of the above

6. The _____ ratio is the ratio of one's after–tax income while unemployed to one's after–tax income while employed.
    a. replacement
    b. sacrifice
    c. benefit
    d. indexation

7. Wages and prices should most clearly be indexed in countries with
    a. high inflation
    b. low inflation
    c. both
    d. neither

8. _____ theory predicts that the business cycle will move predictably with the election cycle in countries with two (or more) party democracies.
    a. political business cycle
    b. insider–outsider
    c. growth
    d. inflation

9. Which of the following is a measure of the political cost of inflation and unemployment?
    a. sacrifice ratio
    b. replacement ratio
    c. misery index
    d. reservation wage

10. The natural rate of unemployment is currently estimated to be about
    a. 0
    b. 2% to 3%
    c. 5% to 6%
    d. 8% to 9%

CONCEPTUAL PROBLEMS

1. Name four ways a person might enter the unemployment pool.

2. Name three ways a person might leave the unemployment pool.

3. What costs are associated with unemployment?

4. Unemployment insurance, because it allows people to spend more time searching for a job than they would otherwise be able to, can increase the natural rate of unemployment. Is this something that policymakers should be concerned with? Explain.

5. Should zero unemployment be a goal? Why or why not?

6. Should zero inflation be a goal? Justify your answer.

TECHNICAL PROBLEMS

1. Suppose that the natural rate of unemployment is 5% for adults and 10% for teenagers. If teenagers make up 40% of the labor force (and adults the other 60%), what is natural rate for the labor force as a whole?

   If the number of teenagers increased to 60% (and the number of adults fell to 40%), how would the overall natural rate change? Would the level of full–employment (*potential*) output be higher or lower than in the previous case?

2. Suppose that in a typical month, 4 people out of every 100 leave their jobs. If 2 of these people remain out of work for 1 month, 1 remains out of work for 3 months, and the last remains out of work (but in the labor force) for 1 year, what is the average duration of unemployment? What is the unemployment rate? *(Hint for calculating the unemployment rate: You need to figure out how many people, out of each 100, will be unemployed in a typical month.)*

8 POLICY

FOCUS OF THE CHAPTER

- This chapter highlights three factors that hinder policymakers: lags, expectations, and uncertainty. It also considers the choice of targets and implementation strategies for particular policy goals.

SECTION SUMMARIES

1. Lags in the Effects of Policy

In practice, it is very difficult to use policy to stabilize output. First, it is necessary to determine whether a disturbance is temporary or permanent (or at least very persistent). If it is temporary, it may be best to do nothing at all—especially if you're using fiscal policy. The effects of the disturbance may have worn off before a policy change is felt, and the policy change may actually *destabilize* output.

There are a number of delays, or *lags*, that make it difficult to implement a policy in any kind of timely manner. First, it takes time to recognize that a policy response is needed at all—the policymaker must identify that there is some problem that needs to be addressed. The amount of time that passes before this happens is called the *recognition lag*. After recognizing that a policy response is needed, it will take more time to decide what policy should be used. This delay is referred to as the *decision lag*. It may take time to implement that policy; if so, then there is also an *action lag*. The recognition, decision, and lags, when grouped together make up the *inside lag*, or the amount of time that passes after a disturbance hits the economy before a policy response is implemented. This will be a *discrete lag*—a fixed amount of time. In contrast, the *outside lag*, or the amount of time required for a policy to have its full effect once it has been implemented, will be a *distributed lag*. These policy effects will be cumulative, gradually rolling through the economy.

Monetary policy has a very short inside lag; with the existing structure of the Federal Reserve System, the decision lag is brief and the action lag nearly zero. Open market operations can be undertaken almost as soon as the decision to use them is made. Fiscal policy has a fairly long inside lag (just imagine Congress debating the adoption of a stabilization policy). For this reason, monetary policy is used more frequently than fiscal policy to stabilize output.

The outside lag associated with monetary policy is longer than the outside lag associated with fiscal policy.

2. Expectations and Reactions

Policymakers do not know the precise values of the multipliers that tell them how strongly their policy will affect aggregate demand. They also do not know how people will react to the implementation of their policy: Will consumers believe that a "permanent" tax cut is really temporary? That a temporary tax cut will last longer than policymakers claim?

Credibility can be a problem for policymakers. If people do not believe the announcements that a government makes, their expectations will be unaffected and they may not respond to policy changes the way that policymakers anticipate.

To make things even more troublesome, the implementation of a policy may itself affect expectations. Lucas, in his *econometric policy evaluation critique* (often referred to simply as the *Lucas critique*), argues that many existing macroeconomic models cannot be used to study the effects of policy changes because the way that people respond to those changes depends on the policy that is being followed.

3. Uncertainty and Economic Policy

Stabilization policy could fail because an unforeseen event, such as a natural disaster or change in consumer preferences, occurs. It could fail also if policymakers use the wrong model to analyze the impact of their policy, or because they use the right model, but with badly estimated parameters. None of us knows enough about the true structure and workings of the economy to predict accurately and confidently all of the effects of any policy.

When we are uncertain about the size of the multipliers associated with different policies, it may be a good idea to use a mix of different policies—mildly expansionary fiscal policy for example, with mildly expansionary monetary policy. With luck, the unexpected effects of both policies will cancel each other out.

The more uncertain we are, the less willing we should be to use activist policy. A combination of active policy and poor information runs the risk of introducing unnecessary fluctuations into the economy.

4. Dynamic Policy and Information Feedback

A policymaker can use either *gradualist* or *cold–turkey* policies to reach an objective. Each has its advantages and disadvantages.

Gradualist policies move the economy slowly toward its target. This is a drawback if you're in a hurry, but it does allow policymakers to monitor a policy's effects as they roll through the economy, and to fine–tune their policy as new information becomes available. Contractionary policies also tend to produce fewer recessionary side effects when they are implemented gradually, as the effects of the contraction are spread out over a longer period of time. Unfortunately gradualist policies can also lack credibility; often they move so slowly it doesn't look as if the government is doing anything at all. And we've seen that people's expectations can play an important role in determining a policy's success or failure.

Cold–turkey policies solve the credibility problem; this is the main rationale for using them. They can produce severe side effects, however, so authorities will usually choose another strategy if one is available.

Policymakers divide variables into several different classes when they formulate and implement policy: *targets*, or a set of variables with some desired value (a real interest rate of 4%, for example, or an inflation rate of 2%); *instruments*, or the variables whose value a policymaker manipulates to achieve these targets (nominal money balances are an example); and *indicators*, a set of variables whose value signals the policy's success or failure. A particular variable, the nominal interest rate for example, can switch categories as policymakers' tactics change—sometimes used as an indicator, other times used as a target.

There are two types of targets: *ultimate* and *intermediate*. An ultimate targets is just what it sounds like—the goal we hope to achieve through the implementation of a policy (2% inflation, for example, or 5% output growth). An intermediate target is something a little trickier; because sometimes these ultimate targets are a little hard to shoot for, an intermediate target is less directly important but easier to measure and attain (2% money growth to correspond to that ultimate goal of 2% inflation, for example).

5. Activist Policy

Proponents of activist policy argue that we should use monetary and fiscal policy to reduce economic fluctuations. While some economists argue against the use of active policy entirely, the authors feel that active policy is appropriate as long as policymakers recognize the uncertainty involved, take into account the lags associated with their policy, and are appropriately modest in their attempts to counteract the effects of disturbances.

Critics of activist monetary policy argue that the monetary authority should be forced to follow rules rather than being able to use policy at its discretion. It is worth noting here that the current chairman of the Federal Reserve, Alan Greenspan, is a very activist policymaker; critics of activist monetary policy would take serious issue with his style of management.

6. Which Target? A Practical Application

Suppose we have two policy goals: first, keep actual GDP close to potential GDP, and second, keep inflation low. What targets should we choose?

REAL GDP: This works really well when we have a good estimate of potential GDP. We can aim straight for a small to zero output gap, and guarantee ourselves low inflation in the bargain. When we don't have a good estimate of potential GDP, however, we can dramatically over– or undershoot. Suppose that the growth rate of potential GDP is only 2%, compared to the 4% we imagine; policymakers end up pushing the economy faster than can be sustained, and produce undesirable inflation.

NOMINAL GDP: This can be safer, because it captures the effects of a policy on both output and inflation. Now if we overestimate the growth rate of potential output, our nominal GDP target limits the potential inflationary side–effects… with nominal growth at, say, 4%, even zero growth in potential output can't produce more than 4% inflation in the long run. (The growth rate of nominal GDP turns out to be roughly equal to the growth rate of real GDP plus the growth rate of inflation.) This still isn't perfect—especially if we *underestimate* the level and/or growth rate of potential output—but it's *safe*.

INFLATION: And then you can just give up on the first goal altogether, and hope it will take care of itself. Some economists believe that it will… others are more doubtful.

7. Dynamic Inconsistency and Rules Versus Discretion

This section argues that well–intentioned policymakers who have the discretion to implement activist policies will be tempted to act, in the short run, in a way that is not consistent with their long–run goals. Suppose, for example, that a policymaker has made a credible commitment to low inflation. The decline in people's inflationary expectations will cause the augmented Phillips curve to shift downwards, enabling expansionary policies to be used with less of an inflationary effect. This changes the output/inflation tradeoff, and taking a fresh look at the situation, the policymaker may at this point be willing to allow a little inflation in exchange for a short-run increase in output and decrease in the rate of unemployment.

When rational, well–intended policymakers find it optimal to deviate from policies (i.e., low inflation) that they have committed to, we say that these policies are *dynamically inconsistent.* Of course, policymakers can't do this sort of thing very often; ultimately it will destroy their credibility, and without credibility the exercise won't work.

KEY TERMS

inside lag	distributed lag
outside lag	econometric model
recognition lag	credibility
decision lag	targets
action lag	instruments
discrete lag	indicators
real GDP target	marginal loss function
inflation target	activist policies
Lucas (econometric policy evaluation) critique	fine tuning
	rules vs. discretion
multiplier uncertainty	activist rules
diversification of policy instruments	dynamic inconsistency
loss function	dynamic programming

TABLE 8 – 1

Year	Percentage Change in Real Money Balances	Year	Percentage Change in Real Money Balances
1979	– 3.1	1990	– 1.5
1980	– 4.4	1991	– 1.1
1981	– 0.5	1992	– 1.4
1982	2.5	1993	– 1.4
1983	7.9	1994	– 2.1
1984	4.1	1995	1.3
1985	4.3	1996	1.8
1986	7.5	1997	3.4
1987	0.0	1998	7.1
1988	1.6	1999	3.6
1989	0.6		

Source: Calculations based on data from the Federal Reserve Economic Data archive

GRAPH IT 8

This Graph It gives you a look at the direction of U.S. monetary policy over the last few decades. The table below provides data on real money balances (currency and checkable deposits, or M2, divided by the CPI) in the U.S. for the years 1979 to 1999. Positive numbers signify expansionary policy; negative ones tell you that the money supply has contracted. Plot the numbers on the graph to your left. Can you explain why the Fed chose to expand or contract in each of these years?

THE LANGUAGE OF ECONOMICS 8

Bear Markets and Bull Markets

The terms "bear market" and "bull market" are frequently tossed about by the media, but are also often confused with one another. Most of you probably know that one of these terms is associated with rising markets and the other with falling markets, but if you're anything like me you can probably never remember which is which. Below you will find both their definitions and, hopefully, a way to remember which of these terms means what.

A *bear market* is a market that is falling. A *bull market* is a one that is growing. Investment analysts are sometimes referred to as "bullish" or "bearish" on certain markets. This refers to their level of optimism—to whether or not they think a market will grow. A *bullish* investor will want to charge ahead and buy. A *bearish* one will want to curl up in his cave and hibernate until the market recovers.

"Bulls" are more optimistic about market performance; bull markets provide a basis for such optimism. "Bears" are more pessimistic. In a falling market, they will be the ones with the most appropriate set of expectations.

REVIEW OF TECHNIQUE 8

Associating Money Growth With Output Growth

The quantity theory of money tells us that $M \times V = P \times Y$, or that in the long run $M \times V = P \times Y^*$. This equation describes a relationship between the *levels* of its constituent variables: M, V, P, and Y. It also, however, implies a relationship between their *rates of change*. There are several ways of deriving this relationship: we could use calculus, which the authors of your textbook have determined to spare you from, or we could use a neat little trick with natural logarithms (see Review of Technique 15 if you need a review of natural logarithms).

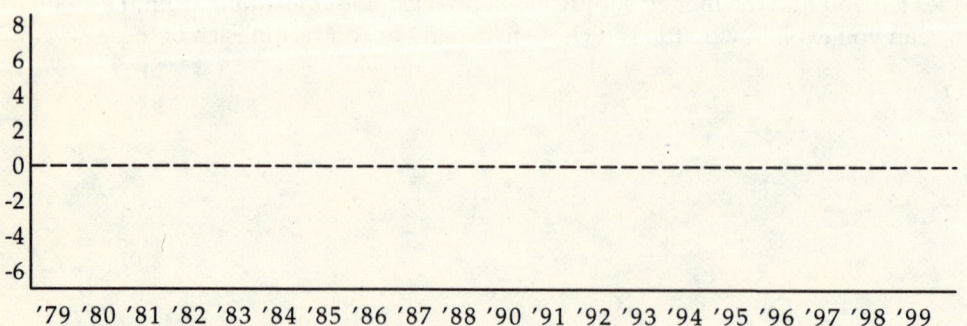

Chart 8-1

There are two properties of logarithms that you need to know for this exercise:

- First, the natural logarithm of a product is the sum of the natural logarithms of the variables that make up that product: $\ln xy = \ln x + \ln y$

- Second, the percentage change in a variable is approximately equal to the change in its natural logarithm: $\%\Delta x \approx \Delta \ln x$

Using these rules, we can show first that $\ln M + \ln V = \ln P + \ln Y$, and then that $\Delta \ln M + \Delta \ln V = \Delta \ln P + \Delta \ln Y$, implying the following relationship:

$$\%\Delta M + \%\Delta V = \%\Delta P + \%\Delta Y$$

or, in the long run:

$$\%\Delta M + \%\Delta V = \%\Delta P + \%\Delta Y^*$$

We also assume that velocity is constant, and eliminate $\%\Delta V$ from both equations. This turns out to be a pretty decent assumption most of the time, and leaves us with two very tractable equations which are "approximately valid most of the time":

$$\%\Delta M = \%\Delta P + \%\Delta Y \quad \text{and} \quad \%\Delta M = \%\Delta P + \%\Delta Y^*$$

These, together with the knowledge that we place inflationary pressure on the economy when we push output above potential output, help us think more quantitatively about targeting.

Consider, for example, a monetary policy rule that expands real money balances at 6% every year. If we believe the price level can't adjust right away to this stimulus ($\%\Delta P = 0$), the first equation tells us that output will increase by the full 6%. We know, however, that in the long run output can't grow any faster than potential output; assuming 4% growth in potential output, the long run effect of our 6% money growth rule will be to expand output by 4% a year, and to raise the inflation rate by 2 percentage points. Our policy is too expansionary, the economy can't handle the stimulus. On the other hand, if potential output grew by 8%, output would either grow by 8% a year with a 2 percentage point decline in the rate of inflation, or it would be limited to 6% growth leave inflation unaffected. In this last case our 6% money growth rule would be *contractionary*.

Nominal GDP targeting has results that are strikingly similar. Say we choose a target of 6% nominal GDP growth. If potential output grows at 4% a year, this target will increase inflation by those 2 percentage points mentioned above. If it grows at 6%, inflation will be unaffected. And with 8% growth in potential output, our policy again turns out to be contractionary, and reduces inflation, probably causing some short run recessions as well.

In the long run our nominal GDP target could be achieved by a constant money growth rule, but it also could be pursued more actively by increasing money growth when nominal GDP falls below 6% and decreasing it when nominal GDP exceeds 6%. You can see why this kind of targeting is pretty safe; as long as we have a realistic idea how fast potential output is growing it's hard for this to cause too much inflation. The risk, of course, is that we're wrong about the growth rate of potential output. It's not an easy number to measure.

Now for real GDP targeting… suppose, for consistency, that we choose 6% real GDP growth as our target. We increase the money supply by 6%, and at first real GDP obliges, increasing also by

6%. In the long run output growth will still be limited by *potential output* growth. The rest of our money expansion will create inflation. If the growth rate of potential output is below our target, output growth will slow and we will have to increase the money supply again. You can see how, repeated, this would lead to an inflationary spiral. It's considerably more dangerous to misjudge the growth rate of potential output with real GDP targeting.

We have seen how to use the quantity theory of money to think through the implications of different policy targets. We have also seen something else, though, and it is something worth noticing: a policy that increases the money supply is not necessarily expansionary. If money grows more slowly than potential output, there is actually a *contraction* taking place. Keep that in mind throughout all the static analysis we do in the next few chapters.

You might also want to go back to the Graph It you just finished and draw a horizontal line representing 4% potential output growth (an estimate). Only the points above the line represent true expansionary policy; all those below it are at least relatively contractionary.

CROSSWORD

ACROSS

1 create difficulties with policy timing
3 tell you how close you are to a policy target
6 policy goals
8 trouble with this might make you use cold-turkey policies
9 has an econometric policy evaluation critique
11 type of lag, eliminated gradually
12 lag between policy implementation and full policy effect
13 lag, time required to notice shock has hit the economy

DOWN

2 lag, time required to implement a policy
3 lag, time between shock and policy response
4 policies that move the economy slowly toward a target
7 used to implement policy
10 lag, time required to determine appropriate policy response

FILL-IN QUESTIONS

1. The time required for policy makers to realize the need for, develop, and implement a policy to counteract an economic disturbance is referred to as the _____ lag.

2. The length of time for this policy to have its full effect is called the _____ lag.

3. The three handicaps of policy making are _____, _____, _____.

4. The amount of time required for policymakers to evaluate and choose a policy that will counteract an economic disturbance is referred to as the _____ lag.

5. Countercyclical policies which require no discretionary action on the part of policymakers are called _____.

6. The _____ lag is much longer for fiscal than for monetary policy.

7. The _____ lag is much shorter for fiscal than for monetary policy.

8. The _____ suggests that the implementation of a policy may itself affect expectations.

9. Rising markets are called _____ markets; falling markets are _____.

10. "_____" are more optimistic than "_____".

TRUE–FALSE QUESTIONS

T F 1. It is quite simple to use monetary and fiscal policies to stabilize output.

T F 2. The world is more complicated than our models suggest.

T F 3. It's always best to target real GDP.

T F 4. Gradualist policies are always better than cold–turkey ones.

T F 5. It can be very difficult to confidently predict the exact effects of a policy.

T F 6. There's no such thing as an activist rule.

T F 7. A variable can never be both an indicator and a target.

T F 8. The implementation of a policy may itself affect people's expectations.

T F 9. If we are uncertain about the size of the multipliers associated with different policies, we should *not* mix them.

T F 10. Even well–intentioned policymakers who have the discretion to implement activist policies will be tempted to act, in the short run, in a way that is not consistent with the long–run goals and interests of the economy.

MULTIPLE–CHOICE QUESTIONS

1. The outside lag associated with monetary policy is:
   a. discrete
   b. distributed
   c. diversified
   d. activist

2. The outside lag associated with fiscal policy is:
   a. discrete
   b. distributed
   c. diversified
   d. activist

3. Which of these is not a part of the inside lag?
   a. implementation
   b. recognition
   c. action
   d. decision

4. It's always best to target:
   a. real GDP
   b. nominal GDP
   c. inflation
   d. people disagree which one's best

5. A policymaker might choose to adopt a "cold–turkey" policy because:
   a. it has a shorter inside lag
   b. he or she has credibility problems
   c. it reduces multiplier uncertainty
   d. the indicators are more reliable

6. When you don't have a good estimate of the growth rate of potential output, it's safer to target:
   a. real GDP
   b. nominal GDP
   c. per–capita GDP
   d. it doesn't matter

7. Which of the following help to determine a policy's effectiveness?
   a. credibility
   b. timing
   c. effect on expectations
   d. all of the above

8. Which of the following does *not* make it difficult for policymakers to stabilize output with fiscal policy?
   a. long inside lag
   b. short outside lag
   c. multiplier uncertainty
   d. long decision lag

9. A policymaker should be more willing to act when he or she believes a shock is:
   a. temporary
   b. discrete
   c. permanent
   d. contractionary

10. Which of the following types of uncertainty hinder effective policy implementation?
   a. multiplier uncertainty
   b. uncertainty about shock's permanence
   c. model uncertainty
   d. all of the above

CONCEPTUAL PROBLEMS

1. What do you think about the "rules vs. discretion" debate? Do you favor rules or discretion?

2. Do you think policymakers should try to "fine tune" the economy? Why or why not?

Part 3

First Models

9 INCOME AND SPENDING

FOCUS OF THE CHAPTER

- This chapter takes a closer look at the way that changes in the goods market affect aggregate demand by examining the link between income and spending—i.e., we use the fundamental national income identity ($Y = C + I + G + NX$) to analyze the way that changes in consumption affect output. We treat both income and consumption as endogenous variables.

- A basic result is that an increase in autonomous spending will increase output by an amount greater than that of the spending increase.

SECTION SUMMARIES

1. Aggregate Demand and Equilibrium Output

The fundamental national income accounting identity, $Y = C + I + G$, states that the *actual* level of output must always equal the sum of all the different sources of aggregate demand. (Notice that we're ignoring net exports for the moment; we'll talk about how to incorporate these into our analysis in chapter 12.) It is easy, however, to imagine a situation in which *planned* levels of output differ from *planned* levels of consumption, investment, and government spending. When this happens, the goods market is not in equilibrium: the quantity of output produced does not equal the quantity demanded. Unintended changes in inventories occur.

These unplanned inventory changes cause firms to increase or decrease their production. The level of output rises or falls accordingly, and brings the goods market back into equilibrium.

2. The Consumption Function and Aggregate Demand

Increased income causes increased consumption. This relationship is captured by the *consumption function*:

$$C = \overline{C} + cY,$$

where c is a number between zero and one, and $\overline{C}$ is positive.

The fraction of each additional dollar of income that is consumed is represented by the variable c in the equation above and called the *marginal propensity to consume* (**mpc**). The fraction that is saved is equal to $(1-c)$, and is called the *marginal propensity to save* (**mps**). Neither the mpc nor the mps can be greater than 1; that would mean that people were consuming or saving an amount greater than their income. The amount that people choose to consume when their income is zero—the variable $\overline{C}$—is positive because people consume out of wealth as well as income.

Since saving $(Y-C)$ is just the difference between income and consumption, saving and consumption cannot be looked at independently. A specific consumption function implies a specific savings function.

If we add a government sector to this model, force individuals to pay taxes ($\overline{TA}$), and allow them to receive transfers ($\overline{TR}$) the consumption function changes slightly:

$$C = \overline{C} + c\,(Y - \overline{TA} + \overline{TR})$$

so that consumption now depends on *disposable*, or after tax, *income (YD)*. If we assume that investment and government spending are exogenously determined, we can write aggregate demand as

$$AD = C + \overline{I} + \overline{G} = \overline{C} + c\,(Y - \overline{TA} + \overline{TR}) + \overline{I} + \overline{G}$$

or, defining a new variable $\overline{A} = \overline{C} + \overline{I} + \overline{G} - c\,(\overline{TA} - \overline{TR})$ as

$$AD = \overline{A} + cY.$$

We can find the level of output for which the goods market is in equilibrium (Y_0) by imposing the requirement $Y = AD$. This can be accomplished graphically, as in figure 9–1, by finding the point at which the lines $Y = AD$ and $AD = \overline{A} + cY$ intersect. It can also be accomplished algebraically, by solving the equation $Y_0 = AD = A + cY_0$. (It turns out that $Y_0 = (1/1-c)\,A_0$)

We can also get this result by setting total saving (government + personal) in our economy equal to planned investment $(\overline{TA} - \overline{TR} - \overline{G}) + S = \overline{I}$, where $S = Y - C$).

3. The Multiplier

A \$1 increase in *autonomous spending* (the term $\overline{A}$ introduced in the previous section), in general, increases GDP by much more than \$1.

Let's follow this \$1 of spending through the economy: The first thing it does is to create one additional dollar of income for those people who helped to produce and sell the goods and

The goods market is in equilibrium when the quantity of output produced is equal to the quantity demanded, or when Y = AD.

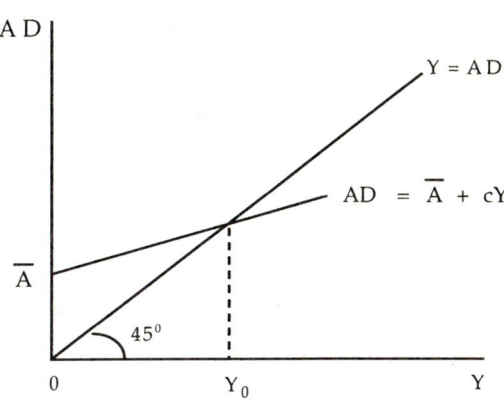

Figure 9 - 1

A GRAPHIC REPRESENTATION OF THE GOODS MARKET EQUILIBRIUM

services it purchased. Once in their pockets, a fraction c of it is spent and a fraction $(1-c)$ is saved, so that an amount $(c \times \$1)$, or $\$c$, goes on to become income for others. They, in turn, spend a fraction c and save a fraction $(1-c)$; an amount $(c \times c \times \$1)$, or $\$c^2$, moves on to become income for still others.

As this process continues, the original $1 spending increase generates an increase in income (and output) of $(1 + c + c^2 + c^3 + ...) \times \$1$, or $(1/(1-c)) \times \$1$, as the **infinite geometric series** $(1 + c + c^2 + c^3 + ...)$ can be written as $1/(1-c)$ when $c < 1$. (This chapter's "Review of Technique" shows why this is the case.)

We call the number $1/(1-c)$ *the multiplier*, as it describes the amount by which that initial $1 is multiplied as it changes hands, and is spent again and again. Note that an increase in the mpc (the variable c) makes this multiplier larger.

4. The Government Sector

In this section we develop a more complete government sector. We assume that the government collects a proportional income tax. Everyone pays the government a constant fraction t of their income, and keeps a fraction $1 - t$. Disposable income is now equal to $(Y + \overline{TR} - tY)$. The consumption function becomes

$$C = \overline{C} + c\,\overline{TR} + c(1-t)Y,$$

and the multiplier

$$\alpha_G = \frac{1}{1 - c(1-t)}.$$

Because it makes the multiplier smaller, so that shocks to autonomous spending have less of an impact on the output and unemployment, the income tax is considered an *automatic stabilizer*. Transfers, because they initially increase aggregate demand by only $c\,\overline{TR}$ (some of the transfer is saved), have a smaller multiplier: $c\,\alpha_G$.

5. The Budget

The *budget surplus* (BS) is defined as the difference between the money that the government takes in and the money that the government spends:

$$BS = \overline{TA} - \overline{TR} - \overline{G}.$$

When a proportional income tax is assumed, as in the previous section, measures of the budget surplus change both because of changes in government policy (*G, t, TR*) and because the level of output changes. We should, therefore, not be surprised to see the budget surplus shrink (or become more negative) in recessions, when output falls.

A negative budget surplus is called a *budget deficit*.

6. The Full–Employment Budget Surplus

The *full–employment budget surplus* (BS*) is a measure of what the budget surplus would be if the economy were at full–employment. It responds to only changes in government policy, and is not affected changes in the output gap. For this reason it can be an indicator of fiscal policy: A full–employment budget deficit, for example, would suggest that fiscal policy is expansionary, or tending to increase output.

KEY TERMS

aggregate demand
equilibrium level of output
consumption function
marginal propensity to consume
budget constraint
marginal propensity to save
disposable income

multiplier
fiscal policy
automatic stabilizer
balanced budget multiplier
budget surplus/deficit
full-employment budget surplus

GRAPH IT 9

This Graph It asks you to verify the following proposition: *A rise in the marginal propensity to consume increases the multiplier, so that a given change in autonomous spending ($\overline{A}$) produces a larger change in GDP.*

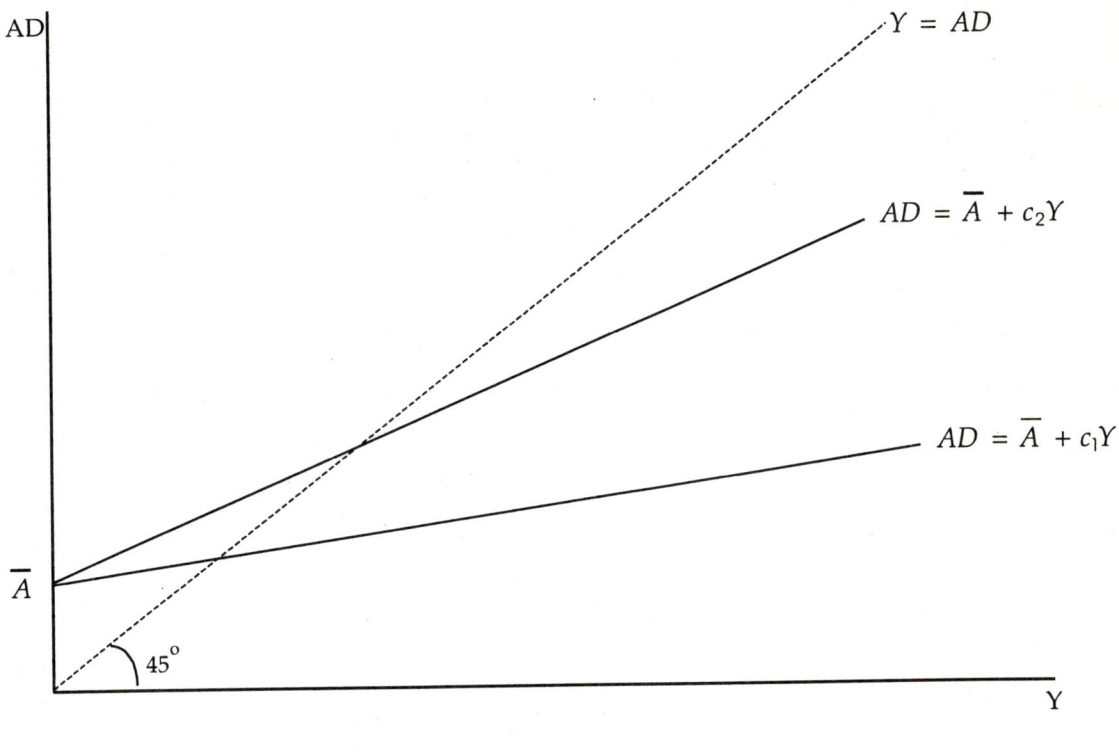

Chart 9 - 1

Chart 9–1 provides you with two AD functions with different mpc's, and with the 45° line that represents the goods market equilibrium (Y = AD). Your task is to shift each of these lines upward by a fixed amount (call it $\Delta \overline{A}$), and to compare the effect of those shifts on the level of output.

The shift in the steeper curve—the one with the higher mpc—should cause a greater increase in the level of output than the shift in the flatter one. Remember to shift both lines upward by the same amount; your result will, otherwise, not be terribly informative. A big shift will make this result easier for you to see.

THE LANGUAGE OF ECONOMICS 9

Autonomous Spending

Autonomous spending is spending that is *exogenously determined*—that is not affected by any of the other variables in our model. In this chapter, this means specifically that it must be independent of income. In the next, we will find that it must be independent of interest rates as well.

Even when a variable itself is endogenously determined—consumption, in this chapter's model, is an example—it may have an exogenous, or autonomous, component.

REVIEW OF TECHNIQUE 9

Infinite Geometric Series

This section shows you how to calculate the sum of an infinite geometric series—a series of the form

$$S = 1 + c + c^2 + c^3 + c^4 + \ldots$$

that goes on forever (i.e., the exponents approach infinity).

Suppose that c is a number between zero and one. When this is the case, there is a useful trick that we can use to find the value of S (the series' sum): We multiply every term in our geometric series by c, creating a new series

$$cS = c + c^2 + c^3 + c^4 + c^5 + \ldots,$$

and then subtract this new series from our original one

$$S - cS = 1 + (c - c) + (c^2 - c^2) + (c^3 - c^3) + \ldots$$

This allows us to solve for S, the sum of the original series:

$$S - cS = 1 + (c - c) + (c^2 - c^2) + (c^3 - c^3) + \ldots$$
$$S - cS = 1 + 0 + 0 + 0 + \ldots = 1$$
$$S(1 - c) = 1$$

or,

$$S = 1 / (1 - c).$$

IN THE QUESTIONS BELOW, WE INCLUDE A GOVERNMENT SECTOR BUT NOT A FOREIGN SECTOR.

FILL-IN QUESTIONS

1. When planned and actual spending are equal, the goods market is in _____.

2. In this chapter's model of aggregate demand, consumption is an _____ variable.

3. A $1 increase in income will increase consumption by $1 times the _____.

4. Consumption, in this chapter, is assumed to be a function of _____.

5. When the goods market is out of equilibrium, there are unintended changes in _____.

CROSSWORD

ACROSS

1. income after taxes, transfers
2. these change when $AD \bullet Y$
5. policy, taxes & spending are tools
6. increase in GDP resulting from a $1 increase in autonomous spending
7. type of tax, an automatic stabilizer
8. goods market equilibrium condition: AD = ___

DOWN

1. negative budget surplus
3. value of balanced budget multiplier
4. type of variable; I, G, & NX in this chapter are examples
6. slope of consumption function

FILL-IN QUESTIONS (continued)

6. The complement of the marginal propensity to consume is the _____.

7. The difference between government expenditure and taxes is called the _____.

8. A(n) _____ is a program, such as unemployment insurance, that reduces the impact of shocks on the economy without any direct government intervention.

9. The difference between the taxes that *would* be taken in, if the economy were at full–employment, and government expenditure is called the _____.

10. The balanced budget multiplier is always equal to _____.

TRUE–FALSE QUESTIONS

T F 1. Raising the income tax rate should increase GDP.

T F 2. An increase in the marginal propensity to consume (mpc) should decrease GDP.

T F 3. An increase in the mpc should decrease savings.

T F 4. An increase in the mpc should increase the equilibrium level of investment.

T F 5. The mpc is an endogenous variable.

T F 6. An increase in disposable income will increase consumption.

T F 7. An increase in disposable income will increase the mpc.

T F 8. An increase in autonomous spending will have no effect on the equilibrium level of output.

T F 9. An increase in the mpc will increase autonomous spending.

T F 10. Output should fluctuate less when automatic stabilizers are present than when they aren't.

MULTIPLE–CHOICE QUESTIONS

1. When we say that investment and government spending are *autonomous*, we mean they are
    a. exogenous variables
    b. endogenous variables
    c. automatic stabilizers
    d. none of the above

2. When aggregate demand is greater than output, there is unplanned
    a. inventory accumulation
    b. inventory reduction
    c. saving
    d. consumption

3. An increase in the mpc will _____ the multiplier.
    a. increase
    b. decrease
    c. not affect
    d. who knows?

4. An increase in the mpc will _____ the mps (marginal propensity to save).
    a. increase
    b. decrease
    c. not affect
    d. who knows?

5. Income taxes _____ the multiplier.
    a. increase
    b. decrease
    c. do not affect
    d. who knows?

6. Government purchases will have _____ effect on output in an economy *without* income taxes than it will be in an economy with them.
    a. a greater
    b. less of an
    c. it depends on the tax rate
    d. it depends on the mpc

7. If the mpc = 0.8 and there are no income taxes, the multiplier will be
    a. 1
    b. 2
    c. 5
    d. 10

8. If the mpc = 0.8 and there are no income taxes, the multiplier relating changes in *transfer payments* to changes in national income will be

   a. 4
   b. 5
   c. 6
   d. 8

9. If the mpc = 0.8 and there is a $0.375 tax levied on each dollar of income, the multiplier will be

   a. 1
   b. 2
   c. 5
   d. 10

10. If the mpc = 0.8 and there is a $0.375 tax levied on each dollar of income, a $40 increase in government purchases will cause tax revenues to _____, and the budget surplus to _____.

    a. increase by $30; rise
    b. increase by $30; fall
    c. increase by $80; rise
    d. increase by $80; fall

CONCEPTUAL PROBLEMS

1. Which will increase output more: a $1 million increase in government spending, or a $1 million increase in government transfers? Why?

2. Which of the following variables are endogenously determined in this chapter's model of aggregate demand? Which are exogenously determined? *(See "The Language of Economics 2" for a review of endogenous and exogenous variables.)*

   a) income
   b) output
   c) disposable income
   d) consumption
   e) investment
   f) autonomous spending

3. Why might the budget deficit be a bad measure of the direction of fiscal policy?

4. In what way is the full–employment budget surplus a better measure of the direction of fiscal policy?

TECHNICAL PROBLEMS

1. Find the savings function that is implied by the following consumption function:
   (Hint: Remember that S = Y – C.)
   $$C = \overline{C} + cY.$$

2. Consider an economy with no income taxes, where the mpc = 0.9.

   (a) What is the value of the multiplier associated with autonomous spending (α_G)?

   (b) How much will output in this economy increase if government expenditures are increased by $100?

   (c) How much will output in this economy increase if government transfers are increased by $100?

3. Now suppose that this economy imposes a proportional income tax, $t = 1/3$.

   (a) What is the value of the multiplier (α_G) now?

   (b) How much will output in this economy increase if government spending rises by $100?

   (c) How will this affect the budget surplus/deficit?

   (d) How will it affect the full–employment budget surplus?

10 MONEY, INTEREST, AND INCOME

FOCUS OF THE CHAPTER

- This chapter introduces the IS–LM model—the heart of short–run macroeconomic theory.

- The simple model of chapter 9 is extended to include the interaction of goods and money markets, which, together, uniquely determine both the interest rate and the position of the AD curve.

- Both investment and the interest rate are now endogenous variables: Investment is a function of the interest rate, which is determined by the equilibrium conditions for goods and money markets.

SECTION SUMMARIES

1. The Goods Market and the IS Curve

This section derives the *IS curve*. The IS curve shows all of the combinations of income and the interest rate for which the goods market is in equilibrium (Y = AD). This equilibrium turns out to be a function of the interest rate because AD is now a function of the interest rate: We develop an investment function, which shows that the level of investment falls when interest rates increase.

Our investment function is written as follows:

$$I = \bar{I} - bi,$$

where i is the real interest rate, $\bar{I}$ is a constant which represents *autonomous investment*, and b is a coefficient which measures the responsiveness of investment spending to changes in the interest rate.

If we imagine that firms borrow the money that they use for investment, it is easy to see why their investment decisions should be affected by the interest rate: higher real interest rates mean more expensive loans, and therefore lower returns on investment opportunities.

107

When we incorporate this investment function into our AD schedule, we find that AD is now a function of the interest rate as well:

$$AD = (\overline{C} + cY) + (\overline{I} - bi) + \overline{G}$$

or, allowing both income taxes and transfers,

$$AD = (\overline{C} + c[(1 - t)Y + TR]) + (\overline{I} - bi) + \overline{G}$$

$$= \overline{A} + c(1 - t)Y - bi$$

where $\overline{A} = \overline{C} + \overline{I} + \overline{G} + c\,\overline{TR}$. $\overline{A}$, as before, represents autonomous spending.

As before, can find the level of output for which the goods market is in equilibrium by imposing the requirement $Y = AD$. The only difference now is that there will be one of these equilibria for each value of i, the real interest rate. We derive the IS curve by allowing the interest rate to vary, and plotting the combinations of i and Y for which the goods market is in equilibrium. This is done graphically in figure 10–1. It is also done algebraically, below:

$$Y = \overline{A} + c(1 - t)Y - bi$$

$$Y - c(1 - t)Y = \overline{A} - bi$$

$$(1 - c(1 - t))Y = \overline{A} - bi$$

or,

$$Y = \frac{1}{1 - c(1 - t)}(\overline{A} - bi),$$

which tells us that the IS curve is negatively sloped. Notice that the term $\frac{1}{1 - c(1-t)}$ is the multiplier (α_G) that we found in the last chapter. An increase in this multiplier—caused either by an increase in the mpc or a decrease in the tax rate—makes the IS curve flatter.*

Just as in chapter 9 a change in autonomous spending changed the equilibrium level of output, an change in autonomous spending here shifts the IS curve—changes the equilibrium level of output for each interest rate. An increase shifts the IS curve outward; a decrease shifts it inward.

---

* The slope of the IS curve is $-\left(\frac{1 - c(1-t)}{b}\right)$, or $-\frac{1}{b\alpha_G}$.

You can show this for yourself by simply writing i as a function of Y (the IS curve is drawn with the interest rate, rather than the level of output, on the vertical axis).

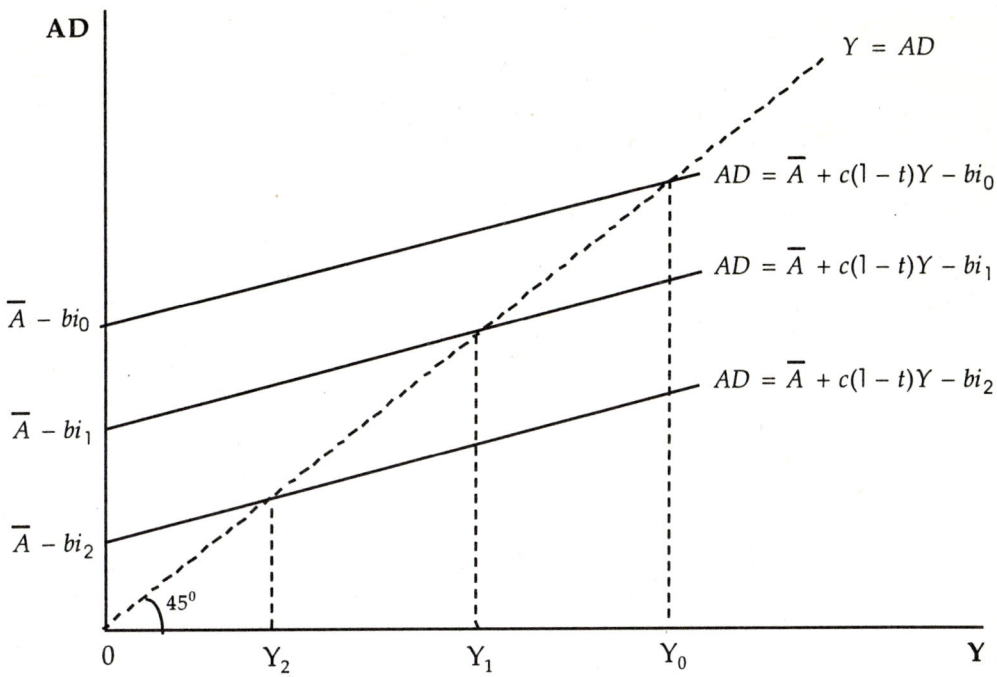

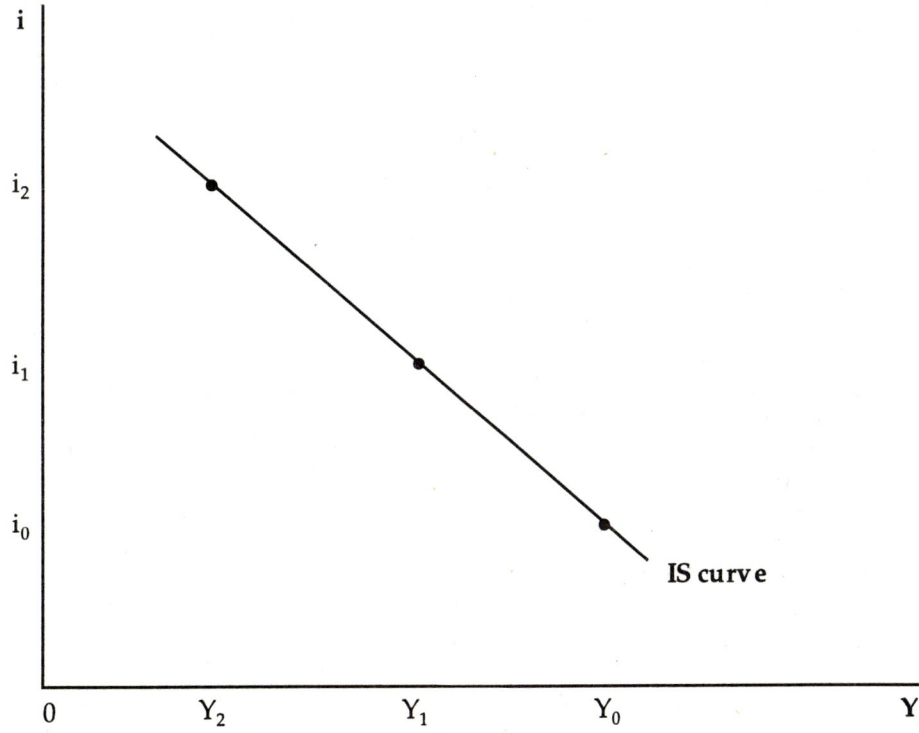

Figure 10-1

DERIVING THE IS CURVE

2. The Money Market and the LM Curve

This section reviews the requirements for equilibrium in the money market, and derives the *LM curve*—the combinations of *i* and *Y* for which the supply of money equals the demand for money.

The demand for money increases when people's incomes rise, and decreases when interest rates rise. The reason for the first is simple: When our incomes rise, we need to hold more money in order to pay for the extra goods we buy. The reason we want to hold less money when interest rates rise has to do with the *opportunity cost of holding money*: when we choose to hold money, rather than keeping our money in an interest bearing asset, we fail to earn the market rate of interest. When real interest rates rise, therefore, the cost of holding money instead of these other assets rises, and we chose to hold less money.

The money demand function is written as follows:

$$L = kY - hi,$$

where k and h are constants which reflect the sensitivity of money demand to changes in income and in the interest rate, respectively. The function *L* represents the demand for *real balances* (M/P). It does not represent the demand for *nominal balances* (M); simple inflation shouldn't affect it.

The supply of real balances is determined by two factors: the money supply, and the price level. The money supply (M) is controlled by a country's central bank (the Federal Reserve System, or "Fed," in the United States). The price level (P), as we have already learned, is determined in both the long and the short run by the interaction of aggregate supply and aggregate demand. We assume, for the moment, that both the money supply and the price level are fixed, so that the supply of real balances is constant at the level *M/P*.

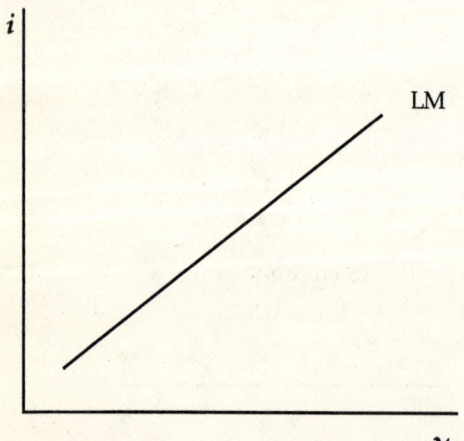

The LM curve shows all of the combinations of output and the real interest rate for which the market for real money balances is in equilibrium.

Figure 10 - 2

THE LM CURVE

The combination of output and the interest rate at which the IS and LM curves intersect is the only one that brings both the goods market and the money market into equilibrium.

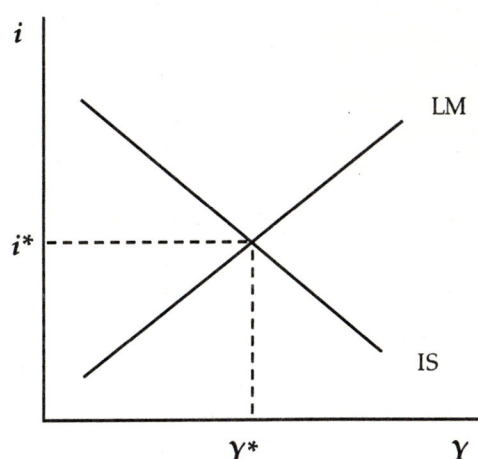

Figure 10 - 3

IS–LM EQUILIBRIUM

We can write the equilibrium condition for the money market (the demand for real balances must equal the supply of real balances) as

$$\overline{M}/\overline{P} = kY - hi.$$

Solving this for i gives us the equation for the LM curve:

$$i = \frac{1}{h}\left(kY - \frac{\overline{M}}{\overline{P}}\right).$$

Notice first that the LM curve is upward–sloping in Y, as the constants k and h are positive.

Notice also that an increase in real money balances ($\overline{M}/\overline{P}$) will shift it outward, or downward, and that a decrease in real balances will shift it inward (upward).

Real balances can change either because nominal balances change (the money supply changes), or because the price level changes. Because the AD curve is graphed in P and Y, however, a change in the price level causes movement along the AD curve rather than a shift in it.

3. Equilibrium in the Goods and Money Markets

The levels of output and the interest rate at which the IS and LM curves intersect are the only ones for which both the goods market and the money market are in equilibrium.

A shift in either curve will change the combination of i and Y at which this equilibrium occurs.

4. Deriving the Aggregate Demand Schedule

This section derives the AD curve by varying the price level for which the LM curve is drawn, and observing the way that this changes the IS–LM equilibrium. The combinations of P and Y that result sketch a downward–sloping AD curve.

Graph It 10 gives you the opportunity to see this for yourself. As you change the price level in order to generate the AD relationship, notice that you are holding the money supply and the level of autonomous spending constant. Any change in these variables, therefore, will cause the AD curve to shift—inward, if the level of income that brings goods and money markets into equilibrium falls, and outward if this level falls.

A change in the price level will just cause a movement along the AD curve.

5. A Formal Treatment of the IS–LM Model (optional section)

Since both the IS and the LM curves are described by linear equations, we can solve these equations simultaneously to find the equilibrium levels of output and the interest rate.

Combining the equations for the IS and LM curves and solving for both Y and i, we find that

$$Y = \frac{\alpha_G}{1 + k\alpha_G(b/h)} \overline{A} + \frac{b\alpha_G}{h + kb\alpha_G} \left(\frac{\overline{M}}{\overline{P}}\right)$$

and

$$i = \frac{k\alpha_G}{h + kb\alpha_G} \overline{A} + \frac{1}{h + kb\alpha_G} \left(\frac{\overline{M}}{\overline{P}}\right).$$

The fraction $\frac{\alpha_G}{1 + k\alpha_G(b/h)}$ is called the *fiscal policy multiplier*. The fraction $\frac{b\alpha_G}{h + kb\alpha_G}$ is called the *monetary policy multiplier*. The equation for Y is also the equation for the AD curve.

KEY TERMS

IS-LM model
IS curve
goods market equilibrium schedule
LM curve
money market equilibrium schedule
real money balances

demand for real balances
central bank
aggregate demand schedule
fiscal policy multiplier
monetary policy multiplier

GRAPH IT 10

The aggregate demand schedule describes the solutions of the IS–LM diagram for different price levels. This Graph It asks you to show how, and why, changes in the prices level affects AD—i.e., why it slopes downward.

Chart 10–1 on the next page lines up an IS–LM diagram with an aggregate demand diagram. We've drawn the IS curve, an LM curve based on the price level P_1, and the equilibrium level of income (Y_1^*) which they mutually determine on the IS–LM diagram. We've marked this same combination of income (Y_1^*) and the price level (P_1) on the AS–AD diagram below it, giving you one point on your AD curve.

You need to draw two more LM curves on the top graph—one for a price level (P_2) greater than P_1, and another for a price level (P_0) less than P_1, and to mark the equilibrium levels of output that they, and the IS curve, determine.

Now drop vertical lines to mark the points (P_0, Y_0^*) and (P_2, Y_2^*) on the aggregate demand diagram. When you connect the three points on the lower graph, you will have an AD curve.

THE LANGUAGE OF ECONOMICS 10

Endogenous Variables Revisited

When we first made the distinction between endogenous and exogenous variables, we had not yet worked with two equation systems. To make sure you are still comfortable with this distinction in the more complicated models you now work with, we provide this brief review.

Endogenous variables, you may remember, are determined *within* a particular model. Typically, the more equations a model involves, the more endogenous variables it is likely to have—the more variables it will determine.

Consider the IS–LM model: We take the price level as given (exogenously determined), and find the levels of output and the real interest rate for which both goods and money markets are in equilibrium. The levels of output and the interest rate are determined endogenously—by the interaction of all the other variables in the model. *Their values can never change unless one of these other variables changes.*

The same is true for the AS–AD model—the price level and the level of output are determined by the level of government spending, the taxes people are required to pay, and the size of the money supply. They are also determined by the position and slope of the AS curve. It is interesting to notice that the interest rate, which varies along the AD curve (look again at Chart 10–1), is also endogenously determined; we cannot change it without first changing the value of some other, exogenous variable. Consumption and investment are also endogenous.

114 CHAPTER 10

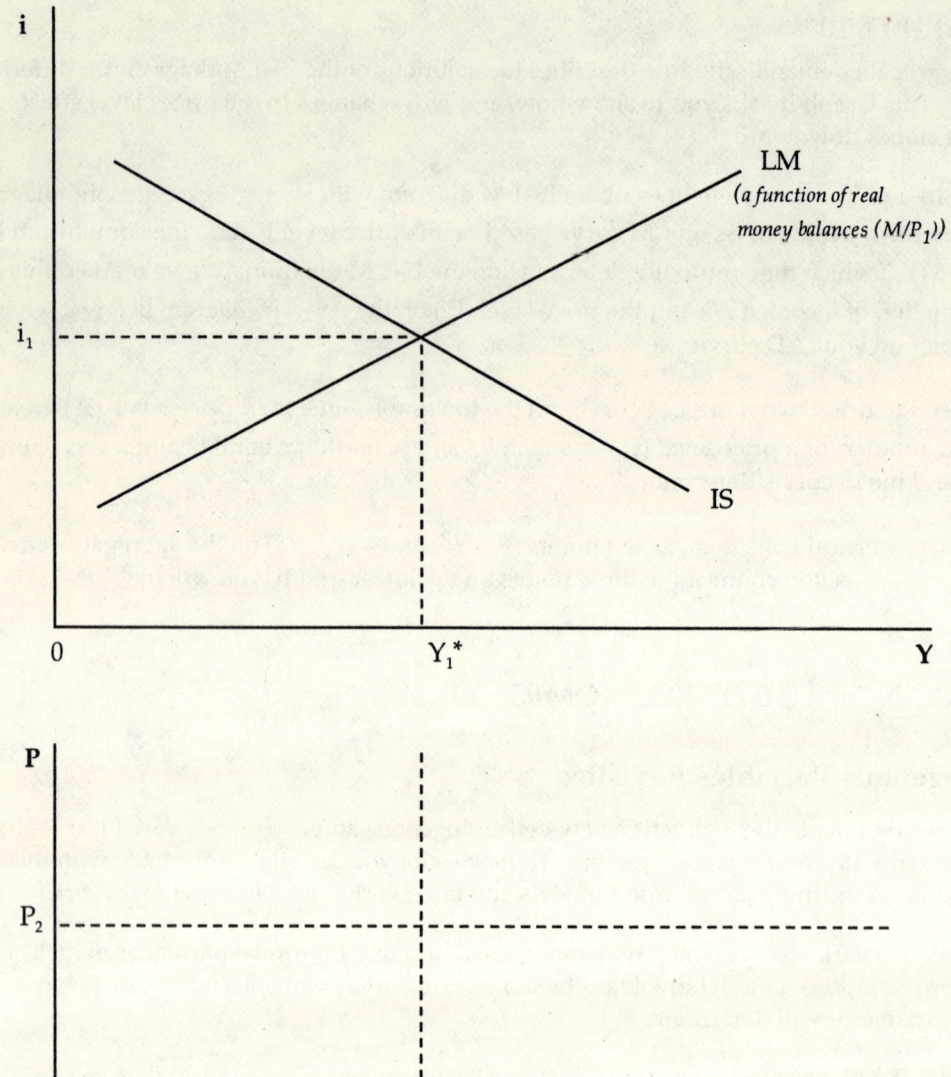

Chart 10 - 4

DERIVING THE AD CURVE

REVIEW OF TECHNIQUE 10

Solving a Two Equation System Graphically and Algebraically

In Review of Technique 5, we learned how to graph a linear equation. In this Review of Technique, we discuss how to find the solution to two linear equations, graphically and algebraically.

Consider the following two equations:

$$Y = aX + b, \quad \text{and} \quad X = -cY + d$$

If we were to graph these, we would draw two curves—one for each equation. In this instance, we would have one upward–sloping and one downward–sloping curve, which, because of their different slopes, would be guaranteed to intersect. (See Figure 10–5, below.)

We would have a very easy time solving these equations graphically: we would simply find the point at which our lines crossed, and the values of X and Y that defined that point. That would be our solution.

Solving these equations algebraically doesn't involve much more than this: We simply impose the assumption (or the requirement) that the values of X and Y are the same in both equations. Once we do this, we can substitute the value of X (or, if we prefer, the value of Y) from one equation into the other, and solve for the remaining variable. For example, we could write:

$$Y = a(-cY + d) + b = -acY + ad + b$$

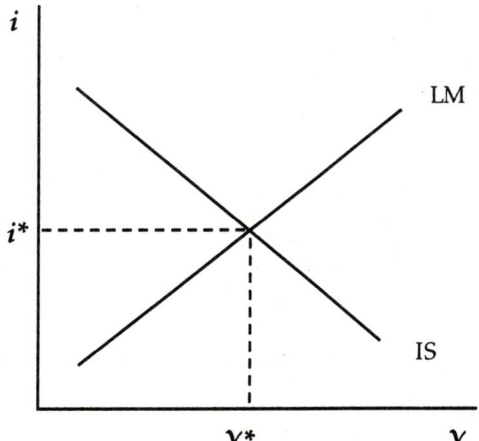

Figure 10 - 5

IS–LM EQUILIBRIUM

and, solve as follows:

$$Y + (ac)Y = ad + b,$$

$$(1 + ac)Y = ad + b,$$

$$Y = (ad + b)/(1 + ac).$$

We could then plug this value of Y into either equation to find the solution for X:

$$X = -c((ad + b)/(1 + ac)) + d,$$

$$X = -c((ad + b)/(1 + ac)) + d((1 + ac)/(1 + ac)),$$

$$X = ((-cad - bc) + (d + cad))/(1 + ac),$$

$$X = (d - bc)/(1 + ac).$$

Algebraic solutions are particularly useful when we need to find quantitative, rather than qualitative solutions—numbers, rather than directions of change.

CROSSWORD

ACROSS

3 number of sections in this chapter
4 policy, shifts LM curve
8 policy, shifts IS curve
11 type of variable, i & Y are examples

DOWN

1 bank, determines monetary policy
2 market, IS curve shows equilibrium
5 type of variable, M & G are examples
6 curve, position determined by IS–LM equilibria
7 its changes shift LM curve but not AD curve
9 same as output
10 market, LM curve shows equilibrium

FILL-IN QUESTIONS

1. The IS curve describes all of the combinations of output and the interest rate for which the _____ market is in equilibrium.

2. The IS curve is downward–sloping because a decrease in the interest rate increases _____.

3. An increase in the marginal propensity to consume (mpc), and hence an *increase* in the multiplier α_G will make the IS curve _____.

4. The LM curve describes all of the combinations of output and the interest rate for which the _____ market is in equilibrium.

5. The LM curve is upward–sloping because when people's income rises, they want to hold more _____. The increase in money demand drives up the interest rate.

6. If money demand is relatively *insensitive* to the interest rate, the LM curve will be quite _____.

7. If money demand is very *sensitive* to the interest rate, the LM curve will be nearly _____.

8. _____ policy shifts the IS curve; _____ policy shifts the LM curve.

9. The interest rate and level of output (under the assumption of a fixed price level) are jointly determined by _____ for goods and money markets.

10. Any change in the equilibrium level of income in the IS–LM model, with the exception of a change in the price level, will cause the _____ curve to shift.

TRUE–FALSE QUESTIONS

T F 1. A change in the price level will shift the IS curve.

T F 2. For a given level of real money balances, there is a positive relationship between interest rates and income along the LM curve.

T F 3. An increase in government spending will shift the IS curve outward *(up and to the right)*.

T F 4. An increase in the money supply will shift the LM curve outward *(down and to the right)*.

T F 5. Decreasing the money supply increases investment.

T F 6. For a given level of output, there can be more than one interest rate for which the goods market is in equilibrium.

118   CHAPTER 10

T   F   7.   For a given level of output there can be more than one interest rate for which the money market is in equilibrium.

T   F   8.   An increase in the tax rate reduces the multiplier.

T   F   9.   The slope of the IS curve cannot be affected by policy decisions.

T   F   10. Equal increases in government purchases and transfers will shift the IS curve by the same amount.

MULTIPLE–CHOICE QUESTIONS

1. Which component of aggregate demand is the main link between goods and money markets?

    a. consumption
    b. investment
    c. government spending
    d. none of the above

2. Which of the following variables can shift the IS curve?

    a. price level
    b. money supply
    c. government spending
    d. none of the above

3. A change in the tax rate will

    a. shift the IS curve
    b. change the slope of the IS curve
    c. both
    d. neither

4. An increase in the price level will

    a. increase real money balances
    b. decrease real money balances
    c. increase nominal money balances
    d. decrease nominal money balances

5. Which of the following variables can shift the LM curve?

    a. price level
    b. money supply
    c. real money balances
    d. all of the above

6. For a fixed price level, a lower money supply leads to

    a. higher income
    b. higher interest rate
    c. both
    d. neither

7. An increase in the mpc will

    a. make the IS curve steeper
    b. make the IS curve flatter
    c. shift the IS curve outward
    d. have no effect on the IS curve

8. When investment is very sensitive to the interest rate, there will be a relatively

    a. steep IS curve
    b. flat IS curve
    c. steep LM curve
    d. flat LM curve

9. The less sensitive money demand is to changes in the interest rate, the more an increase in the money stock will

   a. increase AD
   b. lower interest rates
   c. both
   d. neither

10. Quick adjustment in the money market means that the economy is always on

    a. the IS curve
    b. the LM curve
    c. both
    d. neither

CONCEPTUAL PROBLEMS

1. Name all of the endogenous variables in the AS–AD model.

2. How are the IS–LM and AS–AD models related to each other?

3. What determines the slope of the IS curve? Will it be steeper or flatter in the presence of a proportional income tax?

4. What determines the slope of the LM curve?

TECHNICAL PROBLEMS

1. Suppose that the following equations describe the economy:

$$C = 100 + .8(Y - \bar{T}) \quad \text{(consumption)}$$
$$I = 200 - 1000i \quad \text{(investment)}$$
$$L = \tfrac{1}{2} Y - 7000i \quad \text{(demand for real money balances)}$$

Suppose also that government spending (G) is $550, taxes (T) are $500, and real money balances (M/P) are $900.

(a) Write the formula for the IS curve.
(Hint: When the goods market is in equilibrium, $Y = C + I + G$.)

(b) Write the formula for the LM curve.
(Hint: When the money market is in equilibrium, the supply of real money balances is equal to the demand for real money balances.)

(c) What are the equilibrium levels of output (Y), the real interest rate (i), consumption (C), and investment (I)?

2. Now suppose that the government imposes a proportional income tax, so that

$$C = 100 + .8(Y - tY) \quad \text{(consumption)}$$
$$I = 200 - 1000i \quad \text{(investment)}$$
$$L = \tfrac{1}{2} Y - 7000i \quad \text{(demand for real money balances)}$$

If the $t = .33$ (there is a 33% income tax), government purchases (G) are $700, and the real money supply (M/P) is $500,

(a) What is the formula for the IS curve?

(b) What is the formula for the LM curve?

(c) What is the initial value of the budget deficit?

(d) How large a change in the money supply would be necessary in order to balance the budget?

(e) Why might this be a dangerous strategy for keeping the budget balanced in the long run?

11 Monetary and Fiscal Policy

FOCUS OF THE CHAPTER

- This chapter uses the IS–LM model to look at the ways that fiscal and monetary policy can be used to stabilize the economy. We find that the effectiveness of monetary and fiscal policy depend on the slopes of the IS and LM curves.

- The combination of fiscal and monetary policy in an economy determines both the composition of output and the position of the AD curve.

SECTION SUMMARIES

1. Monetary Policy

The central bank conducts monetary policy by engaging in *open market operations*—by buying and selling bonds. When the Fed sells bonds, it reduces the money supply. People send money to the central bank, which it takes out of circulation; in return, they receive a piece of paper they cannot spend. When the Fed buys bonds, it increases the money supply: people exchange those pieces of paper for money.

An increase in the money supply does not initially affect people's disposable income, or the autonomous component of AD; its initial effect is to lower the interest rate. Because this raises the level of investment without reducing consumption or government spending, aggregate demand then increases. Figure 11–1 uses an IS–LM diagram to show the short-run effect of a monetary expansion.

Monetary policy is most effective when the LM curve is relatively steep, or when the demand for real money balances is not very sensitive to the interest rate (the parameter h in the money demand equation is small). It is also more effective when investment is highly sensitive to changes in the interest rate (the parameter b in the investment function is large), and when the marginal propensity to consume is small—i.e., when the IS curve is relatively flat.

121

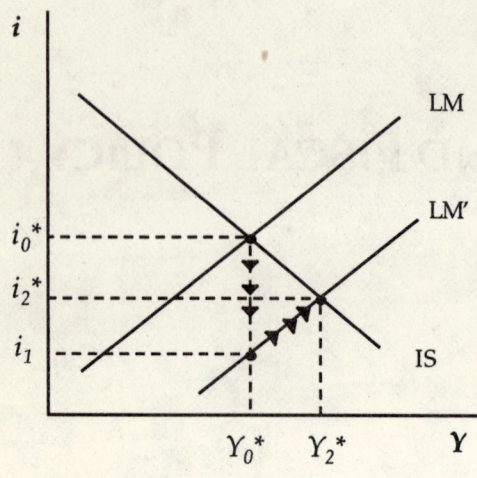 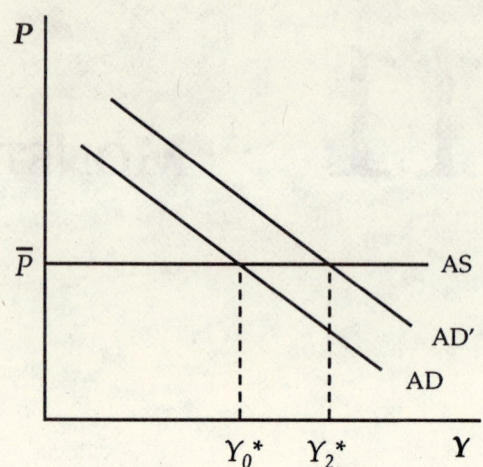

Figure 11 - 1

A MONETARY EXPANSION LOWERS THE INTEREST RATE, SHIFTING THE AD CURVE OUTWARD.

There are two polar cases that have received a lot of attention: The first, called a *liquidity trap*, occurs when people are willing to hold as much money as is supplied (when the money demand curve is horizontal, so that an increase in the supply of real money balances does not affect the interest rate). When the economy is in a liquidity trap, the LM curve is perfectly flat, and changes in the supply of money do not cause it to shift. Because the interest rate does not change, investment demand remains constant, and the level of aggregate demand is not affected.

The second—the *classical case*—occurs when the LM curve is vertical, or when the demand for money is not a function of the interest rate. In this instance, monetary policy is most effective, and fiscal policy cannot affect the level of output at all.

2. Fiscal Policy and Crowding Out

A fiscal expansion—a decrease in taxes, or an increase in either government spending or transfers—directly increases AD, although by less than we might initially expect. An increase in autonomous demand makes people want to hold more money at any given interest rate, shifting the IS curve outward. This increase in money demand, however, drives up the interest rate, which, in turn, reduces the level of investment. One force acts to increase AD; the other pushes back, preventing it from increasing as much as otherwise it would. Figure 11–2 illustrates this.

When a fiscal expansion increases the interest rate and, therefore, reduces investment demand, we say there is *crowding out*. In the classical case (when the LM curve is vertical) there is *full crowding out*—any increase in autonomous spending raises interest rates so much that the corresponding fall in investment prevents AD from increasing at all. Fiscal policy has no effect on output.

There is no crowding out when the economy is in a liquidity trap; an increase in autonomous spending has no effect on the interest rate, and thus no impact on investment. There also need not be any crowding out if the central bank *accommodates* a fiscal expansion by increasing the

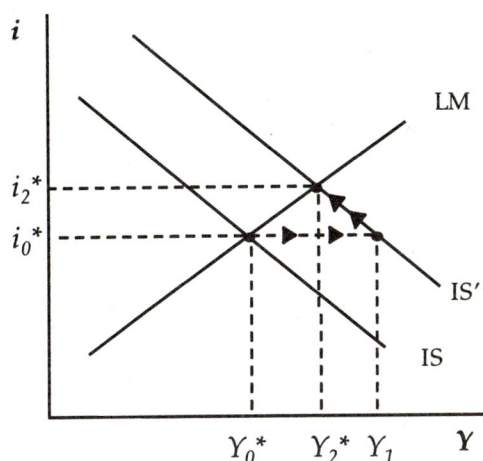 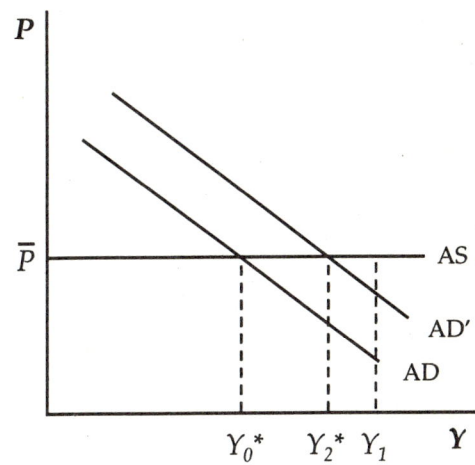

Figure 11 - 2

A FISCAL EXPANSION RAISES THE INTEREST RATE, CROWDING OUT INVESTMENT. THE AD CURVE SHIFTS OUTWARD, BUT NOT BY AS MUCH AS IT COULD.

money supply enough to keep the interest rate at its current level. When the central bank accommodates a fiscal expansion, we also say that they are *monetizing* the budget deficit: it uses some of the money it has taken out of circulation to buy the bonds that the federal government uses to finance its deficit. Figure 11-3 provides an example.

3. The Composition of Output and the Policy Mix

Either fiscal policy or monetary policy can be used to expand aggregate demand. Expansionary fiscal policy, however, discourages investment, while expansionary monetary policy encourages it. Different methods of fiscal expansion affect the composition of output differently. The choice of policy mix—particularly the choice between spending and tax policy—can be made in such a way that other political objectives are accomplished. It is an issue of *political economy*.

4. The Policy Mix in Action

This section provides several historical examples of the ways that the policy mix decision has been made in the real world. It discusses, in particular, the combination of loose (expansionary) fiscal policy with tight (contractionary) monetary policy, and highlights the central bank's ability to combat anticipated as well as existing problems. The connection between the policy and the current or anticipated rate of inflation rate is discussed.

We are reminded of the difference between real and nominal interest rates: The real rate is roughly equal to the nominal rate minus the rate of inflation.

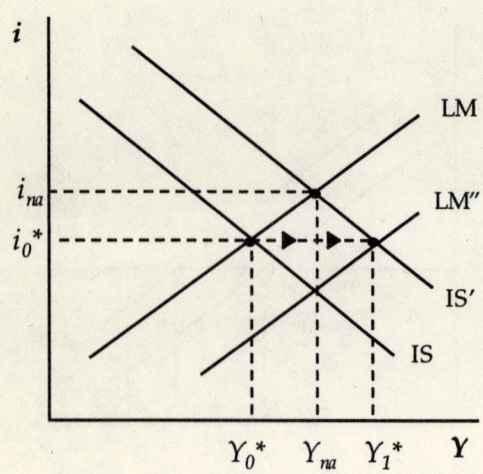 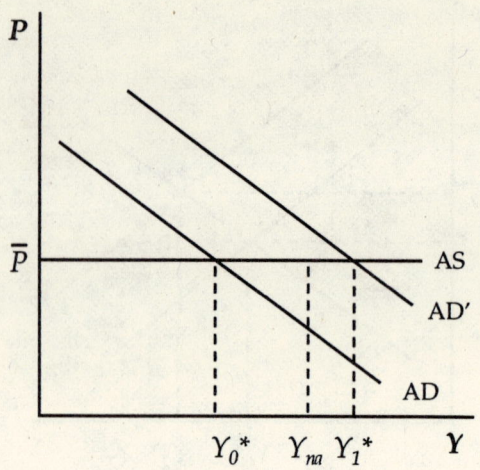

Figure 11 - 3

MONETARY ACCOMMODATION PREVENTS CROWDING OUT.
THE AD CURVE SHIFTS OUTWARD BY THE FULL AMOUNT.

KEY TERMS

open market operations
transmission mechanism
portfolio disequilibrium
liquidity trap
classical case
quantity theory of money
crowding out

monetary accommodation
monetizing budget deficits
investment subsidy
investment tax credit
policy mix
real interest rate
anticipatory monetary policy

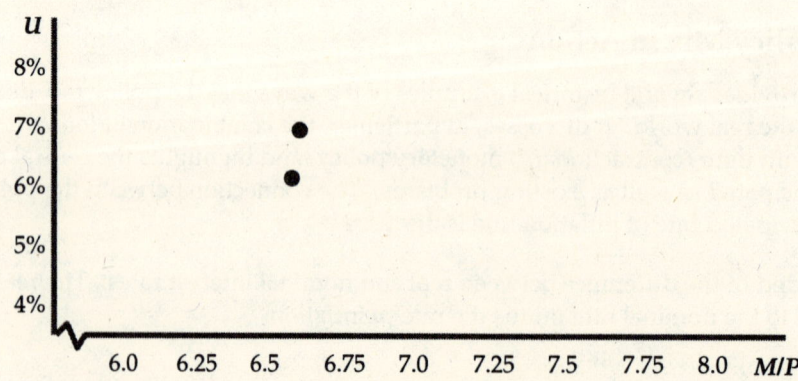

Chart 11 - 1

TABLE 11-1

Year	Unemployment	M1	CPI	Real Money Balances
1986	7.0	724.3	109.6	6.61
1987	6.2	749.7	113.6	6.60
1988	5.5	786.3	118.3	
1989	5.3	792.6	124.0	
1990	5.6	824.6	130.7	
1991	6.8	896.7	136.2	
1992	7.5	1,024.5	140.3	
1993	6.9	1,129.4	144.5	
1994	6.1	1,149.9	148.2	
1995	5.6	1,126.9	152.4	
1996	5.4	1,081.6	156.9	
1997	4.9	1,075.2	160.5	
1998	4.5	1,093.7	163.0	
1999	4.2	1,125.4	166.6	

Source: Economic Data Tables

GRAPH IT 11

Does tight monetary policy put people out of work? You might think that we could answer such a question by simply graphing the unemployment rate against the level of real money balances. This would, of course, be a dangerous way to answer a scientific question; it ignores the influence of fiscal policy on unemployment. As monetary policy seems to have been dominant in recent years, however, we'll throw caution to the winds and do it anyway.

Table 7–1 provides data on the level of unemployment, the nominal money supply, and the price level for the years 1986–1999. You will have to calculate the level of real money balances by hand. This isn't so bad; it just involves dividing some measure of the nominal money supply (we use M1) by another measure of the price level (we use the CPI). After you have calculated the level of real money balances, you should plot the rate of unemployment against it for each year in the sample. We've plotted the first two data points to get you started (see Table 11–1 and Chart 11–

1). You do the rest. Does it look like an increase in the real money supply will reduce the rate of unemployment? (If you fit a line to the points you have drawn, would it slope downward? If so, your answer should be *yes*.)

THE LANGUAGE OF ECONOMICS 11

Stabilization

Usually when economists talk about "stabilizing" the economy, they mean that they want to dampen output fluctuations—reduce the size of recessions and booms, so that the path of output over time is smoother. In an AS–AD framework, this means using fiscal and monetary policy to keep output as close as possible to potential, or full–employment, output.

REVIEW OF TECHNIQUE 11

Working with Multipliers

A multiplier, in general, tells you the amount that some endogenously determined variable increases in response to a 1 unit change in some other exogenously determined variable. It tells you how far a particular curve shifts in response to a change in one of the variables that was held constant when it was drawn.

Take the multiplier

$$\alpha_G = \frac{1}{1-c(1-t)}$$

from in chapter 9, for example: Chapter 9 tells us that a $1 increase in autonomous spending ($\overline{A}$) will increase output by ($1) x ($\alpha_G$), or $\$\left(\frac{1}{1-c(1-t)}\right)$, when the level of investment is held constant.

We can interpret this as a curve shift if we recall from chapter 10 that investment can only remain constant when the interest rate does not change. A $1 increase in autonomous demand, therefore, will increase output by this amount, at each possible level of the interest rate. The IS curve will shift outward by an amount α_G.

Unless the economy is in a liquidity trap, the AD curve will not shift out this far. The multiplier above does not consider the effect that increased demand will have on the interest rate, and therefore on investment. There is another multiplier—one which takes the slopes of both the IS and LM curves into account—that does this.

Even this fiscal policy multiplier (derives in chapter 10, optional section 5), however, does not tell us how much the *equilibrium* level of output increases in response to a given change in autonomous spending. It tells us only how far to shift the AD curve.

While multipliers do tell you how far, and in what direction, to shift various curves, they do <u>not</u> say anything about how these shifts affect the equilibrium values of the models' endogenous variables. Be careful not to jump to conclusions.

CROSSWORD

ACROSS

2 these tell you how far to shift curves
4 type of monetary policy, prevents crowding out
7 expansionary policy; lowers interest rates, increases AD
10 falls when expansionary fiscal policy used
11 LM curve, classical case

DOWN

1 The central bank should ___ the money supply to prevent expansionary fiscal policy from raising the interest rate
3 trap, people will hold as much money as is supplied
5 accommodating a fiscal expansion ___ the budget deficit
6 MPC increases; IS curve gets ___

8 investment demand becomes less sensitive to the interest rate; IS curve gets ___
9 interest rate used in IS–LM diagram

FILL-IN QUESTIONS

1. Monetary policy cannot affect output or the interest rate when the economy is in a _____.

2. Fiscal policy causes complete crowding out in the _____.

3. When money demand is relatively insensitive to the interest rate, the LM curve is _____.

4. When investment is very sensitive to the interest rate, the IS curve is _____.
   (Hint: *when investment is sensitive to the interest rate, is the b large or small?*)

5. When expansionary fiscal policy raises the real interest rate and reduces investment, we say there is _____.

6. The central bank can prevent a fiscal expansion from raising the real interest rate by _____ it.

7. The real interest rate the _____ minus _____.

8. The policy mix that an economy chooses affects the _____ of output.

9. A fiscal expansion _____ investment.

10. The central bank can change the money supply by engaging in _____.

TRUE–FALSE QUESTIONS

T F 1. Monetary Policy is more effective when the LM curve is relatively steep.

T F 2. Fiscal Policy is more effective when the LM curve is relatively flat.

T F 3. Monetary policy is always more effective than fiscal policy.

T F 4. The effectiveness of monetary policy depends only on the slope of the LM curve.

T F 5. Monetary policy first affects AD, and only indirectly affects the interest rate.

T F 6. Expansionary monetary and fiscal policy affect investment differently.

T F 7. A combination of expansionary fiscal and expansionary monetary policy can be used to prevent crowding out.

T F 8. An increase of equal size in transfers and in government spending will shift the IS curve the same distance.

T F 9. An increase in the mpc will make the IS curve steeper.

T F 10. An increase in the mpc will make the IS curve flatter.

MULTIPLE–CHOICE QUESTIONS

1. Fiscal policy is most effective in
   a. the Classical case
   b. a liquidity trap
   c. France
   d. the long run

2. Monetary policy is most effective in
   a. the Classical case
   b. a liquidity trap
   c. Belgium
   d. the neoclassical growth model

3. Fiscal policy is more effective when
   a. investment is relatively sensitive to the interest rate
   b. sensitivity doesn't matter
   c. investment is relatively insensitive to the interest rate
   d. fiscal policy is never effective

4. Monetary policy is more effective when
   a. the IS curve is steep
   b. the IS curve is flat
   c. slope of IS curve doesn't matter
   d. it's never effective

5. Expansionary fiscal policy generally
   a. encourages investment
   b. discourages investment
   c. has no effect on investment
   d. lowers the interest rate

6. Expansionary monetary policy generally
   a. encourages investment
   b. discourages investment
   c. has no effect on investment
   d. raises the interest rate

7. A combination of loose (expansionary) fiscal policy and tight (contractionary) monetary policy
   a. raises Y, lowers i
   b. raises i, lowers Y
   c. raises Y, can't predict effect on i
   d. raises i, can't predict effect on Y

8. Contractionary monetary policy has been used in the past to combat
   a. inflation
   b. recession
   c. unemployment
   d. famine

9. The central bank is able to choose whether or not to _____ a fiscal expansion.
   a. illuminate
   b. prevent
   c. accommodate
   d. run

10. The multiplier $\alpha_G = \frac{1}{1-c(1-t)}$ tells us how far the ____ curve shifts in response to an increase in autonomous spending.
    a. IS
    b. LM
    c. AS
    d. AD

CONCEPTUAL PROBLEMS

1. Will proportional income taxes make monetary policy more effective, less effective, or will their presence have no effect?

2. Will proportional income taxes increase, decrease, or not affect the expansionary effect of an increase in government spending (the amount it raises output) in the short run?

TECHNICAL PROBLEMS

1. How far, and in what direction, will the IS curve shift in response to a $100 increase in government spending?

2. How far, and in what direction, will the AD curve shift in response to a $100 increase in government spending? If the LM curve is upward–sloping, should this AD shift be bigger or smaller than the IS shift in problem 1?

3. How far, and in what direction, will the LM curve shift if the money supply (M) increases $100. (Assume that the price level is constant.)

   Hint: Use the equation for the LM curve: $\overline{M} / \overline{P} = kY - hi$. If you hold i constant and find how much Y changes, this will tell you how far (horizontally) the LM curve shifts.

4. How far, and in what direction, will the AD curve shift in response to this $100 increase in the money supply? Should this AD shift be bigger or smaller than the LM shift in problem 3?

5. Under what conditions will the level of output increase by exactly the same amount as aggregate demand?

6. Under what conditions will the level of output not be affected by changes in aggregate demand (AD shifts)?

7. Suppose that government spending were not simply exogenous. If it increased and decreased with the output gap (the difference between potential output (Y_P) and actual output (Y)) according to the rule

$$G = \overline{G} + d(Y_P - Y),$$

where $d > 0$, what would happen to the slope of the IS curve? Would this make monetary policy more effective or less effective?

12 INTERNATIONAL LINKAGES

FOCUS OF THE CHAPTER

- This chapter provides an introduction to international macroeconomics.

- The IS–LM model is adapted to this new, open economy setting. The effects of fiscal and monetary policy are shown to depend strongly on whether exchange rates are fixed or floating, and on whether capital is more or less mobile (able to move across borders in response to interest differentials).

- The difference between fixed and floating exchange rates is explained, as is the difference between real and nominal exchange rates.

SECTION SUMMARIES

1. The Balance of Payments and Exchange Rates

The *balance of payments* measures the difference between payments entering and payments leaving the country. We break these payments down into payments for goods and services—kept track of in the *current account*—and payments for assets—recorded in the *capital account*.

The current account consists of the *trade balance*—the difference between the money we receive for exporting goods abroad and the money we pay for goods that we import from abroad—of the difference between the value of the services we export and the services we import, and of the difference between the value of the gifts (transfers) that we send to foreigners and those that we receive from them. The current account is in surplus when these transactions cause more money to flow into the country than to flow out of it. It is in deficit whenever they cause more money to flow out of the country than to flow into it.

The capital account keeps track of the sales and purchases of assets like stocks, bonds, land, and bank deposits. There is a capital account surplus whenever the revenue from our sales of these assets exceeds the revenue from our purchases of them.

Both the private sector and the central bank buy and sell assets; the purchases and sales of assets by the central bank are referred to as *official reserve transactions*.

There are some simple guidelines that will help you with balance of payments accounting:

- Any transaction that causes money to flow into a country increases the balance of payments.
- Any transaction that causes money to flow out of a country lowers the balance of payments.
- When the money results from the sale or purchase of goods and services or takes the form of a transfer, the change is recorded in the current account.
- When the money results from the sale or purchase of assets, the change is recorded in the capital account.

The central bank's official reserve transactions must be of exactly the same value as of the balance of payments deficit. When more money is leaving the county than is entering it, the central bank must exchange the domestic currency on its way out for the foreign currency in which other countries prefer to be paid. This decrease in official reserves represents a balance of payments deficit. Conversely, an increase in official reserves indicates a balance of payments surplus.

The central bank can only run down its reserves by so much until it runs out. A balance of payments deficit, therefore, is unsustainable. It could increase its reserves indefinitely, but is unlikely to want to do so; it will have to print money with which to purchase this currency, driving down its real interest rate and, eventually, over time, creating a great deal of inflation. The balance of payments is equal zero in equilibrium.

In order to understand how central banks finance balance of payments surpluses and deficits, we must first distinguish between fixed and floating exchange rates. Under a *fixed exchange rate* regime, the central bank is obligated to maintain a given rate of exchange between its currency and others. For example, if Germany's currency were fixed relative to that of the US—let's say at 4 marks (DM) per dollar ($)—the Bundesbank (Germany's central bank) would be obligated to buy or sell an unlimited amount of US dollars at that price. To prevent this price from changing, the Bundesbank would have to *intervene* in the foreign exchange market—to buy dollars with marks when the exchange rate falls below 4 DM/$ (i.e., to 3 DM/$), and sell dollars (in exchange for marks) when it rises above 4 DM/$ (i.e., to 5 DM/$). Figure 12–1 uses a simple supply/demand diagram to show you how this works.

In a *flexible (floating) exchange rate* regime, the central bank is not obligated to maintain any particular exchange rate. When it chooses not to intervene at all, we say that the exchange rate follows a *clean float*. In this case, official reserve transactions are zero; the exchange rate adjusts so that the current account and the capital account sum to zero. When the central bank does periodically intervene in the foreign exchange market, we say that the exchange rate follows a *managed*, or *dirty float*. In both fixed and floating regimes, central banks are only able to intervene when they have enough reserves. The Bundesbank, in the example above, can only sell as many dollars as it has. When it runs out, it will have to allow the price of the mark to fall (or, equivalently, the price of the dollar to rise from 4 DM/$ to, for example, 5 DM/$). Under a flexible exchange rate regime, a reduction in the value of a currency is called a *depreciation*, and an increase in value an *appreciation*. Under a fixed exchange rate regime, this reduction in value is called a *devaluation*, this increase a *revaluation*..

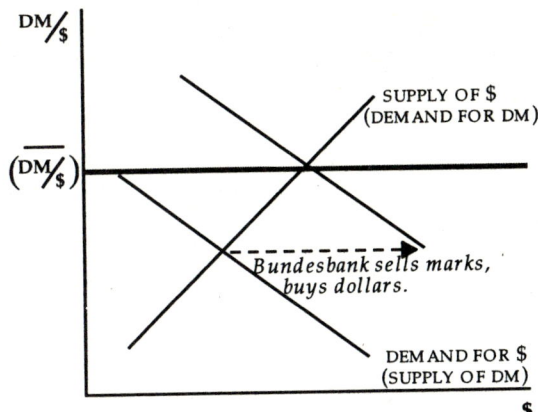

Figure 12 – 1

GERMANY'S CENTRAL BANK INTERVENES TO PREVENT THE VALUE OF THE MARK FROM FALLING.

Under a fixed exchange rate regime, the central bank has to intervene in the foreign exchange market in order to prevent its exchange rate from rising or falling.

Exchange rates are typically quoted as the amount of foreign currency that it takes to buy one unit of the domestic currency (the price of the domestic currency). From the perspective of the US, the exchange rate between the US and Germany should be quoted in marks per dollar (DM/$), the exchange rate between the US and Japan in yen per dollar (¥/$), and the exchange rate between the US and Great Britain in pounds per dollar (£/$). A decrease in the exchange rate makes the domestic currency more valuable—it costs fewer dollars to buy one unit of the foreign currency—and the foreign currency less valuable.

2. The Exchange Rate in the Long Run

In the long run, the exchange rate between two countries is determined by the relative purchasing power of their currencies—the amount that a given quantity of the one country's currency can buy in each.

Relative purchasing power is measured by the ***real exchange rate*** (R), defined as

$$R = \frac{eP_f}{P},$$

where P is the domestic price level, P_f is the foreign price level, and e is the nominal exchange rate, measured in units of domestic currency per unit of foreign currency. (*Note that this is contrary to convention: usually we measure nominal exchange rates in units of foreign currency per unit of domestic currency.*) **Purchasing power parity** (PPP) exists when the same basket of goods can be purchased both at home and abroad for the same amount of domestic currency, or when the real exchange rate is equal to 1.

We believe that, over long periods of time, nominal exchange rates will adjust in order to bring the purchasing power of one country's currency into line with the purchasing power of other currencies, so that purchasing power parity will be achieved.

3. Trade in Goods, Market Equilibrium, and the Balance of Trade

This section adds net exports (NX) to the IS–LM model. Domestic spending no longer determines domestic output; instead, spending on domestic goods—both by domestic residents and by the residents of other countries—does.

Spending by domestic residents ($A = C + I + G$) includes spending on imported goods by consumers, by investors, and by the government, and excludes the value of the goods that we export, making our previous measure of aggregate demand ($AD = C + I + G$) inadequate. To convert this into a measure of spending on domestic goods, we have to include the value of the goods that we export to other countries, and exclude the value of the goods that we import from other countries. We do this by adding net exports (exports– imports) to the aggregate demand equation:

$$AD = C + I + G + NX.$$

We assume, as in chapter 10, that spending by domestic residents depends on their income (Y) and on the real interest rate (i): $A(Y, i) = C(Y - \overline{T}) + I(i) + \overline{G}$.

We also make some assumptions about exports and imports:

- Exports (X) increase when other countries' income (Y_f) rises, and when there is a real depreciation in the home country (when the real exchange rate rises): $X(Y_f, R)$.

- Imports (Q) increase when the home country's income (Y) rises, and fall when it experiences a real depreciation (when the real exchange rate rises): $Q(Y, R)$. The increase in the demand for imports that results from a 1-unit increase in domestic income is called the *marginal propensity to import*.

These assumptions allow us to conclude that net exports rise when the real exchange rate rises, fall when domestic income rises, and rise when foreign income rises:

$$NX(Y, Y_f, R) = X(Y_f, R) - Q(Y, R).$$

We can now write a more precise equation for aggregate demand:

$$AD = A(Y, i) + NX(Y, Y_f, i),$$

and, imposing the requirement for goods market equilibrium ($Y = AD$), for the IS curve:

$$Y = A(Y, i) + NX(Y, Y_f, i).$$

An increase in foreign income and a real depreciation of the domestic currency both cause the IS curve to shift to the right.

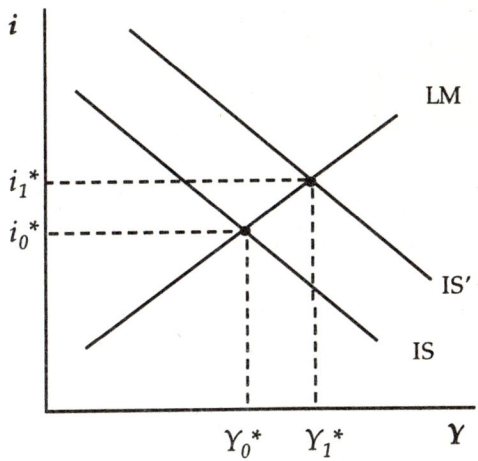

Figure 12 - 2

The fact that a fraction of domestic income is spent on foreign goods reduces the multiplier α_G and makes the IS curve steeper than it would be in a closed economy. As before, expansionary fiscal policy will shift the IS curve outward (though, because our multiplier is smaller, not as far as it did in Chapter 10). An increase in foreign income will also, now, cause an outward shift in the IS curve. So will a real depreciation.

Our policies can have *repercussion effects*—they can affect income in other countries as well as income in our own country. Expansionary fiscal policy increases income both at home and abroad: When our income rises, we import more goods from other countries. This causes their incomes to rise, so that they, in turn, import more of our goods. Everyone shares in the expansion. Everyone is better off. *This not true of changes in the real exchange rate: a real depreciation of our currency increases our income and reduces income abroad.*

4. Capital Mobility

Interest rates, once they have been adjusted for the risk associated with changes in the exchange rate, tend to be very similar across countries with well–developed capital markets when capital is highly mobile (able to flow easily across borders). If they get very far out of line, they create an opportunity for speculators to make a substantial profit by taking their money out countries with low interest rates and investing it in countries with high interest rates. This causes the higher interest rate to fall, as more funds become available to investors, and the lower rate to rise, as the funds that local investors have been using are sent abroad.

We assume, in this chapter, that capital is *perfectly mobile*—able to move between countries quickly, with low transaction costs, and in unlimited amounts. Capital will therefore flow into a country whenever its interest rate is even a little above the world interest rate, and out of it whenever its interest rate is at all below the world interest rate, affecting the capital account and, therefore, the balance of payments. This has serious implications for the use of fiscal and monetary policy in open economies.

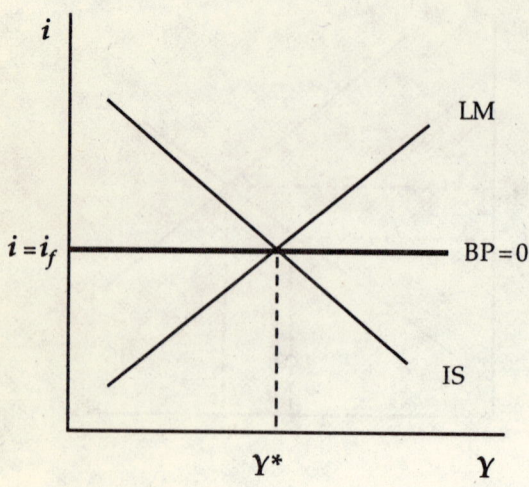

Figure 12 - 3

THE MUNDELL–FLEMING MODEL

> *The Mundell–Flemming model imposes the requirement that the balance of payments surplus be 0, or that domestic interest rates be fixed at the prevailing world rate, on the standard IS–LM model.*

The economy is in *external balance* when the balance of payments surplus is zero:

$$BP = NX(Y, Y_f, R) + CF(i - i_f) = 0.$$

Net exports represent the current account surplus in this equation. Net capital flows (flows into the country minus flows out of the country) measure the capital account surplus. Note that, by choosing an appropriate real interest rate, we can create a capital account surplus that exactly offsets a current account deficit, or vice versa.

The economy is in *internal balance* when output is at its full–employment level. The next two sections help us to understand how fiscal and monetary policy can be used to keep the economy in both internal and external balance under different exchange rate regimes.

5. The Mundell–Flemming Model: Perfect Capital Mobility Under Fixed Exchange Rates

We have already noted that when capital is highly mobile the slightest difference between domestic and international interest rates generates immense capital flows, which force them back into line. *The Mundell–Flemming model imposes the requirement that the balance of payments surplus be zero, or that domestic interest rates be fixed at the prevailing world rate, on the standard IS–LM model.* By requiring that the country be in external balance, we are able to see which policies are *also* able to bring it into internal balance—to bring output as close as possible to its full–employment level.

We have also noted that when a country's exchange rate is fixed the central bank must intervene in the foreign exchange market to keep it at its agreed–upon level. In a small open economy, when capital is perfectly mobile, this means that the central bank must keep the domestic interest rate at the same level as the world interest rate at all times, so that capital has no incentive to flow either

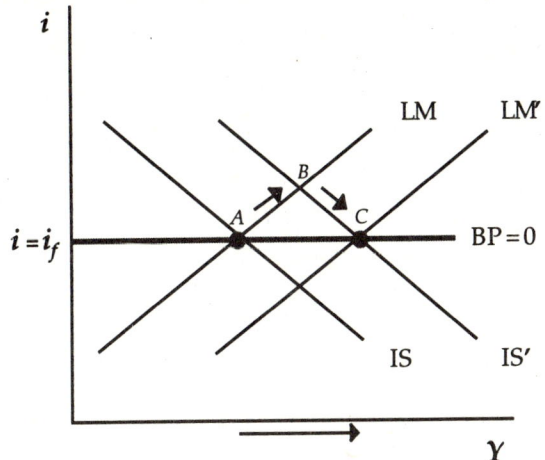

Figure 10 - 4

THE MUNDELL–FLEMING MODEL WITH
FIXED EXCHANGE RATES

> *Fiscal policy can affect output when exchange rates are fixed because the central bank is obligated to accommodate it—to use monetary policy to reverse its effect on domestic interest rates.*

in or out of the country. This obligation prevents the central bank from using monetary policy to stabilize output, as it can affect output only by changing the interest rate.

Fiscal policy is thus the only tool the government of a small open economy can use to bring its economy into internal balance, when its exchange rate is fixed relative to that of some other country… at least when capital is perfectly mobile, and exchange rates are fixed.

6. Perfect Capital Mobility and Flexible Exchange Rates

The Mundell–Flemming model can be used with flexible as well as fixed exchange rates. The major difference is that when nominal exchange rates are flexible, the central bank has no obligation to keep domestic interest rates equal to foreign ones. The LM curve does not adjust to keep the balance of payments surplus equal to zero. Instead, capital flows into and out of the country in search of the highest return, raising demand for the domestic currency when real interest rates at home exceed those abroad, and lowering it when real interest rates at home cannot compete with those abroad. Any change in currency demand will cause the nominal exchange rate to change. This, in turn, will change net exports and therefore the position of the IS curve. Thus it is the IS curve that shifts to keep domestic interest rates equal to foreign ones, when capital is perfectly mobile and exchange rates are flexible.

Let's work through an example:

First, suppose that we begin with the country in both internal and external balance, so that output is equal to potential output and the balance of payments surplus is equal to zero ($i = i_f$). Exchange rates are flexible; capital is perfectly mobile. If the central bank increases the money supply, the LM curve will shift outward and domestic interest rates will fall below foreign interest rates. This is unsustainable: Capital will immediately flow out of the country, increasing the demand for

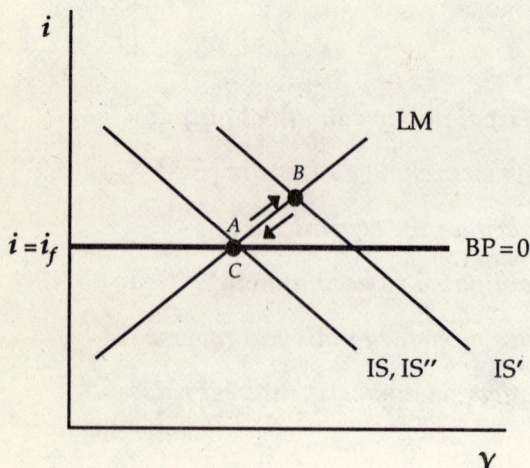

Figure 10 - 5

THE MUNDELL–FLEMING MODEL WITH
FLOATING EXCHANGE RATES

Fiscal policy cannot affect output when exchange rates are flexible because its use creates interest differentials which ultimately counteract the effect of the policy.

other currencies and decreasing the demand for the domestic currency. As a result, the domestic currency will *depreciate*. Goods produced abroad will look more expensive to domestic residents; goods produced domestically will appear less expensive to foreigners. Imports will fall. Exports will rise. The IS curve will shift outwards. Output is now greater than potential output; the balance of payments surplus is still zero.

Notice that while net exports rise at home, they fall for the rest of the world; we improve our own standard of living at the expense of everyone else's. For this reason, depreciation–induced output growth has been called a *beggar–thy–neighbor policy*.

Despite its less–than–flattering nickname, this sort of depreciation can be mutually beneficial when countries are at different stages in the business cycle: increasing AD at home and decreasing it abroad may not be a bad thing if the home country is in recession and whatever foreign countries are affected are subject to inflationary pressures.

It is only truly bad when countries have highly synchronized business cycles, so that its contractionary effect on other countries' aggregate demand is truly unwelcome. Then it may encourage retaliation—set off a cycle of *competitive depreciation*, as each country tries to reduce the value of its own currency in order to increase its exports and raise output.

Notice that fiscal policy cannot affect output when exchange rates are flexible unless the central bank chooses to accommodate it; because expansionary fiscal policy raises the domestic interest rate, it causes the domestic currency to appreciate and net exports to fall, reversing the initial IS shift and leaving the economy right where it started (though with a higher nominal exchange rate).

KEY TERMS

globalization
open economy
trade
finance
balance of payments
current account
net investment income
trade balance
capital account
balance-of-payments surplus
fixed exchange rate system
reserves
intervention
European exchange rate mechanism (ERM)
European Monetary Union (EMU)
target zone
flexible (floating) exchange rate

clean floating
managed (dirty) floating
devaluation/revaluation
currency depreciation
currency appreciation
purchasing power parity (PPP)
real exchange rate
marginal propensity to import
repercussion effects
perfect capital mobility
interest differential
external balance
internal balance
Mundell-Fleming model
beggar-thy-neighbor policy
competitive depreciation

GRAPH IT 12

Does an increase in the exchange rate really reduce exports? By how much? This Graph It gives you the opportunity to answer these questions.

Table 12–1 provides you with data on the real value of US exports and the real trade–weighted value of the US dollar* for the years 1990-1995. Your task is to convert this data into natural logs (there should be a *ln* function on your calculator), and then to graph the natural log of US exports against the natural log of the real value of the dollar for each year. When you are finished, you will have produced a *scatterplot*. Each year will be represented by a single point.

If a real appreciation of the dollar actually does cause US exports to fall, you should expect the points that you have plotted to form a downward–sloping line; the slope of this line will give you an estimate of the percentage decline in US exports that results from a 1% increase in the value of the dollar.

Does an increase in the exchange rate really reduce exports? What do you think?

(*Note:* We graph this data in log form so that we can look at percentage changes in our variables instead of absolute ones. Review of Technique 15 provides a brief overview of natural logarithms.)

---

* This compares the dollar to a weighted average of other currencies. Weights are determined by volume of trade, so that countries which trade with the US frequently and in large volume are more heavily represented than countries with whom it trades less.

TABLE 12-1

Year	Real Exports	Natural Log of Real Exports	Real Value of the dollar*	Natural Log of the Dollar
1990	564.4	6.34	86.0	4.45
1991	599.9	6.40	86.5	4.46
1992	639.4		83.4	
1993	658.2		90.0	
1994	712.0		88.7	
1995	775.4		82.5	

* March 1973 = 100.

Source: Economic Data Tables

THE LANGUAGE OF ECONOMICS 12

Accommodation

Typically, when we refer to a policy as "accommodating" we mean that it relaxes whatever barriers prevent a shock from having its full effect.

Expansionary monetary and fiscal policy can be used to accommodate negative supply shocks—to allow their full impact on wages and prices to be felt at once, so that output need not deviate from potential output during the adjustment period.

Monetary policy can also be used to accommodate a fiscal expansion: By increasing the money supply just enough to prevent interest rates from rising, the central bank can prevent the crowding out that a fiscal expansion would ordinarily cause. Notice that when exchange rates are fixed, the central bank is *required* to accommodate both expansionary and contractionary fiscal policy, whereas when exchange rates are floating it can choose whether or not it wishes to.

REVIEW OF TECHNIQUE 12

Interpreting Changes in Real and Nominal Exchange Rates

When a nominal exchange rate is written in the conventional manner—in units of foreign currency per unit of domestic currency—an increase in the exchange rate makes the domestic currency more valuable and the foreign currency less valuable. Those who hold the domestic

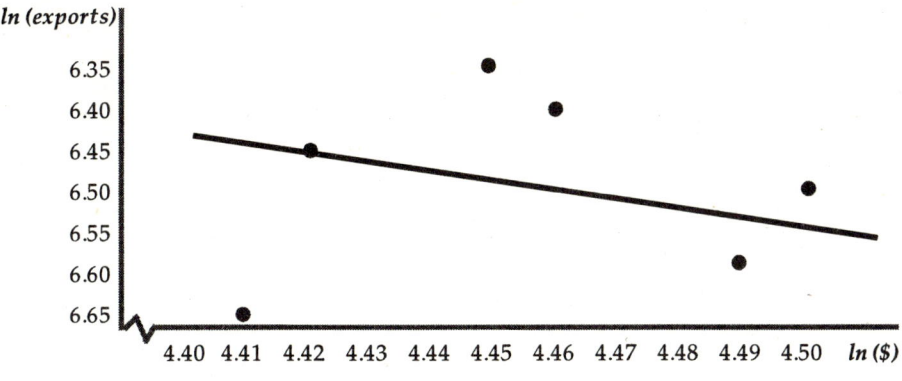

Chart 12-1

currency are able to buy more foreign currency when the exchange rate rises; correspondingly, those who hold the foreign currency cannot buy as much domestic currency.

Consider the following example: Between 1985 and 1986, number of yen that 1 US dollar could purchase fell from 238.47 to 168.35. This constituted a 29% decline in the US's exchange rate with Japan—a considerable depreciation of the dollar. Notice that this decline in the value of the dollar constituted an increase in the value of the yen; the number of dollars it could buy rose from (1/238.47), or .0042, to (1/168.35), or .0059. One currency cannot depreciate without causing another to appreciate.

This book expresses the real exchange rate in a somewhat counter–intuitive manner: The real exchange rate is equal to the nominal exchange rate (written in units of *domestic* currency per unit *foreign* currency) times the ratio of the foreign price level to the domestic price level:

$$R = \frac{eP_f}{P}.$$

Its value is not expressed in expressed in terms of any currency. Instead, the real exchange rate shows the number of domestic goods that can be exchanged for a "basket" of foreign goods. When the real exchange rate increases, it means that this basket of foreign goods can be exchanged for more domestic goods, or that the foreign currency is more valuable in real terms. It can purchase more goods and services. The domestic currency is *less* valuable in real terms; it cannot purchase as many goods and services. An increase in the real exchange rate, then, causes a real depreciation of the domestic currency and a real appreciation of the foreign currency.

The fact that real and nominal exchange rates are expressed in different terms can be confusing, but if you stop to remember that we have used a different convention for the real and nominal exchange rates, you should be okay. Let's put everything together:

- An increase in the (conventionally defined) nominal exchange rate represents an appreciation of the domestic currency and a depreciation of the foreign currency.

- If both the domestic price level and the foreign price level are fixed, as this chapter assumes, this increase in the nominal exchange rate causes the real exchange rate to fall (recall that the formula for the real exchange rate uses an unconventional form of the nominal exchange rate—one written in units of the domestic currency per unit of foreign currency).

- The domestic currency appreciates in real terms. The foreign currency depreciates in real terms.

Notice that the change in the domestic and foreign currencies are consistent across real and nominal exchange rates. It is only the direction of change of the real and nominal exchange rates that appear, at first, to be inconsistent.

CROSSWORD

ACROSS

3 type of currency float, central bank does intervene in foreign exchange markets
5 curve that shifts in Mundell-Fleming model to keep domestic interest rates equal to foreign interest rates when the exchange rate is fixed
6 type of balance, current and capital accounts exactly offset one another
7 curve that shifts in Mundell-Fleming model to keep domestic interest rates equal to foreign interest rates when the exchange rate is floating
8 account that keeps track of capital flows related to payments for goods and services
(continued next page)

FILL-IN QUESTIONS

1. Under a _____ *exchange rate* regime, the central bank is obligated to intervene in the foreign exchange market, buying and selling foreign currency as necessary in order to maintain a particular exchange rate.

2. Under a _____ *exchange rate* regime, the central bank is not obligated to do this.

3. When the number of pesos that can be exchanged for $1 rises, the value of the peso _____ and the value of the dollar _____.

4. When the number of yen that can be exchanged for $1 falls, the value of the yen _____ and the value of the dollar _____.

5. Under a floating exchange rate regime, an increase in the value of a currency is called an _____ ; under a fixed exchange rate regime, it is called a _____.

6. Under a floating exchange rate regime, a decrease in the value of a currency is called a _____ ; under a fixed exchange rate regime, it is called a _____.

7. A depreciation–induced change in the trade balance is also called a _____ policy.

ACROSS (CONTINUED)

9. increase in value of a currency when exchange rate is floating
10. type of currency float, central bank does not intervene in foreign exchange markets

DOWN

1. increase in value of a currency when exchange rate is fixed
2. decrease in value of a currency when exchange rate is fixed
3. decrease in value of a currency when exchange rate is floating
4. type of economy assumed in this chapter
7. type of balance, output equals potential output

8. When real interest rates are higher in one country than in the rest of the world, capital will flow _____ that country, _____ the demand for its currency and causing its exchange rate (expressed in units of foreign currency per unit of domestic currency) to _____.

9. It is these capital flows which prevent domestic interest rates from rising above or falling below international rates, or which keep countries in _____.

10. When a country's currency depreciates, we expect that country's imports to _____ and its exports to _____.

TRUE–FALSE QUESTIONS

T F 1. When the US imports more goods and services than it exports, the current account is in deficit.

T F 2. When the current account is in deficit and the balance of payments surplus is equal to zero, the capital account must be in surplus.

T F 3. An increase in official reserves indicates a balance of payments surplus.

T F 4. All policies that increase domestic output reduce output in other countries.

T F   5.   All policies that increase domestic output raise output in other countries.

T F   6.   Policies that increase domestic output never affect output in other countries.

T F   7.   When a country has fixed exchange rates and capital is perfectly mobile internationally, monetary policy is ineffective (cannot be used to stabilize output).

T F   8.   When a country has fixed exchange rates and capital is perfectly mobile internationally, fiscal policy is ineffective (cannot be used to stabilize output).

T F   9.   When a country has flexible exchange rates and capital is perfectly mobile internationally, monetary policy is ineffective (cannot be used to stabilize output).

T F   10. When a country has flexible exchange rates and capital is perfectly mobile internationally, fiscal policy is ineffective (cannot be used to stabilize output).

MULTIPLE–CHOICE QUESTIONS

1. In which of the following cases will official reserve transactions always be zero?

   a. clean float
   b. dirty float
   c. managed float
   d. fixed exchange rate

2. Which of the following is <u>not</u> a part of the capital account?

   a. trade balance
   b. official reserve transactions
   c. asset sales by the private sector
   d. asset sales by the central bank

3. If we export more goods and services than we import, and neither give nor receive any gifts, the

   a. current account will be in deficit
   b. capital account will be in deficit
   c. current account will be in surplus
   d. capital account will be in surplus

4. Which of the following is <u>not</u> a part of the current account?

   a. trade balance
   b. official reserve transactions
   c. money sent to other countries as aid
   d. b and c

5. Relative purchasing power is measured by

   a. official reserve transactions
   b. the balance of payments
   c. the real exchange rate
   d. the nominal exchange rate

6. An economy is in internal balance when (the)

   a. balance of payments surplus is zero
   b. output equals potential output
   c. domestic interest rates = foreign ones
   d. current account = the capital account

7. An economy is in external balance when (the)

   a. balance of payments surplus is zero
   b. output equals potential output
   c. domestic interest rates = foreign ones
   d. current account = the capital account

8. A real depreciation causes a country's exports to

   a. rise
   b. fall
   c. has no effect
   d. who knows?

9. An increase in foreign income will cause a country's

   a. exports to rise
   b. exports to fall
   c. imports to rise
   d. imports to fall

10. An increase in domestic income will cause a country's

    a. exports to rise
    b. exports to fall
    c. imports to rise
    d. imports to fall

CONCEPTUAL PROBLEMS

1. When exchange rates are fixed and capital is perfectly mobile, will monetary or fiscal policy be better able to stabilize output? Why?

2. How would your answer to the previous question change if exchange rates were flexible rather than fixed?

3. Why might a country choose to have fixed rather than flexible exchange rates? Why might it not?

4. What are the possible political and economic dangers of using a real depreciation to stimulate domestic output? Might it be a better idea in some situations than in others? Explain.

5. Name 10 different currencies and the countries in which they are used.
   (*Try to do it without looking at the list in the appendix.*)

TECHNICAL PROBLEMS

1. Which of the following transactions will increase the US's balance of payments? Which will decrease it? Note whether each will be recorded in the current account or the capital account.

   a) The sale of 2 airplanes to Greece.
   b) The purchase of 100 tins of caviar from Russia.
   c) The sale of 3,000 shares of General Motors (a US auto maker) stock to investors abroad.
   d) The sale of Rockefeller Center to Japanese investors.
   e) $1,000,000,000 sent by the US as foreign aid to Israel.
   f) The purchase of 1,000,000 acres of the Brazilian rainforest by US conservationists.
   g) The purchase of a haircut and a manicure in the US by a German tourist.

2. If an economy without proportional income taxes has a marginal propensity to consume of 0.9, and if its imports (Q) and exports (X) are given by the functions:

$$Q = \overline{Q} + 0.1(Y - \overline{T}), \quad X = \overline{X}$$

what is the multiplier for government spending? (Assume that exchange rates are fixed.)

3. What would this multiplier be if an income tax (τ) of 0.25 were imposed?

*4. Now let's consider a world with only two countries, whose exchange rates are fixed relative to each other. Suppose that Country A has a marginal propensity to consume of 0.9 (as in the problem above), and imports (Q_A):

$$Q_A = \overline{Q}_A + 0.1(Y_A - \overline{T}_A),$$

that Country B has a marginal propensity to consume of 0.8 and imports (Q_B):

$$Q_B = \overline{Q}_B + 0.1(Y_B - \overline{T}_B)$$

and that neither have proportional taxes. What is the multiplier for government spending in Country A? What is the multiplier for government spending in Country B?

Part 4

Behavioral Foundations

13 Consumption and Saving

FOCUS OF THE CHAPTER

- Consumption is the largest component of aggregate demand.

- The amount that we consume today depends not only on our current income, but also on our wealth and our expectations of future income.

- Because people try to spread their resources out over their lifetimes, transitory changes in income do not affect their consumption very much at all. Permanent changes in income do.

SECTION SUMMARIES

1. The Life–Cycle/Permenant Income Theory of Consumption and Saving

The life–cycle and permanent income theories tell a very similar story, and for that reason have been grouped together in this textbook. Both are based on the notion that people try to smooth consumption over their lifetimes—that they borrow when their income is low and save when their income is high in order to maintain a constant level of consumption over the years. They really only differ in the way that they model the decision–making involved in this process.

The *life–cycle theory* of consumption assumes that consumption is a function of both wealth and our average lifetime income, and that we have different *marginal propensities to consume* out of each: a high marginal propensity to consume out of income, and a low marginal propensity to consume out of wealth, which we try to spread out evenly over our lifetimes. It emphasizes the demographic aspect of saving behavior—people's tendency to borrow against their future income when they are young, save for retirement when they are older, and to live off of their savings after they retire.

The *permanent income theory* suggests that people form expectations of the income they will receive over their lifetime, divide it by the number of years during which they expect to live, and consume an amount equal to that each period. When their actual income is below their *permanent income*, they borrow or draw down their savings. When their actual income exceeds their permanent income, they save. For this reason temporary changes in people's incomes do not affect their consumption very much; the benefits of a windfall gain today get spread out over an entire lifetime.

It is interesting to note that, in both of these models, changes in people's expectations—either their expectations regarding their future income or their expectations regarding their time of death—can strongly influence their consumption patterns.

2. Consumption Under Uncertainty—the Modern Approach

Modern consumption theory both emphasizes the link between income uncertainty and changes in consumption and takes a slightly more formal approach to modeling the way that people decide how much to consume. Here, consumption does not change unless something causes people's *expectations* to change. Changes in people's consumption, as a result, should not be predictable.

The empirical predictions of modern consumption theory have not been validated. Consumption seems to respond both too strongly to predictable (read *expected*) changes in income, and not strongly enough to unexpected changes in income—characteristics which are referred to, respectively, as *excess sensitivity* and *excess smoothness*.

Excess sensitivity could well be the result of *liquidity constraints*—constraints on people's ability to borrow money that force them to finance their consumption entirely out of current income. It could also result from *myopia*—a short-sightness that prevents people from learning or caring about the future, and hence from forming good expectations of their lifetime incomes.

Excess smoothness could well result from *precautionary*, or *buffer-stock saving*: saving intended to provide inheritances for children or grandchildren, or to leave something in the bank for a future rainy day.

3. Further Aspects of Consumption Behavior

Barro–Ricardo equivalence, also called *Ricardian equivalence*, follows directly from the Life-Cycle/Permanent Income Hypothesis. Under Ricardian Equivalence, it doesn't matter whether deficits are financed through increased taxes or the accumulation of debt. Debt financing merely postpones taxes to a future date, and, under some stringent conditions, is identical to current taxation.

There are two main theoretical objections to this proposition, however. First, people have finite lifetimes, and because of this do not need to worry about taxes that are postponed into the very distant future. The second objection echoes one we have already heard: people may very well be liquidity constrained. If this is the case, a tax cut today—even one that people know they'll have to pay back in 5 years—can be of real benefit to people, since they wish to consume more than their current income allows. Note that this is consistent with one of our explanations for excess sensitivity.

The household savings rate in the United States is one of the lowest found in industrialized countries. Our net saving rate—the rate at which we are adding to our wealth—and our national (government plus private) savings rate are remarkably low as well. Most private saving is done by the business sector, in the form of retained earnings (earnings not paid out to stockholders/owners). Why is this? One reason may be demographics: we have an aging population. The U.S. also has a very well developed financial sector; it may be that residents of the U.S. have an easier time borrowing to finance large purchases, and don't need to save in order to pay for them with cash. These explanations do not fully explain low U.S. saving, but they do help close the gap.

Arguments have been made that policy measures that increase the rate of interest on savings accounts will increase household saving. Empirical evidence, however, suggests that changes in interest rates have had little impact on household saving in the US. It may be that we're all just more myopic, and don't like to save as much as others.

KEY TERMS

life-cycle hypothesis
permanent income hypothesis
lifetime utility
lifetime budget constraint
marginal utility of consumption
random-walk model of consumption
excess sensitivity
excess smoothness
liquidity constraint

myopia
buffer-stock saving
government saving
private saving
business saving
personal saving
Ricardian (or Barro–Ricardo) equivalence
liquidity constraints
operations bequest motive

TABLE 13 – 1

Permanent Income (YP)	Total Income (Y)	Consumption* (C = cYP)
$500	$400	$400
$500	$500	$400
$500	$600	$400
$1,000	$900	$800
$1,000	$1,000	$800
$1,000	$1,100	$800

* We assume that c, the marginal propensity to consume, is 0.8

GRAPH IT 13

This graph It allows you to see for yourself why the marginal propensity to consume might appear to be too small in estimates based on cross–sectional data (data that takes a "slice" of the current population instead of following a few select individuals through time).

Table 13–1 provides data for a hypothetical cross–section of the population. There are six individuals in our sample; three have one level of permanent income, and three have another. Each person is experiencing a different level of good or bad fortune, so that their actual income does not equal their permanent income.

Graph each point in the sample, and find the line that best fits the group as a whole. Does the *mpc* appear too small? Does the consumption function appear to have a positive intercept? This is an example of what statisticians call an "errors in variables" problem. Our estimate of the marginal propensity to consume is biased (wrong) because we have plotted consumption against the wrong variable.

What variable does life–cycle/permanent–income theory suggest we *should* have placed on the horizontal (or "x") axis?

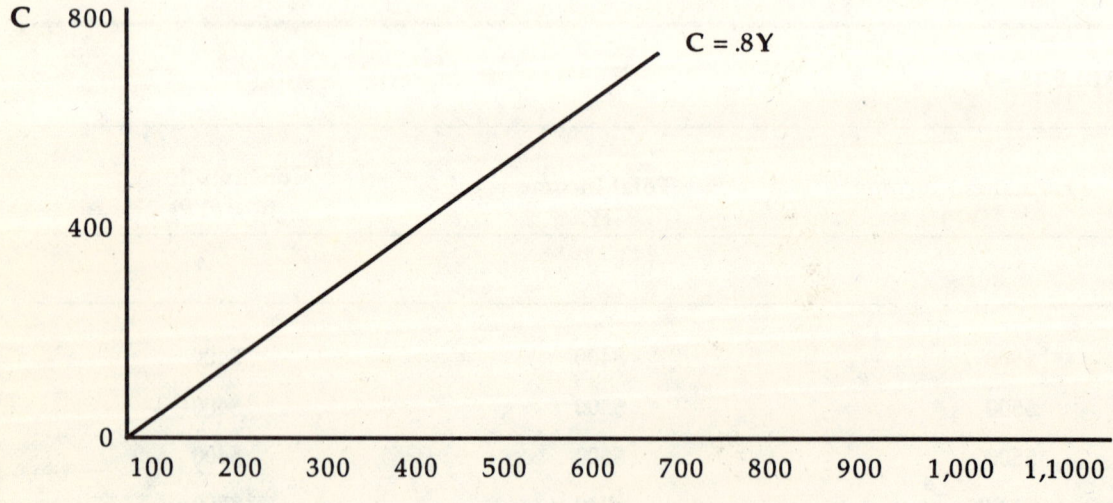

Chart 13 - 1

THE LANGUAGE OF ECONOMICS 13

Theories and Hypotheses

All theories begin as hypotheses—ideas, proposed relationships, statements about what might be. If you told a friend, for example, that you believed there were life on other planets, you would be making a *hypothesis*. If you thought that perhaps humans had evolved from seaweed, you would be making another hypothesis.

Not all hypotheses are true, and not all hypotheses become theories. A theory is nothing more than a hypothesis, or set of hypotheses, that seem to provide a good description of the world. The theory of general relativity was once a hypothesis; so was the belief that the sun orbited the Earth. The latter, obviously, is not considered a theory today.

REVIEW OF TECHNIQUE 13

Errors in Variables

"Errors in variables" is a phrase borrowed from statistics to describe a problem that arises when we try to test theories and hypotheses. Often we cannot find precise measures of the variables that we wish to look at; there are no universally accepted measures of the depreciation rate, for example, and there are so many different measures of the interest rate and the money supply that it's hard to know which one to use. Often there are no good measures: think of trying to measure intelligence or courage, for example.

An errors–in–variables problem occurs when we use a variable that we *can* measure in place of a more appropriate variable that we can't—actual instead of permanent income, for example, or IQ test scores in place of intelligence. Substituting variables in this way can *bias*—introduce systematic errors into—our estimates.

Consider the consumption function: The permanent–income hypothesis suggests that consumption is most appropriately expressed as a function of permanent income (YP)

$$C = cYP.$$

If we substitute actual income for permanent income when actual income (Y) is given by the function

$$Y = YP + YT,$$

where YT is the transitory deviation of actual income from permanent income, and try to estimate c (the marginal propensity to consume), our estimate $\tilde{c}$ will be *biased downwards*:

$$C = \tilde{c}Y = \tilde{c}(YP + YT).$$

Note that $\tilde{c}$ here will be a weighted average of the marginal propensities to consume out of permanent and transitory income and therefore, because the marginal propensity to consume out of transitory income is small, too low.

CROSSWORD

ACROSS

1. Idea, possibility
5. Type of "walk"; modern theory says consumption should take one
7. Consumption exhibits excess smoothness; it does not change enough in response to ___ changes in income
8. Type of income, mpc is small
10. Appears to be higher in the short run than in the long run
12. Life–cycle hypothesis
13. Permanent income hypothesis

DOWN

2. Type of saving; meant to guard against "rainy days"
3. Type of income, mpc is large
4. Type of constraint; people cannot borrow enough to support consumption at permanent income levels
6. When we say consumption exhibits excess sensitivity, we mean that it changes too much in response to this kind of change in income
9. Type of earnings; not paid out to owners/stockholders
11. Do most of the saving in the US

FILL-IN QUESTIONS

1. The _____ theory of consumption assumes that people try to smooth consumption over their lifetimes, and make consumption decisions based on the income they expect to earn over their lifetimes.

2. When people's actual income exceeds their permanent income, they _____.

3. The marginal propensity to consume out of permanent income is _____ than the marginal propensity to consume out of transitory income.

4. The life–cycle hypothesis suggests that the marginal propensity to consume out of income is _____ than the marginal propensity to consume out of wealth.

5. The life–cycle/permanent income theory of consumption implies that consumption should follow a _____.

6. The marginal propensity to consume depends on the number of years they spend _____ relative to the number of years they spend _____.

7. The _____ hypothesis highlights the way that demographic changes affect national saving.

8. Purchases of _____ are very sensitive to changes in the interest rate.

9. The permanent–income hypothesis suggests that saving should change slightly over the business cycle, rising in _____ and falling in _____.

10. Young people anticipating high incomes in the future will want to _____ to increase their current level of consumption.

TRUE–FALSE QUESTIONS

T F 1. Consumption is the largest component of aggregate demand.

T F 2. The life–cycle and permanent–income hypotheses make very different claims about the way that people make consumption decisions.

T F 3. The long–run mpc appears to be higher than the short–run mpc.

T F 4. Consumption appears to change too much in response to predictable changes in income.

T F 5. Consumption appears to change too much in response to *unpredictable* changes in income.

T F 6. The life–cycle hypothesis suggests that countries with higher proportions of retired individuals should see savings rise.

T F 7. People may save more than the life–cycle/permanent income theory suggests because they wish to leave inheritances for their children.

T F 8. People may not be able to smooth consumption as much as the life–cycle/permenant income theory suggests because they are liquidity constrained.

T F 9. Changes in the rate of interest paid by savings accounts have a strong impact on household savings.

T F 10. Most of the saving in the US is done by households.

MULTIPLE-CHOICE QUESTIONS

1. Estimates of long-term consumption opportunities based on expectations of lifetime income are called _____ income.
   a. disposable
   b. adjusted
   c. permanent
   d. transitory

2. Characteristic of consumption; consumption changes too much in response to predictable changes in income.
   a. liquidity constraint
   b. excess sensitivity
   c. excess smoothness
   d. myopia

3. Characteristic of consumption; consumption does not change enough in response to unpredictable changes in income.
   a. liquidity constraint
   b. excess sensitivity
   c. excess smoothness
   d. myopia

4. Constraints on people's ability to borrow money at the market interest rate are referred to as
   a. liquidity constraints
   b. budget constraints
   c. myopia
   d. bequests

5. Saving for a rainy day (precautionary saving) is referred to as
   a. bequest saving
   b. myopic saving
   c. buffer-stock saving
   d. excess saving

6. Most of the saving in the US is done by
   a. businesses
   b. households
   c. the government
   d. children

7. Which of the following is the largest component of aggregate demand?
   a. consumption
   b. investment
   c. government spending
   d. net exports

8. The life-cycle/permanent-income theory of consumption is associated with the
   a. Keynesian school
   b. Monetarist school
   c. neither
   d. both

9. The life-cycle hypothesis suggests that wealth during a person's working years should.
   a. increase
   b. decrease
   c. not change, on average
   d. all be spent

10. Which of the following groups of people should have the highest rate of saving?
    a. college students
    b. children
    c. people who have retired
    d. people approaching the end of their working lives

CONCEPTUAL PROBLEMS

1. Why do modern theorists argue that, if the life–cycle/permenant income theory of consumption is correct, consumption should follow a random walk?

2. How do you think longer life–spans will affect people's saving patterns? Explain.

3. How should an increase in the interest rate affect people's permanent income?

4. Are you liquidity constrained?

TECHNICAL PROBLEMS

1. If the typical urban consumer expects to work for 30 years and live 10 years beyond retirement, how should a $100 tax cut on labor income affect consumption? Does your answer depend on whether the tax cut is temporary or permanent? Disregard any multiplier effects.

2. Will expansionary fiscal policy be more or less effective when people are liquidity constrained? Justify your answer.

14   INVESTMENT SPENDING

FOCUS OF THE CHAPTER

- Investment is the most volatile sector of aggregate demand; changes in investment account for much of the change in GDP.

- The three types of investment are *business fixed investment*, *residential investment*, and *inventory investment*.

- Investment is the flow of spending that adds to the physical stock of capital.

- Investment demand is the primary link between monetary policy and aggregate demand. Increased interest rates reduce investment because capital becomes more expensive.

SECTION SUMMARIES

1. The Stock Demand for Capital and The Flow of Investment

Businesses use machinery, equipment, and structures to produce output. Together, these make up the stock of *business fixed capital*. This section develops a theory of the *desired capital stock*—the capital stock which firms would like to have in the long run. Because it takes time to order and install new capital, firms do not always have this desired capital stock; investment—the flow of new machinery into the capital stock—closes the gap between the desired capital stock and the actual capital stock.

Manufacturers consider three factors when they decide how much capital they want to have: the amount of output they expect to sell, the amount that one more unit of capital will increase their output (the *marginal product of capital*), and the amount that it will cost them to use that unit of capital (the *rental*, or *user*, *cost of capital*).

More capital always enables more output to be produced. Each additional unit of capital costs the same amount to use, but each additional unit also contributes less and less to production. This combination of constant marginal cost and diminishing marginal product means that there will be some point at which it is no longer sensible for firms to buy capital; eventually, the marginal benefit that they derive from their capital will fall below the marginal cost of employing it. Firms will therefore accumulate capital as long as the marginal benefit of their doing so exceeds the marginal cost. The capital stock will be at its optimal or desired level when the marginal benefit of employing an additional unit of capital (i.e., the marginal product of capital) is exactly equal to the marginal cost.

The rental cost of capital is little more than the expected real interest rate (r)—the opportunity cost associated with using their funds to buy capital instead of bonds. There is also a cost, however, that firms must incur if they wish to keep the capital they have already installed in good working order; capital *depreciates*, or wears out, over time. We write the rental cost of capital (rc), then, as

$$rc = r + d$$

or, imposing the *Fischer relationship*,

$$rc = (i - \pi^e) + d.$$

We use the expected real interest rate instead of the actual one because uncertainty regarding future inflation translates into uncertainty regarding the real rate of interest that assets pay when they held over time; we only ever really *know* that real interest rate when we look back on it and can measure the difference between the nominal rate of interest and the rate of inflation. Capital is assumed to depreciate at a constant rate (d).

This rental cost must be adjusted to account for the effect of taxes: The capital stock will really be at its optimal, or desired level when the *after–tax marginal product of capital* is equal to the *after–tax rental cost*. Higher corporate tax rates raise the rental cost of capital, and, as a result, reduce the desired capital stock. **Investment tax credits** do the opposite: Because they allow firms to deduct a fraction of their investment expenditures each year, they *reduce* firms' rental cost of capital.

Fiscal policy can therefore affect the desired capital stock by changing either the corporate tax rate or the investment tax credit. Both monetary and fiscal policy can also affect the desired capital stock through their effect on the real interest rate.

The **q theory of investment** restates the marginal benefit equals marginal cost rule in more easily quantifiable terms. It points out that that the price of a company's stock, because it represents a claim on the stream of profits that company's capital is expected to generate, is a measure of the value of that capital. Likewise, the amount of money that would be required to replace all of the capital that a firm owns is a measure of that firm's cost of capital.

Looking at the ratio of the market value of a firm (the number of shares of stock it has issued times the market value of those shares) to that firm's replacement cost of capital,

$$q = \frac{\text{market value of firm}}{\text{replacement cost of firm's capital}},$$

then, should tell us something about ratio of marginal benefits to marginal costs: A q greater than 1 suggests that the benefit of acquiring new capital exceeds the cost, or that the firm should invest more. A q smaller than one suggests that the cost of acquiring new capital is greater than the benefit, or that the firm should *disinvest*—allow its capital stock to fall. A *q* exactly equal to 1 suggests that the firm has exactly the right amount of capital, or capital is at its desired level.

The rate of investment depends on the difference between the actual capital stock (*K*) and the desired capital stock (*K**). The *flexible accelerator model* is based on the notion that firms with larger gaps between their actual and desired capital stocks should be investing more than firms whose actual capital stock is closer to its desired level. It assumes that firms try to close some fraction, λ, of this gap each period, or that

$$I = K - K_{-1} = \lambda(K^* - K_{-1}),$$

where K_{-1} represents the capital stock that the firm had at the end of the previous period. If you're not comfortable working with lagged terms, don't worry. This chapter's Review of Technique goes over them with you.

2. Investment Subsectors—Business Fixed, Residential, and Inventory

Business fixed investment is investment's largest subsector, and a leading indicator of business cycle fluctuations. It is also closely linked to firms' *retained earnings*—profits not paid out to stockholders—as many firms, especially smaller ones, are unable to obtain all of their funding from outside sources. This inability to borrow at prevailing interest rates is called *credit rationing*, and forces firms to consider their available funds as well as market-determined interest rates when they make investment decisions.

The irreversibility of many types of investment complicates things as well. Many types of capital are difficult to disassemble and reallocate once they have been installed; this forces firms to worry about future as well as current profitability when choosing to install a particular type of capital.

People in the trenches frequently make decisions using *discounted cash flow analysis*, basing their investment decisions on some estimate of the current value of an expected future stream of profits.

Residential investment is really just additions to housing supply, and is driven by both real and nominal interest rates, and by the demand for existing structures. Specifically, investment in housing occurs when the quantity of homes demanded exceeds the existing stock of housing, driving up the price of buying or renting a home. Housing demand falls when interest rates–especially mortgage rates—rise, and when people's incomes fall. For the latter reason, housing demand is especially sensitive to the effects of monetary policy, and tends to move with the business cycle, rising in booms and falling in recessions.

Inventory investment is the accumulation of raw materials held for use in production, unfinished goods currently in the middle of the production process, and finished goods held by firms in anticipation of future sale. It is also the most volatile type of investment. Unintended inventory accumulation occurs when sales fall unexpectedly, and is a signal to firms to decrease production. Intended inventory accumulation occurs when firms anticipate an increase in the demand for their good in the near future. Unintended inventory accumulation is a signal of recession; intended inventory is a signal that a boom is anticipated.

162 CHAPTER 14

To reduce the cost of storing inventories, many firms have been adopting *just–in–time inventory management* techniques, bringing production more closely into line with sales and keeping fewer inventories on hand. Inventories are moving less over the business cycle as a result.

4. Investment and Aggregate Supply

Investment is a component of aggregate demand, but doesn't it also increase potential output? In the long run, yes. Investment is one of the most effective ways to expand capacity. In fact, countries which invest a substantial fraction of their output appear to grow much faster than countries which do not. But the supply–side effects of any type of investment are rarely felt in the short run, so don't worry too much about trying to take them into account.

KEY TERMS

business fixed investment	real interest rates
residential investment	q theory of investment
inventory investment	flexible accelerator model
investment	credit rationing
capital stock	discounted cash flow analysis
desired capital stock	accelerator model
marginal product of capital	inventory cycle
rental (user) cost of capital	just-in-time inventory management

GRAPH IT 14

Investment is a small but volatile sector; its changes are responsible for much of the variation in aggregate demand. This Graph It asks you show that changes in aggregate demand closely follow changes in investment—that the relationship between investment volatility and aggregate demand volatility is very strong.

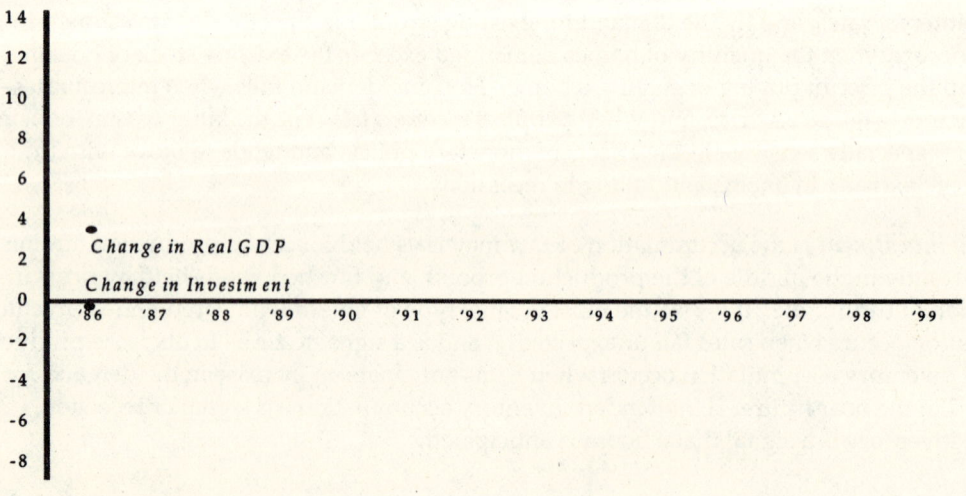

Chart 14 - 1

Table 14–1 provides data on GDP and gross investment. Your task is to find the percentage change in each of these variables from year to year, and to plot each, individually, on Chart 14–1.

TABLE 14 – 1

Year	Real GDP	Gross Private Domestic Investment	% Change in Real GDP	% Change in Investment
1985	5,717.1	863.4		
1986	5,912.4	857.7	3.42	- 15.4
1987	6,113.3	879.3		
1988	6,368.4	902.8		
1989	6,591.8	936.5		
1990	6,707.9	907.3		
1991	6,676.4	829.5		
1992	6,880.0	899.8		
1993	7,062.6	977.9		
1994	7,347.7	1,107.0		
1995	7,543.8	1,140.6		
1996	7,813.2	1,242.7		
1997	8,159.5	1,393.3		
1998	8,515.7	1,566.8		
1999	8,875.8	1,669.7		

Source: See Economic Data Table B

THE LANGUAGE OF ECONOMICS 14

Investment

Investment, as it is used in macroeconomics, does *not* refer to the accumulation of interest–bearing assets. It does not refer to the purchase of stocks and bonds.

Investment is the accumulation of physical, and sometimes human capital. New home construction, the purchase of new machinery, and the accumulation of inventories are all types of physical investment. Education and health maintenance are both types of investment in *human capital* (not discussed in this chapter). Investment in human capital is not usually measured by national income accounts.

REVIEW OF TECHNIQUE 14

Working with Lagged Variables

When we introduce lags into a model, it becomes *dynamic* instead of *static*. Past events can affect the values of present variables; current events can affect the values of future variables.

A *lagged variable* is just a variable valued in an earlier period. Lags are represented by time subscripts: Last period's income, for example, might be represented by Y_{-1}. The "−1" indicates a one–period lag—tells us to use last period's value instead of this period. Last period's capital stock can be represented by K_{-1}; the difference between last period's capital stock and the desired capital stock as $K^* - K_{-1}$.

Although you may not know it, you've already worked with lags. You've found the rates of change of a number of variables by applying the formula

$$\left(\frac{x - x_{-1}}{x_{-1}}\right) \times 100.$$

You've learned about random walks (or, if you haven't, can by reading Review of Technique 8), which are characterized, in their simplest form, by the equation

$$y = y_{-1} + \varepsilon.$$

You have also, whether or not you knew it at the time, worked through a number of dynamic processes. You did so when you derived the government purchases multiplier. You did when you looked at the way that capital accumulated over time in the neoclassical growth model. And you did when you examined the way that past and expected future income interacted to determine people's permanent income.

You're an old hand at this. It's hardly worth going over.

CROSSWORD

ACROSS

4 Rise unexpectedly at the beginning of recessions, fall unexpectedly at the beginning of booms

5 Occurs when capital wears out/becomes outmoded over time

6 Cost of capital, real interest rate plus rate of depreciation

8 The accumulation of financial ___ does not constitute investment

9 Type of variable, capital is an example

DOWN

1. Accelerator model, assumes that firms try to close a constant fraction of the gap between their actual and desired capital stock each period
2. Type of investment, tracks housing construction
3. Primary link between monetary policy and aggregate demand
7. When interest rates rise, housing demand

FILL-IN QUESTIONS

1. The three principal types of investment are _____, _____, and _____.

2. The machinery, equipment, and structures used in production are a part of _____ investment.

3. The rental cost of capital is equal to the real interest rate plus the rate of _____.

4. The rental cost of capital is also called the _____ cost of capital.

5. The _____ model assumes that firms try to close some fraction of the gap between their desired and actual capital stock each period.

6. _____ inventory management techniques reduce the number of inventories kept on hand, bringing production more closely into line with sales.

7. The government can subsidize firms' investment by giving them _____.

8. The _____ theory of investment restates the "marginal benefit equals marginal cost" rule in more easily quantifiable terms.

9. _____ consist of raw materials held for use in production, unfinished goods, and finished goods held by firms in anticipation of future sale.

10. Investment, because it adds to the capital stock, increases _____.

TRUE–FALSE QUESTIONS

T F 1. Investment is the most volatile sector of aggregate demand.

T F 2. Rising interest rates increase investment.

T F 3. Rising GDP increases investment.

T F 4. Investment is a stock variable.

T F 5. Investment is the primary link between monetary policy and aggregate demand.

T F 6. Expansionary monetary policy increases investment.

T F 7. Rising interest rates reduce investment.

T F 8. Unexpectedly high sales cause inventories to fall.

T F 9. The actual capital stock adjusts gradually to the desired capital stock.

T F 10. The adoption of just–in–time inventory management techniques have caused inventories to fluctuate less over the business cycle.

MULTIPLE–CHOICE QUESTIONS

1. An increase in the corporate tax rate _____ investment.
   a. increases
   b. decreases
   c. has no effect
   d. could be any of the above

2. An increase in the investment tax credit _____ investment.
   a. increases
   b. decreases
   c. has no effect
   d. could be any of the above

3. Which of the following is *not* a type of investment?
   a. purchase of a machine
   b. accumulation of inventories
   c. construction of new home
   d. purchase of stock or bond

4. An increase in the rate of depreciation _____ the rental cost of capital.
   a. increases
   b. decreases
   c. has no effect
   d. who knows?

5. An increase in the rate of depreciation _____ the desired capital stock.
   a. increases
   b. decreases
   c. has no effect
   d. who knows?

6. An increase in the real interest rate _____ the rental cost of capital.
   a. increases
   b. decreases
   c. has no effect
   d. could be any of the above

7. An increase in the real interest rate _____ the desired capital stock.
   a. increases
   b. decreases
   c. has no effect
   d. could be any of the above

8. Which of the following measures of the benefit to a firm of acquiring capital?
   a. market value of firm
   b. replacement cost of capital
   c. user cost of capital
   d. rate of depreciation

9. Expansionary monetary policy _____ investment.
   a. increases
   b. decreases
   c. does not affect
   d. who knows?

10. Expansionary fiscal policy, *when* it is accommodated, _____ investment.
    a. increases
    b. decreases
    c. does not affect
    d. who knows?

CONCEPTUAL PROBLEMS

1. Why does an increase in the real interest rate reduce the desired capital stock?

2. Why does an increase in the rate at which capital depreciates reduce the desired capital stock?

3. Why do we use real instead of nominal interest rates in our formula for the rental cost of capital?

TECHNICAL PROBLEMS

1. If the desired capital stock is $20,000, the current level of the capital stock is $12,000, and a firm wishes to close half of the gap between them each period, what does the flexible accelerator model suggest will be next period's level of investment? What will be the level of investment the year after that?

2. Assume that the desired capital stock is determined by the equation $K^* = 0.25Y/rc$. The nominal interest rate is 12%. The rate of inflation is 6%. Capital depreciates at a rate of 10% per year.
   a) If income is $16,000, what is the desired capital stock?
   b) What will be the desired capital stock if income doubles?
   c) What will be the desired capital stock if, instead, the rental cost of capital doubles?

3. Consider a publicly held firm with 1 million shares of common stock, each priced at $35. If the replacement value of this firm's capital stock is $50 million, should it acquire any new capital? Why or why not? How would your answer change if the price of this company's stock rose to $80 per share?

15 THE DEMAND FOR MONEY

FOCUS OF THE CHAPTER

- We all hold money—either in currency, in our pockets, or as deposits in a bank. In studying the demand for money, we try to discover why people hold money, and what determines the amount of money they hold.

- Our main goal is to find some function that tells us the amount of money people will hold for a known level of income and a known interest rate. You will recall, no doubt, that we need to know this in order to form the LM curve.

- Both theory and empirical evidence suggest that an increase in people's incomes makes them want to hold more money, and that an increase in the interest rate makes them want to hold less.

SECTION SUMMARIES

1. Components of the Money Stock

Money consists of the stock of assets held as cash, checking accounts, and other, closely related assets, *not* generic wealth or income. There are four different measures of the money supply: *M1*, *M2*, *M3*, and *L*. *M1* consists of those assets that are the most *liquid*—most easily used to pay for goods and services. *L* consists of those assets that are least liquid, but which can still be converted into a form that creditors will accept. The components of each measure of money are listed below:

- *M1* currency, demand deposits, travelers checks, and other checkable deposits
- *M2* *M1* plus shares in money market mutual funds, money market deposit accounts, savings deposits, and small time deposits
- *M3* *M2* plus repurchase agreements, Eurodollars, large time deposits, and institutional money market mutual fund holdings

> L   M3 plus savings bonds, bankers acceptances, commercial paper, and short–term Treasury securities

2. The functions of Money

Money has traditionally been thought to have four functions:

> *A medium of exchange.* Money is used to pay for goods and services, and enables us to avoid the "double coincidence of wants" required in a barter economy.
>
> *A store of value.* Money retains its value over time; money we receive today can be stuck under our mattresses or placed in our checking account and used to purchase goods and services at a later date.
>
> *A unit of account.* Prices are quoted in dollars and cents rather than chickens, avocados, or visits to the dentist.
>
> *A standard of deferred payment.* Money is used in long–term transactions; you might borrow $100 from a friend, for example, and promise to pay him back $105 at a later date.

The most important thing to know about money is that *it is whatever people generally accept as a payment for goods and services.* As such, it can take many forms.

3. The Demand for Money: Theory

Why would we ever choose to hold money instead of some other, interest–bearing asset? Keynes suggested three different motives:

> *The transactions motive.* We wish to avoid having to cash in another asset every time we make a purchase. (Imagine what a nuisance that would be!)
>
> *The precautionary motive.* "Just in case." We never know our spending plans exactly; it pays to keep a little extra money around in case the urge for a hot fudge sundae hits at a time when your stock broker is playing golf and cannot liquidate any of your assets.
>
> *The speculative motive.* While money doesn't have a very high return, it is less risky than other assets. Speculative demand for money is actually demand for a safe asset.

An increase in the rate of return on other assets reduces the demand for money, whatever one's motive for holding it. An increase in the amount of uncertainty we have about our future spending plans increases the people's demand for money, when that demand is based on the precautionary motive.

We model the demand for real rather than nominal money balances here (M/P rather than M); we assume that, because people hold money for its purchasing power, they do not care about their nominal money holdings. For this to be true, people must be free of *money illusion*—the belief that changes in nominal wages and prices are meaningful.

4. Empirical Evidence

Empirical research has settled four key points about money demand:

1) When the real interest rate increases, the demand for real money balances falls.
2) When income increases, money demand also increases.
3) It takes time for money demand to fully adjust to changes in income and the interest rate.
4) If the price level doubles, so will nominal money demand. Real money demand will be unaffected; there is no money illusion.

High inflation can also induce people to hold less money. With sufficiently high rates of inflation, people may not wish to hold financial assets at all, holding food and other goods instead. This is called a *flight out of money*.

5. The Income Velocity of Money

The *income velocity of money* is the number of times the stock of money is turned over, or reused each year to finance all of the purchases that occur. If people purchased \$1,000,000 of goods and services in a particular year, and the (nominal) money supply were \$1,000,000, for example, the velocity of money would be equal to 1; each dollar would be used an average of one time. If people purchased \$1,000,000 of goods and services in a particular year, and the (nominal) money supply were \$500,000, the velocity of money would be equal to 2; each dollar would be used an average of two times.

The income velocity of money is defined as:

$$V = \frac{P \times Y}{M} = \frac{Y}{M/P}$$

The *quantity theory of money* uses this definition to explain how and why the price level and the money stock are connected:

$$M \times V = P \times Y.$$

The classical incarnation of this theory assumes that both V and Y are fixed and, based on those assumptions, argues that any change in the money supply will cause a proportional change in the price level.

Appendix

The Baumol–Tobin formula for the transactions demand for money,

$$M^* = \sqrt{\frac{tcY}{2i}}$$

uses some basic intuition and a small bit of math to find a formula for the amount of money people want to hold for the purpose of buying goods and services.

First, notice that a person's average balance (M) over a given period will be equal to 1/2 the amount of money they spend over that period divided by the number of times (n) they convert their other assets into money (e.g., withdraw cash from their savings account):

$$M = \frac{Y}{2n}$$

Next, observe that the opportunity cost of holding money is equal to the value of the next best opportunity—the rate of interest (i) paid by other assets. Each transfer is also assumed to cost an amount tc.

The total cost of holding average balances Y/2n, then is:

$$(n \times tc) + \frac{iY}{2n}$$

The best number of transactions is, of course, the one that minimizes this total cost. That number (n^*), it turns out, is given by the following formula:

$$n^* = \sqrt{\frac{iY}{2tc}}.$$

Plugging this into our original equation $M = Y/2n$, we find that people will find it optimal, or best to hold average money balances

$$M^* = \sqrt{\frac{tcY}{2i}}.$$

KEY TERMS

money
M1
M2
M3
liquidity
medium of exchange
store of value
unit of account
standard of deferred payment
real balances
money illusion
transactions motive

precautionary motive
speculative motive
portfolio
risky asset
interest elasticity
income elasticity
flight out of money
income velocity
quantity theory of money
quantity equation
classical quantity theory

GRAPH IT 15

It's about time for a loose, relaxing exercise… don't you think? This Graph It asks you to demonstrate the essential principles of precautionary money demand by drawing some loose wiggles on Chart 13–1.

The idea behind the precautionary demand for money is that you want to hold enough so you don't have to keep running to the bank, but don't want to hold too much because of the opportunity cost. We've drawn a wiggley line representing a particular cash need. Assuming that we don't want to run out of money more than twice during the period on the graph, we took a straightedge and drew a dashed line as low as possible, with the wiggle peeking over it no more than twice. This solid line shows the precautionary demand for money.

Your task is to draw a new cash–need wiggle, with the cash needs generally having higher peaks. Then use a straightedge to draw in the money–demand line that is consistent with your not wanting to run out of money any more than twice during the period covered by the graph.

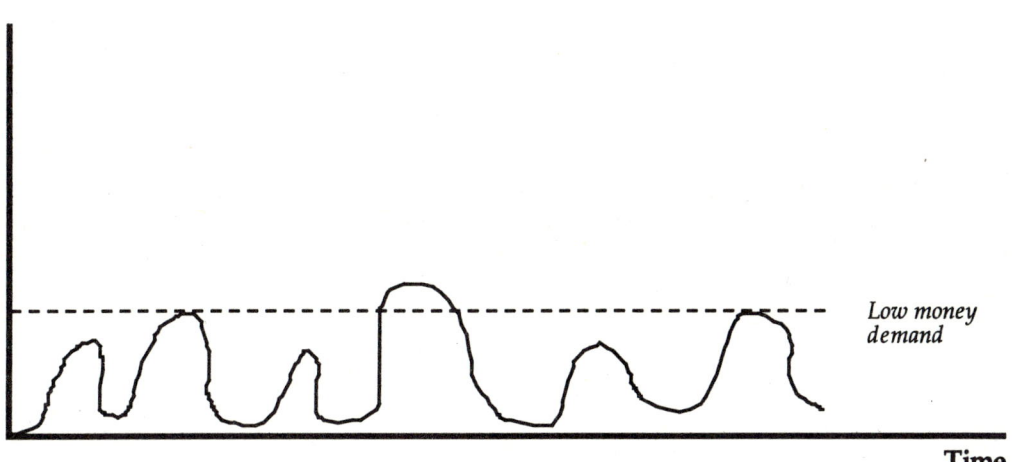

Chart 15 - 1

THE LANGUAGE OF ECONOMICS 15

Liquidity

An asset is *liquid* when it can be converted into goods or services quickly, at low cost, and with low risk. Cash is the ultimate liquid asset; it can be directly exchanged for goods and services anywhere. Checking accounts, or "demand deposits," are quite liquid too.

Stocks and bonds are less liquid. Both take time to sell, and therefore cannot as easily be used to buy goods or services. The prices of stocks and bonds also fluctuate. Imagine having to sell a share of stock every time you get a haircut or buy groceries; you might have to sell at a loss, simply to finance your purchase. Having to regularly convert either of these assets into goods and services would involve considerable *risk*.

Ironically, one of the least liquid assets is a lake full of water. Lakes couldn't possibly be easy to sell on short notice.

REVIEW OF TECHNIQUE 15

Working with Natural Logarithms

Before the days of calculators, tables of logarithms were used to speed up calculations. Today that is no longer necessary; few of us do our calculations by hand.

Natural logarithms are still useful, however, because they are intimately connected to percentage changes: *the change in the natural log of a variable is approximately equal to the percentage change of that variable*. This is particularly useful when graphing one variable against another. If you graph the natural log of y (ln y) against the natural log of x (ln x), for example, the slope of your line will tell you the amount that y changes, in percentage terms, when x rises by 1%.

A natural logarithm is formally defined as follows:

$$X = \ln Y \quad \text{if and only if} \quad Y = e^x,$$

where e is an irrational number (i.e., it goes on forever) approximately equal to 2.71828. Taking the natural log of the function e^x gives you x; raising e to the power ln x also gives you x (e^x and ln x are *inverse functions*).

There are some rules that will help you to work with natural logs:

1) $\ln(xy) = \ln x + \ln y$

2) $\ln(x/y) = \ln x - \ln y$

3) $\ln(x^y) = y \times \ln x$

4) $\ln(1 + x) \cong x$ (the symbol $\cong$ means " approximately equal to")

FILL-IN QUESTIONS

1. The assets which form M1 are _____ liquid than the assets which form M2.

2. Savings accounts are _____ liquid than Treasury bonds.

3. Holding money to reduce the risk associated with your portfolio of assets is an example of the _____ motive.

CROSSWORD

ACROSS

2. Motive for holding money, people do not want to convert illiquid assets into cash every time they make a purchase
5. Role of money, medium of ___
7. Motive for holding money, just in case
9. Type of deposit, included in M2 but not M1

DOWN

1. Included in M1
3. Motive for holding money, reduces portfolio risk
4. Measures number of times the average dollar changes hands in a year
6. Role of money, unit of ___
8. Role of money, store of ___

FILL-IN QUESTIONS (CONTINUED)

4. Holding money because you're worried that something may come up that requires you to spend it is an example of the _____ motive.

5. Holding money in order use it to buy goods and services is an example of the _____ motive.

6. Ice cubes would not be a very good form of money because they would be a terrible _____.

7. Giant stone slabs might not be the best form of money because they would not be a very convenient _____.

8. When high inflation induces people to hold goods instead of assets, we say there is a _____.

9. The equation $M \times V = P \times Y$ is called the _____ equation.

10. The _____ of money measures number of times the average dollar changes hands each year.

TRUE–FALSE QUESTIONS

T F 1. Cash is the most liquid asset of all.

T F 2. Stocks are the most liquid asset of all.

T F 3. An increase in income raises money demand.

T F 4. Money demand adjusts immediately to changes in both income and the interest rate.

T F 5. M1 is more liquid than M3.

T F 6. M3 is more liquid than L.

T F 7. People will hold as much money as they can get their hands on.

T F 8. It is always better to hold more money than less.

T F 9. If the money supply grows more quickly than output, it will cause inflation.

T F 10. When the real interest rate increases, the demand for real money balances falls.

MULTIPLE–CHOICE QUESTIONS

1. Currency is contained in
   a. M1
   b. M2
   c. M3
   d. all of the above

2. T–bills (3-month Treasury bonds) are contained in
   a. M1
   b. M2
   c. M3
   d. all of the above

3. Which of the following is the most liquid?
   a. M1
   b. M2
   c. M3
   d. L

4. Which of the following is the least liquid?
   a. M1
   b. M2
   c. M3
   d. L

5. Which of the following is the most commonly used measure of money?
   a. M1
   b. M2
   c. M3
   d. L

6. Which of the following is not a function of money?
   a. medium of exchange
   b. unit of account
   c. store of value
   d. measure of greed

7. People will want to hold less money if there is/are
   a. high inflation
   b. low interest rates
   c. money illusion
   d. all of the above

8. In the long run, an increase in the money supply causes
   a. high real interest rates
   b. high output
   c. inflation
   d. all of the above

9. Money is:
   a. bills and coins
   b. bills, coins, and bank accounts
   c. anything people can exchange for goods and services.

10. In classical quantity theory,
    a. output is fixed
    b. velocity is fixed
    c. the price level can vary
    d. all of the above

CONCEPTUAL PROBLEMS

1. Why do *you* hold money? (How many of the motives for holding money can you identify with?)

2. What do you know of, aside from bills and coins, that has been used as money over the years?

TECHNICAL PROBLEMS

1. If nominal GDP is $1,000,000 and the money supply (as measured by M2) is $500,000, what is the income velocity of money?

2. If output grows at an average of 3% per year and the money supply grows at an average of 8% per year, what must be the rate of inflation?

3. If you earn $100,000 per year, you pay $1.50 to withdraw money from your banking account, and the interest rate is 6%, how much money does the Baumol–Tobin model of the transactions demand for money suggest you will want to hold?

16 THE FED, MONEY, AND CREDIT

FOCUS OF THE CHAPTER

- This chapter develops the concept of fractional reserve banking, and explores the process by which the Federal Reserve controls the money supply.

SECTION SUMMARIES

1. Money Stock Determination—the Money Multiplier

The money supply is made up mostly of deposits at financial institutions, which the Fed cannot control directly. Those institutions, however, keep some of their money on reserve at the Fed, and occasionally borrow money from it. The Federal Reserve can decide how many reserves those banks are required to keep on hand. It can determine the rate of interest it charges on the money it lends to banks (called the *discount rate*). Moreover, it can control the number of bills and coins circulating in the economy. Thus it has a number of *instruments* that it can use to control the money supply.

The currency circulating through the economy and the reserves kept for banks by the Fed make up the *monetary base*, and are also called *high–powered money*. The bills and coins that are held by the public are considered a part of the money supply. The currency which banks keep on reserve is *not*.

The *money multiplier* (*mm*) is defined as the ratio of the money supply to the stock of high–powered money (the monetary base), and is given by the formula:

$$mm \equiv \frac{1 + cu}{re + cu},$$

where *cu* is the *currency–deposit ratio*—the ratio of currency to bank deposits—and *re* is the *reserve ratio*—the ratio of bank reserves to bank deposits.

The money supply (*M*) is therefore given by the equation

$$M = \left(\frac{1 + cu}{re + cu}\right)H,$$

where H is the stock of high-powered money. An increase in reserve ratio makes the money multiplier smaller, increasing the amount of high-powered money required to support a given money supply. An increase in the currency-deposit ratio makes the money multiplier bigger, so that a given stock of high-powered money can support a larger money supply.

Banks often hold more money in reserve than they are required to—loan out less than they could. Because reserves do not earn interest, banks try to minimize the amount of *excess reserves* they hold. They try especially hard when interest rates are high; because of this, increases in the interest rate can, to a limited extent, reduce the reserve ratio and increase the money multiplier.

The *Federal Deposit Insurance Corporation (FDIC)* insures bank deposits, so that depositors get paid even if their bank fails. *Bank runs*—a rush by depositors to withdraw their money because they believe others will do so—can cause the currency-deposit ratio, and therefore the money supply, to fall.

2. The Instruments of Monetary Control

The Fed mostly uses *open market operations*—the purchase or sale of government bonds—to increase or decrease the monetary base, and, as a result, the money supply. By buying assets and paying for them with its own liabilities, the Fed can create as much money as it wants to.

It can also increase the money supply by lowering the *required reserve ratio*—the amount fraction of a bank's deposits that it is required to keep on reserve—or by decreasing the *discount rate*, which would enable banks to hold fewer excess reserves.

The Federal Reserve does not generally print money. It is not required to finance government budget deficits by buying bonds.

3. The Money Multiplier and Bank Loans

This section presents an alternative way to understand the way that the money multiplier translates a change in the monetary base into a change in the money supply.

An open market purchase increases transfers money from the Fed to individuals, who either hold it as cash or deposit it in a financial institution. If it is deposited in a financial institution, the reserves of that institution immediately rise by the amount of the deposit. This increases the reserve ratio; the bank now has more excess reserves. To reduce these excess reserves, it lends out more money. The person receiving the loan either deposits it in the bank, or gives it to someone else who deposits some or all of it in the bank. *The money supply has now increased by more than the amount of the open market purchase.* The bank's reserves increase by the amount of the deposit; again, its excess reserves rise and it must make more loans to drive them back down. This process repeats and repeats until all banks are holding exactly the amount of reserves they want to; the money supply increases again with every repetition. The bank's reserves, of course, increase to reflect the increase in the value of its deposits. The reserve ratio itself does not necessarily change.

The money multiplier summarizes the total expansion of the money supply created by this process; it describes the amount that a $1 increase in the monetary base increases the total money supply.

4. Control of the Money Stock and Control of the Interest Rate

The Fed can use monetary policy to achieve a specific interest rate or to achieve a specific money supply, but cannot use it to achieve both objectives unless they happen to coincide. The money demand function determines the real interest rate that is associated with each level of real money balances.

On a day-to-day basis, the Fed can control interest rates more accurately than it can control the money supply.

5. Money Stock and Interest Rate Targets

If most shocks to output are the result of unexpected changes in the IS curve, the Fed will stabilize output more effectively in the short run by trying to keep the money supply constant than it will trying to keep the interest rate constant.

If most shocks to output are the result of unexpected changes in the LM curve, the Fed will stabilize output more effectively in the short run by trying to keep the interest rate constant.

Monetarists argue that, because increases in the money stock eventually lead to increases in the price level, it is a mistake to target interest rates rather than money. The only way to avoid inflation over long periods of time is to keep the money supply growing at a moderate pace.

6. Money, Credit, and Interest Rates

The Fed can have credit targets as well as money stock or interest rate targets; it can use monetary policy to achieve a particular level of debt in non-financial sectors. Debt appears to have an even stronger link to GDP than money.

Those who support credit targets argue that interest rates can be an unreliable indicator of the state of the economy when there is credit rationing—when individuals cannot borrow as much as they want to at the existing interest rate.

7. Which Targets for the Fed?

There are two sorts of targets: *ultimate targets*, or variables whose behavior the Fed ultimately cares about, and *intermediate targets*, variables whose behavior is linked to that of the ultimate targets. The Fed only tries to achieve its intermediate targets because achieving them helps it to aim its policy more accurately toward its ultimate targets.

The ideal intermediate target is a variable that the Fed can control accurately, that has a known, exploitable relationship with its ultimate target. Monetary base targets are necessarily intermediate; we only care about the monetary base because it affects interest rates, and, as a result, output and the rate of inflation. Inflation and GDP are ultimate targets.

Critics of the Fed argue that it should choose targets which it can be held accountable for achieving or failing to achieve. Others believe that the Fed can be trusted, and prefer the board of governors to exercise its judgment about what policies will best achieve the dual objectives of low inflation and high output.

KEY TERMS

credit
fractional reserve banking
high-powered money
monetary base
money multiplier
currency-deposit ratio
reserve ratio
bank run
disintermediation
Federal Deposit Insurance Corporation (FDIC)
required reserves
excess reserves

open market operation
discount rate
required-reserve ratio
foreign exchange market intervention
federal funds rate
credit targets
credit rationing
ultimate target
intermediate target
instrument(s)
monetary-base targeting
inflation targeting
nominal GDP targeting

TABLE 16 – 1
First Balance Sheet

FRED				BANK			
ASSETS		*LIABILITIES*		*ASSETS*			*LIABILITIES*
Deposit	$200	None		Reserves	$200	$200	Deposit
				(Required	$20)		
				(Excess	$20)		
		$200	Net Worth				
	$200	$200			$200	$200	

GRAPH IT 16

Graph It 16 asks gives you the chance to use balance sheets to illustrate the multiple expansion of deposits that occurs in fractional–reserve banking systems. To make things simple, we assume that there's only one bank and one person, whom we'll call Fred.

Fred begins by making a $200 deposit. The bank begins with that $200 on reserve. We assume that the required reserve ratio is 10%, and that the bank prefers not to hold any excess reserves. Table 16–1 (located on the previous page) shows the bank's balance sheet at this point.

Fred then decides to borrow $180 from the bank; he wants to go fishing. This being an especially nice bank (most would never give anyone a loan for such a frivolous reason), it agrees to loan him the entire amount. Fred signs the loan agreement and the bank credits his account with $180. Fill in the blanks in Table 16–2 to reflect this new state of affairs.

TABLE 16 – 2
Second Balance Sheet

FRED				BANK			
ASSETS		*LIABILITIES*		*ASSETS*		*LIABILITIES*	
Deposit	$ ____	$180	Loan	Reserves	$200	$ ____	Deposit
				(Required	$ ____)		
				(Excess	$ ____)		
		$ ____	Net Worth				
$ ____		$ ____		$ ____		$ ____	

Fishing being a costly activity, Fred decides to take out *another* loan! This ridiculously agreeable bank agrees to loan him all its excess reserves. He signs the agreement; the bank credits his account. Fill out Table 16–3 to show everyone's assets and liabilities now.

TABLE 16-3
Third Balance Sheet

FRED				BANK			
ASSETS		*LIABILITIES*		*ASSETS*		*LIABILITIES*	
Deposit	$____	$____	Loan	Reserves	$____	$____	Deposit
				(Required	$____)		
				(Excess	$____)		
		$____	Net Worth				
	$____	$____			$____	$____	

Clearly, this process could go on forever. Use what you've learned about the money multiplier to fill out Table 16–4: the balance sheet reflecting the final multiple–expansion of deposits and the position of zero–excess reserves.

TABLE 16-4
Final Balance Sheet

FRED				BANK			
ASSETS		*LIABILITIES*		*ASSETS*		*LIABILITIES*	
Deposit	$____	$____	Loan	Reserves	$____	$____	Deposit
				(Required	$____)		
				(Excess	$0)		
		$____	Net Worth				
	$____	$____			$____	$____	

THE LANGUAGE OF ECONOMICS 16

The Fed

"The Fed" is really a nickname for the Federal Reserve System—a network of twelve regional banks which share responsibility for supervising and regulating financial institutions and providing bank services to member banks and the federal government, and the government agency, the Board of Governors of the Federal Reserve, which oversees them.

The Board of Governors consists of 7 members, nominated by the President and confirmed by the Senate, who serve 14-year terms. Its chairman and vice-chairman—two of these members—serve a 4 year term and can be reelected. The Board of Governors has sole authority over changes in reserve requirements, and must approve any change in the discount rate made by any regional bank. It also forms a portion of the Federal Open Market Committee (FOMC)—the group of people who supervise open market operations. The other members of the FOMC are the president of the New York Fed and 4 presidents of the other 11 regional banks who cycle through on a rotating basis. In practice, the Chairman of the Fed has almost total discretion over monetary policy in the US.

You can learn more about the Fed on the Web at http://www.federalreserve.gov.

REVIEW OF TECHNIQUE 16

Reading a Balance Sheet

It is important in life, as well as in economics, to be able to read a balance sheet. Balance sheets are really nothing more than tables which show the assets and liabilities of agents in the economy, and are useful to work through because they force you to think through every element of a transaction. By completely writing out all balance sheet changes, one can make two special checks—one for *vertical balance*, and one for *horizontal balance*.

For vertical balance, all of the changes on a given balance sheet must be the same. Either assets and liabilities will change by the same amount or one asset (liability) may rise by the same amount that another liability (asset) falls.

For horizontal balance, the changes in the total amount of a particular asset must sum to zero over every balance sheet in the economy. This is because *one person's asset is another's liability*. You should be careful when checking for horizontal balance: It is true, for example, that if a person withdraws money from a bank the total amount of money in the bank is lower. This decrease in the person's *assets*, however, is matched by a decrease in the bank's *liabilities*.

Every transaction and combination of transactions must show both vertical and horizontal balance. Tables 16–1, 16–2 and 16–3 in this chapter's Graph It are examples of simple balance sheets.

CROSSWORD

ACROSS

2. Open market transactions, discount rate, required reserve ratio
4. Organization that insures bank deposits (initials)
6. Money ___, consists of currency reserves plus bank deposits
7. A type of target, the money base is an example
9. Part of Fed that sets targets, directs monetary policy (initials)
11. Current chairman of the Fed

DOWN

1. A type of target, inflation and output are examples
3. Ratio, fraction of bank deposits held in reserve
5. People who argue that debt has a stronger link to output than money favor these kinds of targets
8. Rate Federal Reserve charges banks for short-term loans
10. Nickname for the Federal Reserve

FILL-IN QUESTIONS

1. A bank's total reserves are made up of both _____ and _____ reserves.
2. The interest rate charged by the Fed to member banks is called the _____.
3. The rate that one bank charges another to borrow its deposits at the fed is called the _____.
4. The ratio of the money supply to the money base is called the _____.
5. The money base is also called the stock of _____.
6. The ratio of currency to bank deposits is called the _____.
7. The ratio of bank reserves to bank deposits is called the _____.

8. The _____ insures bank deposits, so that depositors get paid even if a bank fails.

9. The Fed mostly uses _____ to control the money supply.

10. The money supply increases more than the monetary base when the Fed buys bonds because of _____ banking.

TRUE–FALSE QUESTIONS

T F 1. An increase in high–powered money increases the money supply.

T F 2. An increase in the public's desire to hold currency instead of deposits increases the money supply.

T F 3. An increase in the required reserve ratio increases the money supply.

T F 4. An increase in the amount of excess reserves that banks hold increases the money supply.

T F 5. An increase in income increases the money supply.

T F 6. An increase in the discount rate increases the money supply.

T F 7. An open market purchase of bonds by the Fed increases the money supply.

T F 8. The Fed increases the money supply when it buys foreign currency.

T F 9. Inflation increases the money supply.

T F 10. A decrease in taxes increases the money supply.

MULTIPLE–CHOICE QUESTIONS

1. Which of the following are examples of ultimate targets?
   a. money base
   b. credit
   c. output
   d. none of the above

2. Which of the following are examples of intermediate targets?
   a. inflation
   b. output
   c. credit
   d. none of the above

3. The money multiplier is
   a. zero
   b. one
   c. greater than one
   d. could be any of the above

4. If the currency–deposit ratio is 1/2 and the reserve–deposit ratio 1/4, the money multiplier will be

   a. 0.75
   b. 0.25
   c. 1
   d. 2

5. Monetary policy is determined by the

   a. FDIC
   b. FOMC
   c. SEC
   d. EPA

6. The Chairman of the Board of Governors of the Federal Reserve is

   a. Alan Greenspan
   b. Milton Friedman
   c. Paul Samuelson
   d. John Maynard Keynes

7. The primary instrument of monetary control is

   a. the discount rate
   b. the required reserve ratio
   c. open market transactions
   d. foreign exchange intervention

8. Which can the Fed control most accurately on a day–to–day basis?

   a. interest rates
   b. the monetary base
   c. output
   d. inflation

9. Which of the following instruments of monetary control does the fed use *least* often?

   a. the discount rate
   b. the required reserve ratio
   c. open market transactions
   d. it uses them all equally

10. Interest rates can be an unreliable indicator of monetary policy if there is

    a. money illusion
    b. inflation targeting
    c. credit rationing
    d. disintermediation

CONCEPTUAL PROBLEMS

1. Why might banks wish to hold excess reserves?

2. How can the Fed increase the money supply?

3. Why do monetarists argue that it is a mistake to target the interest rate rather than the money base?

4. What targets do *you* think the Fed should use, and why?

*5. Can you name 3 former chairmen of the Federal Reserve? Comment on their performance and, if possible, their reasons for leaving office.

TECHNICAL PROBLEMS

1. If the public becomes suspicious of the banking system and decides to hold more of its money in cash, what will happen to the money base, to interest rates and, in the short run, to output?

2. Will the Fed better stabilize output when most changes are the result of unexpected shocks to the LM curve by targeting the money base or the interest rate? Show, using IS–LM analysis.

3. How much will a $1 increase in the money base increase the supply of money if the currency–deposit ratio is 0.2 and the reserve ratio is 0.1?

17   Financial Markets

FOCUS OF THE CHAPTER

- Financial markets are the vehicle through which macroeconomic affect the lives of everyday people; fluctuations the stock market directly affect people's pensions and incomes; changes in interest rates affect our ability to buy a home, or a car.

- This chapter examines the behavior of three markets: the bond market, the stock market, and the market for foreign exchange.

- All of these markets are *forward–looking*; asset prices reflect people's expectations of future returns. As a result, changes in these asset prices are *unpredictable*.

SECTION SUMMARIES

1.   Interest Rates—Long–Term and Short

There is more than one interest rate in the economy; bonds of different maturities, in particular, have different interest rates. The relationship between the interest rates paid on bonds of differing maturity is called the *term structure of interest*.

Interest rates on long–term bonds are typically higher than interest rates on short–term bonds. Because holding one long–term bond is equivalent to holding a series of short–term bonds, *the interest rate on long–term bonds is equal to the average of the current interest rate on short–term bonds and expected future short–term interest rates, plus a term premium which compensates the holder for the risk associated with holding long– rather than short–term bonds*. Long–term bonds are typically perceived as riskier than short–term bonds because of their greater price volatility (variation in price).

The *expectations theory of the term structure* highlights the way that people's expectations of future short–term interest rates affect current long–term interest rates. The text observes that term premia vary over time.

The *yield curve* shows the relationship between interest rates on assets of different maturities. Because long–term interest rates are typically higher than short–term interest rates, the yield curve is usually upward-sloping. A downward-sloping yield curve implies that people must expect short–term interest rates to fall in the future; this is sometimes a recessionary signal.

Boxes 17–2 and 17–3 work through the details of calculating the *net present value* of assets whose payoff occurs in the future, and discuss the relationship between the net present value of a bond's *coupon payments* plus *face value* and its price. Increases in interest rates are shown to reduce bond prices—particularly *long–term* bond prices.

2. The Random Walk of Stock Prices

Because in an efficient market stock prices are based on all of the information that people have regarding a firm's profit opportunities, and, therefore, the value of the dividends that will be paid to stockholders, they should only change when new information becomes available. Changes in the price of a stock should, therefore, be completely unpredictable—stock prices should follow a *random walk*. (See Review of Technique 8 if you're not quite sure what a random walk is.)

While the stock market is probably not 100% efficient, changes do tend to be unpredictable. The random walk model appears to describe the behavior of stock prices fairly well.

Note that because stocks and bonds are substitutes, rising interest rates cause stock prices to fall.

3. Exchange Rates and Interest Rates

As we have noted in Chapters 12 and 21, the exchange rate is affected by interest differentials between countries. When a country's after–tax real interest rates are higher than the real interest rates that can be realized on assets of comparable risk that can be found in other parts of the world, capital will flow into that country, causing its currency to appreciate.

Uncovered interest parity states that domestic interest rates should be able to exceed foreign interest rates only by the amount that the domestic currency is expected to depreciate, or that

$$\frac{e_{t+1} - e}{e} = i - i^*,$$

where i represents the domestic interest rate, i^* the foreign interest rate, and e the nominal exchange rate *measured in units of domestic currency per unit of foreign currency*, so that an increase in e indicates a depreciation of the domestic currency.

KEY TERMS

maturity (or term) of bond
term structure of interest
arbitrage
term premium
expectations theory of the term structure
yield curve

net present value
coupon
face value
consol (or perpetuity)
random walk
uncovered interest parity

GRAPH IT 17

This Graph It asks you to draw the yield curve for the hypothetical set of assets provided by Table 17–1. What must people expect to happen to interest rates in the near future?

TABLE 17–1
Hypothetical yields on bonds of different maturity

Maturity	Interest Rate
3 mo.	5.6
1 yr	7.1
5 yr	9.5
10 yr	12.4

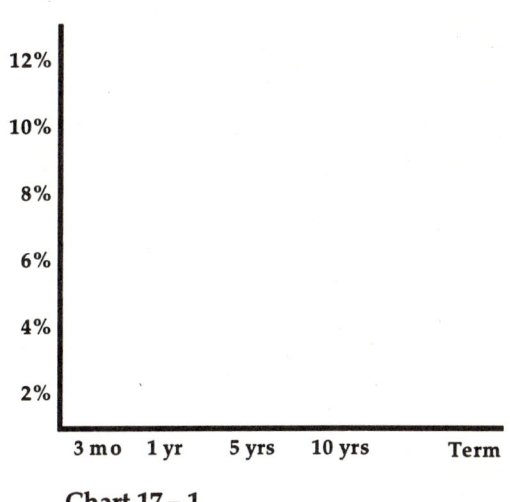

Chart 17–1

THE LANGUAGE OF ECONOMICS 17

Arbitrage

People who engage in *arbitrage* conduct riskless transactions by simultaneously buying and selling an asset in different markets—buying at a lower price, and selling at a higher one. It is arbitrage activities like this which the prices of assets in different markets from diverging.

Arbitrage activities occur in all markets, but some provide classic examples. Arbitrage in foreign exchange markets is one of these: Suppose that the dollar is selling in one place for 5.1 DM, and in another for 5.2 DM. An arbitrageur would buy dollars in the first and immediately sell those dollars in the second. She or he would make a riskless profit while simultaneously performing a public service—bringing prices into line. Because this arbitrageur's purchase of dollars would increase demand in the first market, the price of the dollar in that market will rise. Because his or her sale of dollars in the second market would increase supply, the price of the dollar in that market will fall. Soon they will be equal, and the *arbitrage opportunity* (the opportunity to make this sort of riskless transaction) will have disappeared.

It is perhaps easiest to observe this process at the supermarket: people leave longer lines at the checkout counter and add themselves to the back of shorter lines. This keeps all of the lines at the supermarket roughly the same length… and the people who realize the arbitrage opportunities very happy.

194 CHAPTER 17

REVIEW OF TECHNIQUE 17

Compound Interest

When the interest on a debt is allowed to accumulate, and the interest on that interest, and the interest on *that* interest, the size of the debt rises quickly. Anyone with an outstanding balance on their credit card knows this firsthand.

The interest you are paid on your savings account accumulates in this same way: If you start off with P dollars, invest them at a rate r for t years and let the interest accumulate, you end up with an amount FV given by the following formula:

$$FV = P(1 + r)^t$$

If you would like to know the amount of time it will take to make your money double, a good rule of thumb is the "rule of 72's": The approximate number of years required for an investment to double when its interest is allowed to accumulate this way can be found by dividing the number 72 by the interest rate. With an interest rate of 10%, for example, your money would double in just over 7 years.

CROSSWORD

ACROSS

2 Curve, shows relationship between interest rates on assets of different maturity

4 A bond that never matures (lasts forever)

7 An increase in interest rates causes stock prices to ___

9 Stocks and bonds are

ACROSS (CONTINUED)

10 Stock prices take this sort of a walk

DOWN

1 An increase in interest rates ___ bond prices

3 Changes in stock prices should be unpredictable when the stock market is

5 Amount of time remaining until a bond expires

6 Periodic payment made to the holder of a bond

8 Premium, compensates the holder for the risk associated with holding long- rather than short-term bonds

FILL-IN QUESTIONS

1. The relationship between the interest rates paid on bonds of differing maturity is called the _____.

2. Long–term bond are typically perceived as _____ than short–term bonds because of their greater price volatility.

3. The _____ curve shows the relationship between interest rates on assets of different maturities.

4. Periodic payments made to bond–holders are called _____ payments.

5. The amount that a bond pays its holder upon expiration is called its _____.

6. Changes in the price of a stock should be completely _____.

7. The relationship between exchange rates and interest differentials described in this chapter is called _____.

8. Domestic interest rates should exceed foreign interest rates only by the the amount that the domestic currency is expected to _____.

9. The time remaining before a bond expires is referred to as the term, or _____ of the bond.

10. _____ involves the simultaneous sale and purchase of an asset at different prices, in different markets.

TRUE–FALSE QUESTIONS

T F 1. Term premia appear to vary over time.

T F 2. The yield curve is usually downward–sloping.

T F 3. When interest rates rise, so do bond prices.

T F 4. When interest rates rise, so do stock prices.

T F 5. Financial markets are interesting in and of themselves, but have little to do with macroeconomics.

T F 6. Fluctuations in the prices of stocks and bonds have little effect on regular people's incomes.

T F 7. Asset prices should be easily predictable.

T F 8. Asset prices reflect people's expectations of future returns; only new information should make them change.

T F   9. It is sometimes, but not always, a recessionary signal when interest rates on long–term bonds are lower than interest rates on short–term bonds.

T F   10. People's expectations of future short–term interest rates affect current long–term interest rates.

MULTIPLE–CHOICE QUESTIONS

1. Which of the following compensates bond–holders for the risk associated with holding long– rather than short–term bonds?

   a. yield curve
   b. coupon
   c. perpetuity
   d. term premium

2. A bond which never matures is called a

   a. consol
   b. perpetuity
   c. coupon
   d. (a) and (b)

3. The amount that a bond pays when it expires called its

   a. coupon
   b. face value
   c. return
   d. (b) and (c)

4. The maturity of a bond is also called its

   a. term
   b. coupon
   c. face value
   d. return

5. The yield curve is usually

   a. upward–sloping
   b. downward–sloping
   c. flat
   d. there is no "usual" slope

6. A down–ward sloping yield curve is _____ a recessionary signal.

   a. sometimes
   b. never
   c. always
   d. its actually an expansionary signal

7. Stock prices should follow a.

   a. distributed lag
   b. random walk
   c. predictable pattern
   d. cycle

8. If domestic interest rates exceed foreign interest rates, uncovered interest parity suggests that people must expect the domestic currency to

   a. depreciate
   b. appreciate
   c. collapse
   d. it suggests nothing of the kind

9. Long term bonds are riskier than short–term bonds because of their

   a. coupon variation
   b. unpredictable face value
   c. greater price volatility
   d. term premium

10. Which of the following prevents asset prices from diverging (one asset from having many different prices)?
    a. monetary policy
    b. compound interest
    c. net present value
    d. arbitrage

CONCEPTUAL PROBLEMS

1. Why is a downward–sloping yield curve sometimes a recessionary signal?

2. Why isn't a downward–sloping yield curve *always* a recessionary signal?

3. Why shouldn't changes in asset prices be predictable?

4. What effect would you expect an increase in interest rates to have on stock prices? Explain.

TECHNICAL PROBLEMS

1. If the current rate of interest on 3 month treasury bills is 6%, and is expected to rise 1/2 of a percentage point each quarter (every 3 months), what should be the rate of interest on a 1 year Treasury bond? (Assume that the term premium is zero.)

2. If the current rate of interest on a 1 year treasury bond is 8%, and if the rate of interest on 3 month treasury bills is expected to remain at 6%, what must be the term premium for a 1 year bond?

3. If the dollar is expected to depreciate 2% relative to the yen, what does the uncovered interest parity relationship suggest should be the difference between US and Japanese interest rates?

Part 5

Big Events, International Adjustments, and Advanced Topics

18 THE ECONOMICS OF DEPRESSION, HYPERINFLATION, AND DEFICITS

FOCUS OF THE CHAPTER

- In this chapter we revisit the time period which gave birth modern macroeconomics: the Great Depression. We examine the role that both monetary and fiscal policies played in its beginnings, its continuation, and our ultimate recovery from it.

- We also examine the link between money growth and inflation in normal business cycles and in hyperinflations. A variety of policy responses to hyperinflation are reviewed; the necessity of stabilizing government budget deficits in hyperinflationary economies is emphasized.

- The US budget deficit is examined in some detail. There is a brief discussion of the national debt.

SECTION SUMMARIES

1. The Great Depression: The Facts

The Great Depression began just before the infamous stock market crash of September 1929, and, fueled by large–scale bank failures that caused an immense decline in the money supply, lasted until the end of 1941 when the US entered World War II. Unemployment averaged 18.8% between 1930 and 1941, and was reached a high of 24.9% in 1933. Net investment was negative between 1931 and 1935. Output fell nearly 30% between 1929 and 1933. The consumer price index fell almost 25%. The stock market declined an astounding 85% between the crash of September 1929 and June 1932.

Because the federal government in the mid–1930's was worried about balancing the budget, federal state and local fiscal policies were actually contractionary between 1932 and 1934, exactly opposite what was needed. President Roosevelt's "New Deal," often credited with pulling the U.S. out of the Great Depression, actually wasn't expansionary at all. A number of institutional changes, however, were made during Roosevelt's first term: the Federal Deposit Insurance Corporation (FDIC) was created to supervise banks and insure bank deposits; the Securities and Exchange Commission (SEC) was established to regulate the securities industry; and the Social Security Administration was set up so that the elderly would not have to rely on savings to finance their retirement. These changes were all viewed as potentially stabilizing, and all of them have persisted to this very day. Many economists, however, give credit to the bombing of Pearl Harbor and the subsequent entry of the US into World War II for our eventual victory over the Great Depression.

Due in part to the collapse of the international financial system and the widespread adoption of "beggar–thy–neighbor" trade policies, the Great Depression was a virtually worldwide phenomenon. Many countries weathered it much better than the U.S., perhaps because they were more willing to adopt expansionary fiscal policies.

2. The Great Depression: The Issues and Ideas

Early Keynesians believed that the depression was a consequence of contractionary fiscal policy, and argued that the only effective remedy for it was fiscal expansion. They gave very little weight to monetary factors, claiming that expansionary monetary policy could not have triggered an economic recovery because the US economy was in a liquidity trap. Interest rates were close to zero, and they believed that any monetary expansion would be absorbed without significantly changing them.

Monetarists, notably Milton Friedman and Anna Schwartz, took a different view. They believed that the Fed's failure to help struggling banks and to prevent the decline of the domestic money stock was responsible for the severity of the depression, and made quite a persuasive argument.

Although Keynesian and Monetarist explanations of the Great Depression were originally held to be at odds with one another, there is no inherent conflict between them. Everyone behaved ineptly during the 1930's; there is plenty of blame to go around.

It is interesting to note that the stock market crash of October 19, 1989 was much worse in percentage terms than the crash of September 29, 1929. Unlike the crash that heralded the beginning of the Great Depression, however, "Black Monday" did not even cause a mild recession. The Fed acted instantly, allowing the federal funds rate to drop severely. After a few days, the economy returned to normal.

3. Money and Inflation in Ordinary Business Cycles

The link between money growth and inflation is not as tight in the short run as it is in the long run, in part because money growth can affect output in the short run, in part because low levels of inflation can be a fiscal as well as a monetary phenomenon. Hyperinflation, however, is indisputably a result of excessive money growth. It is an unfortunate reality, however, that it is easier to create a hyperinflation than it is to stop one.

4. Hyperinflation

Although there is no consensus on what constitutes a hyperinflation, a working definition is an annual rate of inflation that exceeds 1,000%. Hyperinflationary countries all appear to suffer from large budget deficits and high rates of money growth. Because inflation increases the measured deficit, economists often look instead at the *inflation–adjusted deficit*:

$$\text{total deficit} - (\text{inflation rate} \times \text{national debt})$$

This subtracts the component of the interest payments on the debt that are attributed directly to inflation.

The *heterodox approach to stabilization* combines monetary, fiscal, and exchange rate policies with incomes policies; it constitutes a coordinated attack on inflation, and offers the possibility of deflation without recession. But like all other policies that need to affect people's expectations in order to work, this heterodox approach must be *credible*. For countries with debt–driven hyperinflation, this often means a strong commitment to debt reduction. Nobody's going to believe the government will stop printing money until the problems that made it necessary have been dealt with.

This highlights a very important fact: the *sacrifice ratio*, or the percentage decline in output resulting from a one percentage–point reduction in the rate of inflation, can be reduced through the implementation credible policies. Central bank credibility can be an immensely powerful tool.

5. Deficits, Money Growth, and The Inflation Tax

The government can finance its deficits in two ways: it can either sell bonds, or persuade the central bank to increase the monetary base. The Fed is said to *monetize* a deficit whenever it purchases some of the bonds that the Treasury sells to finance that deficit. If it does not do this, the fiscal expansion behind the deficit will drive up interest rates; if it does, it runs the risk of causing inflation. Evidence is mixed on whether the Federal Reserve even partially monetizes US deficits.

Creating high–powered money serves as an alternative to taxation. The revenue collected through money creation is referred to as *seigniorage*. The total amount of seigniorage that can be collected is given by the formula

$$\text{inflation tax revenue} = \text{inflation tax rate} \times \text{real money base}$$

As the growth rate of money becomes large, the real money stock falls to zero; the government cannot collect an arbitrarily large amount of tax revenue simply by printing money. The "inflation tax" appears to be quite low in industrialized countries, where the money base is small relative to the size of the economy. Countries with less developed financial sectors, where people hold large amounts of currency, appear able to generate more revenue by printing money.

6. Budget Deficits: Facts and Issues

Government expenditures consist of both *mandatory and discretionary outlays*. Mandatory outlays consist of spending made under entitlement programs; Medicaid, Social Security, and Aid to Families with Dependent Children are examples. In the US, discretionary spending must be approved by congress; it includes defense spending and foreign aid.

Defense spending as a fraction of GDP has declined in the US since the end of the Cold War. Entitlement spending is nearly double what it was in the 1960's, and interest payments on the national debt have become a significant component of government expenditure. Most of the federal government's revenues come from taxes. The government's revenues hasn't changed very much as a percentage of GDP over the last 30 years; its expenditures have soared. Social security taxes contribute more to federal revenue today than anytime in the recent past; revenue from corporate income taxes, as a percentage of GDP, has fallen by half since the 1960's.

Structural deficits measure the size that the budget deficit would be if output were at its full-employment level. *Cyclical deficits* are the difference between actual structural deficits. The deficit is typically broken into two components: the *primary*, or *non-interest deficit*, and interest payments on the public debt. During periods of low inflation, nearly half of the nominal interest payments on the debt may be offset by inflation.

The national debt of the US, well over $5 trillion, seems like a great burden. In per capita terms, however, that amounts to only $20,000 per person. The debt ratio—the ratio of debt to income—is less than 1; we could pay back the entire debt using less than 1 year's output. And most of it does not even need to be paid back; we owe the bulk to ourselves. Still, an increasingly large portion of the national debt is owned by foreigners. That portion represent a tax burden that future US taxpayers will have to carry. Because it places an upward pressure on interest rates, the debt can also lower investment and may decrease our potential for long-term growth.

7. Social Security

The US currently uses a *pay-as-you-go* social security system, in which the taxes of paid by those generations who are currently working are used to funds payments made to retirees. Due to declines in population growth, at some point in the near future we will either have to raise the social security tax or reduce the amount of benefits paid to each retiree. The US does not face this problem alone; a vast number of countries will soon have to address the same problem.

Suggested social security reforms include increasing the age at which people can get social security benefits, taxing all social security benefits received in excess of contributions, and reducing cost-of-living increases by changing the way inflation is measured. Other suggestions include placing a part of the Social Security Trust Fund in a diversified portfolio of stocks and bonds, and allowing individuals to substitute investment in private retirement accounts for part of their social security contributions.

KEY TERMS

Great Depression
New Deal
Keynesian revolution
quantity theory of money
velocity of money
hyperinflation
inflation–adjusted deficit
heterodox approach to stabilization
credible policy
credibility bonus
inflationary inertia
sacrifice ratio
government budget constraint

monetization
seigniorage
inflation tax
mandatory outlays
discretionary outlays
entitlement programs
government purchases
transfer payments
primary (non–interest) deficit
debt–income ratio
intergenerational accounting
pay–as–you–go (social security) system

GRAPH IT 18

This Graph It gives you a chance to look at what happened to output during the Great Depression. Table 18–1 provides data on US real GDP between 1929 and 1942. Your task is to find and plot the percentage change in output for each year.

You might also try graphing the *level* of output during this period. Although a chart is not provided for you, you could easily make one.

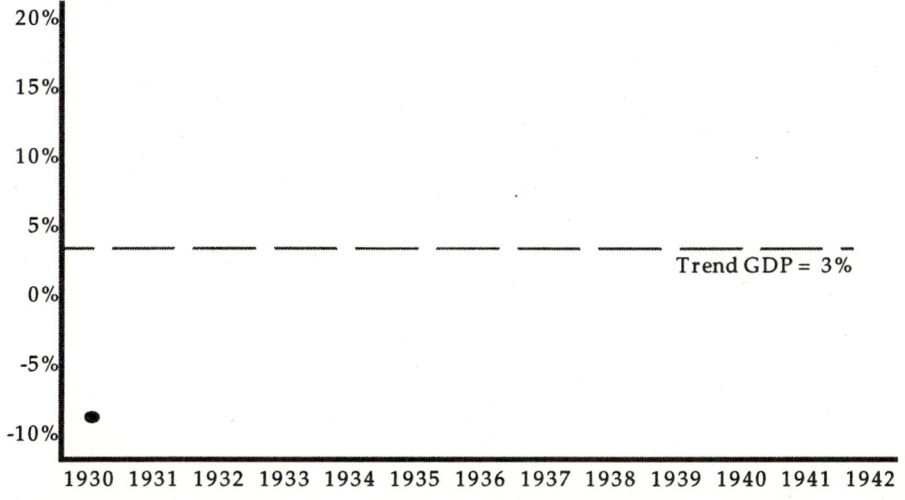

Chart 18 - 1

TABLE 18 – 1

Year	GDP	Percent change from previous year
1929	790.9	—
1930	719.7	– 9.0
1931	674.0	
1932	584.3	
1933	577.3	
1934	641.1	
1935	698.4	
1936	790.0	
1937	831.5	
1938	801.2	
1939	866.5	
1940	941.2	
1941	1,101.8	
1942	1,308.9	

Source: Bureau of Economic Analysis (National Income and Product Accounts)

THE LANGUAGE OF ECONOMICS 18

Debts and Deficits

Debts and deficits are frequently confused. Both appear to be in levels, and both seem to be a problem. What is the difference between them, and how are they related to one another?

The primary difference is that debt is a *stock* and the deficit is a *flow* into that stock. Budget deficits, when they are not *monetized*, add to the debt. Budget surpluses reduce the debt, as all of the money that the government does not spend can be used to buy back the bonds the Treasury has issued on that debt.

It is more useful to look at the debt–income ratio than at the absolute level of the debt. While the national debt of the United States, for example, is clearly greater than that of Italy *in absolute terms*, it represents a much smaller fraction of output. If both countries were to completely pay off their debts, the US would find it less of a burden: the US national debt, as of 1996, was 69.2% of GDP. Italy's was roughly 121%.

REVIEW OF TECHNIQUE 18

Dynamic Expectations

When expectations are based on current or lagged variables, they change over time to reflect the impact of new information. This Review of Technique works through simple model with dynamic expectations.

Suppose that permanent income is given by the formula:

$$YP = Y^e$$

where Y^e is the average amount of money you expect to earn each year for the rest of your life. Suppose also that your expectations regarding this stream of income are given by the formula

$$Y^e = \tfrac{1}{2}(Y + Y_{-1})$$

and that consumption, investment, and government spending are as follows:

$$C = \tfrac{1}{2} YP = \tfrac{1}{2} Y^e = \tfrac{1}{4}(Y + Y_{-1})$$

$$I = 1000$$

$$G = 0$$

Table 18–2 traces out, for a few periods, this process of expectational adjustment and show the effect that it has on consumption. We use the national income accounting relationship $Y = C + I + G$, or, more precisely,

$$Y = \tfrac{1}{2}(Y + Y_{-1}) + 100$$

to track the way that income changes over time.

Do you see how changes in people's expectations of future income affect their consumption patterns?

Table 18–2

Period	Y	Y_{-1}	Y^e	C	I	G
0	1,400.00	1,000.00	1,200.00	600.00	1000.00	0
1	1,600.00	1,400.00	1,500.00	750.00	1000.00	0
2	1,750.00	1,600.00	1,675.00	837.50	1000.00	0
3	1,837.50	1,750.00	1,793.75	896.88	1000.00	0

(Note: The function that we have used to represent these expectations is not a realistic one. If we were building a more careful model, we would want people's expectations to be formed <u>rationally</u>—to take into account all available information about the economy.)

FILL-IN QUESTIONS

1. Hyperinflations have historically tended to occur in the aftermath of _____.

2. Wage and price controls are referred to as _____.

3. The revenue collected through money creation is called _____.

4. The creation of high–powered money in order to generate revenues is referred to as an _____.

5. The Fed is said to _____ a deficit when it buys some or all of the bonds that the treasury sells to finance that deficit.

6. The _____ deficit subtracts the component of the interest payments on the national debt that are attributed directly to inflation.

7. A _____ approach to stabilization consists of the simultaneous use of monetary, fiscal, exchange rate, and incomes policies.

8. The government can finance its budget deficits in two ways: it can either _____ or _____.

9. Rising markets are called _____ markets; falling markets are _____.

10. Countries with hyperinflation often have large, persistent _____.

TRUE–FALSE QUESTIONS

T F 1. The Great Depression was specific to the US; everyone else was just fine.

T F 2. Fault for the Great Depression has been attributed to both bad fiscal and bad monetary policy.

T F 3. Monetary policy was expansionary during the early years of the Great Depression.

T F 4. Fiscal policy was clearly expansionary during the early years of the New Deal (1932-1934).

T F 5. The stock market crash of October 1989 wasn't nearly as bad as the one of 1929.

T F 6. The link between money and inflation is stronger in the short run than in the long run.

T F 7. Wage and price controls are an effective way to halt inflation.

T F 8. A heterodox approach to stabilization offers the possibility of deflation without recession.

T F 9. Policy credibility has no effect on sacrifice ratio.

T F 10. The US has one of the largest debt–income ratios in the world.

MULTIPLE–CHOICE QUESTIONS

1. The length and severity of the Great Depression was the fault of
   a. monetary policy
   b. fiscal policy
   c. neither
   d. both

2. The depression of the 1930's was a _____ phenomenon.
   a. US
   b. North American
   c. western
   d. global

3. The Great Depression begin, in the US, in
   a. 1929
   b. 1931
   c. 1933
   d. 1935

4. The Great Depression ended, in the US, in
   a. 1935
   b. 1939
   c. 1941
   d. 1945

5. Credit for the end of the Great Depression in the US is given to
   a. monetary authorities
   b. the "New Deal"
   c. US entry into WWII
   d. stock market recovery

6. Which of the following agencies was not created by Roosevelt's "New Deal" reforms?

   a. FDIC
   b. FOMC
   c. SEC
   d. Social Security Administration

7. Keynesian theory, during the 1960's, was dubbed the

   a. New Economics
   b. New Deal
   c. Great Depression
   d. "beez-neez"

8. Which of the following annual rates of inflation would be called a hyperinflation?

   a. 10%
   b. 100%
   c. 1000%
   d. (b) and (c)

9. There is a stronger link between the rate of money growth and the nominal rate of inflation in the

   a. long run
   b. short run
   c. steady–state
   d. no difference

10. Hyperinflations are usually ended through

    a. currency reform
    b. reduced budget deficits
    c. tight monetary policy
    d. all of the above

CONCEPTUAL PROBLEMS

1. Why do you think the US stock market crash of October 1989 didn't cause another depression? Were we lucky, or did we do something right?

2. Explain why each of the following situations might lead to hyperinflation. Can you think of any historical examples in which they've done exactly this?

   a) A government cannot meet its debt obligations (does not have sufficient revenues to repay the interest on its debt).

   b) A country is assessed war reparations that force its government to run huge budget deficits.

   c) A government lacks either the power or the necessary infrastructure to collect taxes.

3. How can the creation of high–powered money can be a source of government revenue?

4. Do you think that the US national debt is a burden? Do our high levels of debt risk triggering a hyperflation?

TECHNICAL PROBLEMS

1. How much inflation tax revenue would be generated in a country with a real money base of $1,000 and an inflation rate of 1000%?

2. How much inflation tax revenue would be generated in a country with a real money base of $500 and an inflation rate of 1000%?

3. What happens to the real money base, over time, when the growth rate of money becomes large? Given this, do you think that seigniorage is good way to generate revenue?

19 INTERNATIONAL ADJUSTMENT AND INTERDEPENDENCE

FOCUS OF THE CHAPTER

- This chapter extends the open economy analysis of Chapter 12 by allowing the domestic price level to change. Methods and strategies of foreign exchange intervention are explored in greater depth.

SECTION SUMMARIES

1. Adjustment Under Fixed Exchange Rates

In our discussion of fixed exchange rate regimes in Chapter 12 we assumed that the central bank would take preventative action to insure that balance–of–payments problems never occurred. In reality, this is a little idealistic. Central banks can, and do, finance temporary payments imbalances. This section asks what happens when one of these imbalances proves less temporary than the central bank had hoped.

In order to finance a payments imbalance, a central bank must regularly intervene in the currency market, buying or selling foreign exchange. In a balance–of–payments deficit, the demand for foreign currency exceeds the supply and the central bank must step in regularly to make up the difference. It is limited by its reserves and cannot keep this up forever; ultimately it must devalue its currency. But if it chooses not to do this there is an automatic adjustment process that takes effect: the decline in the central bank's reserves caused by its currency market intervention gradually erode the stock of high–powered money and reduce aggregate demand. As long as the central bank does not try to offset this by buying domestic bonds (*sterilizing* its intervention) this will eventually repair the payments imbalance. If the payments imbalance occurs with output at or below potential output, a decline in wages and prices may also have to occur to bring the economy back into internal balance. This will reduce the real exchange rate (remember it's the nominal exchange rate that's fixed) and add a bit back to aggregate demand by raising net exports. This slow return to internal and external balance is called the *classical adjustment process*.

A combination of *expenditure switching policies*—policies which shift demand between domestically produced goods and goods produced in other countries—and *expenditure reducing (or expenditure increasing) policies*—policies which decrease (or increase) aggregate demand—

213

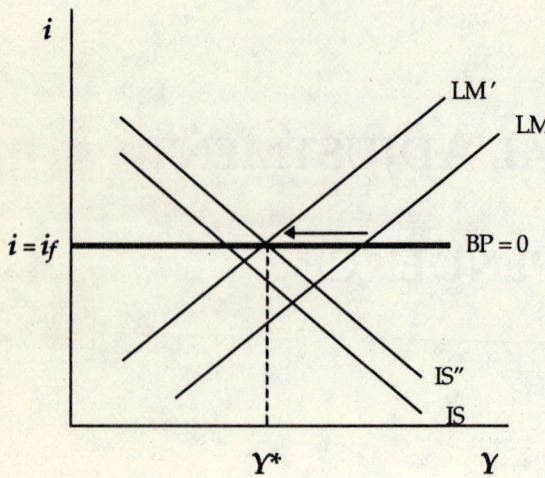

Figure 19-1

ADJUSTMENT TO A PAYMENTS IMBALANCE IN THE MUNDELL–FLEMING MODEL

Your textbook provides a different graph; this is an alternative way to visualize the adjustment process.

can achieve internal and external balance both more quickly and with much less pain than the classical adjustment process. We have already observed that devaluation could have corrected the payments imbalance described above (the IS curve would have shifted outwards as a result of net export increases); contractionary monetary policy could have done the same. Both of these in combination could achieve the joint goals of internal and external balance quickly and with less pain than automatic adjustment allows. Import taxes could be used in place of or in combination with devaluation to raise net exports.

Some countries faced with the threat of frequent devaluation find it easier to fix their real exchange rate than their nominal one. They do this by implementing a *crawling peg*—regularly devaluing their nominal exchange rate to make up for changes in foreign and domestic prices. This devaluation occurs at a rate approximately equal to the inflation differential between the country and its trading partners.

2. Exchange Rate Changes and Trade Adjustment: Empirical Issues

In order for a nominal devaluation to be successful (i.e., to resolve a payments imbalance), it must be accompanied by a real devaluation—a decline in the real exchange rate. This means that there can be no changes in foreign or domestic prices that negate the effect of the nominal devaluation. This section asks whether nominal devaluations are usually associated with real devaluations, and, on a slightly different subject, whether a decline in the relative price of domestic goods really does improve the trade balance.

The first question has a fairly straightforward answer: nominal devaluations do seem to cause real devaluations as long as the monetary authority resists the impulse to accommodate the price increases they create.

The answer to the second question is somewhat more complex: Because it takes some consumers—and some producers—time to adjust to changes in relative prices, the initial effect of a real devaluation is to *increase* the amount of money spent on imported goods. It is only later that a decline in the relative price of domestic goods improves the trade balance.

The text raises one final point about overvalued currencies: If a currency is overvalued for long enough, it may permanently reduce the competitiveness of domestic firms in the international marketplace. Domestic firms may lose foreign market share, or be driven out of markets altogether. Trade patterns may change permanently.

3. The Monetary Approach to the Balance of Payments

The monetary approach to the balance of payments is based on the belief that most balance of payments deficits are caused by excessive monetary growth. Sterilization operations may contribute to this problem, as they prevent the monetary contraction and subsequent rise in interest rates that would ordinarily result from the central bank's attempt to maintain an overvalued exchange rate. Higher real interest rates would, of course, attract foreign capital and add to the current account, reducing the balance of payments deficit.

Proponents of the monetary approach argue that devaluation can only reduce or eliminate a balance of payments deficit in the short run—that the increase in net exports it causes will lead to a monetary expansion, increasing aggregate demand, driving up the price level and causing a real appreciation of the currency so that the economy ends up right back where it started.

The authors of the textbook do not entirely agree with this analysis. They point out that when a currency is overvalued because of persistent deficits and a high rate of unemployment, a devaluation may actually speed up the adjustment process.

It is also worth noting that, even if a nominal devaluation does work only the short run, its effect on a country's competitive position could still be permanent because of the permanent effects discussed in the previous section.

4. Flexible Exchange Rates, Money, and Prices

This section makes a fairly obvious argument: monetary policy can affect output only temporarily. Eventually, prices will adjust and bring the economy back into internal balance. Real money balances will rise or fall, returning to their original level; as will the real exchange rate. Net exports will be unaffected.

Because prices and exchange rates do not change at the same rate, however, there are some interesting effects that occur during the adjustment process. One of these is *exchange rate overshooting*—a tendency of the exchange rate to move beyond the point of its long-run equilibrium and then, after time, gradually return. Imagine a rubber band. You stretch it—perturb it from its equilibrium—and then let go and allow it to snap back. Anyone who has spent enough of their childhood playing with rubber bands knows that the rubber band will snap too far backwards, and will hit their finger. The rubber band, like the exchange rate, overshoots its equilibrium position… much to the dismay of whomever is holding it.

5. Interest Differentials and Exchange Rate Expectations

We have argued that capital mobility should prevent interest differentials from developing. How then can we explain why there *are* differences in tax- and risk-adjusted real interest rates across countries?

The answer, of course, is that real interest rates are not the only component of an asset's return; because its holder is ultimately concerned with the asset's return *valued in his or her own currency*, and must therefore worry about changes in the exchange rate.

The return on a foreign asset is equal to the rate of interest that it pays (i_f), measured in units of the foreign currency, plus the change in the value of that currency ($-\Delta e/e$)*. The expected return on that asset is that same rate of interest (i_f) plus the *expected* change in the value of the foreign currency ($-\Delta e/e$). With perfect capital mobility, therefore, we should expect:

$$i = i_f - \Delta e/e.$$

Interest rates can differ across countries because of anticipated changes in the exchange rate. Oddly, this means that exchange rate expectations, because of the way that they affect international capital flows and, therefore, actual exchange rates, can be self-fullfilling. If enough people expect the British pound to depreciate, money will flow out of Great Britain in search of higher expected returns, causing the pound to depreciate.

6. Exchange Rate Fluctuations and Interdependence

The present system of foreign exchange, for most countries, is one of **dirty floating**. Central banks intervene from time to time in order to influence the exchange rate. It is often argued that governments ought to intervene in foreign exchange markets to smooth out temporary fluctuations; unfortunately, it has proven nearly impossible to figure out which fluctuations are temporary and which are permanent.

Intervention in foreign exchange markets, even when it fails to affect the exchange rate, can still be effective if it affects people's expectations—perhaps by implying a commitment on the part of the government to some announced policy change. This expectational effect may be the only reason that sterilized intervention can affect the exchange rates; because sterilization prevents foreign exchange market intervention from having any effect on domestic interest rates, there are many who question its ability to affect the exchange rate at all.

Spillover effects result both from international capital flows and from the way that trade imbalances affect price levels in different countries. The authors note that some of the problems associated with such effects could be eliminated if countries better coordinated their policies, but also find most countries unwilling to give up the amount of independence that would entail.

---

* Here we use standard notation for the nominal exchange rate; *e* is written in units of foreign currency per unit of domestic currency, so that a depreciation of the domestic currency/appreciation of the foreign currency increases it.

7. The Choice of Exchange Rate Regimes

This section presents several alternatives to fixed exchange rates. You have already heard about the crawling peg—an exchange rate that devalues or revalues at a constant rate to make up for differences in the inflation rates between it and its trading partners. There is also a variation on the fixed exchange rate called a *target zone*, a fixed band in which an exchange rate is allowed to float. For increased credibility there are *currency boards*, in which the domestic currency is 100% backed by foreign reserves, and there is the outright adoption of another country's currency (we call this *dollarization*, although the currency adopted need not be the dollar). Beyond this, there is the option of taking a flexible exchange rate and subjecting it to periodic *joint intervention* when it gets away from what is deemed its appropriate value—the ultimate dirty float.

KEY TERMS

automatic adjustment mechanisms
classical adjustment process
expenditure-switching policies
expenditure-reducing (-increasing) policies
internal and external balance
tariff
World Trade Organization (WTO)
International Monetary Fund (IMF)
devaluation
real devaluation
crawling peg
wage-price spiral
sticky real wages

J-curve effect
hysteresis effects
monetary approach
domestic credit
domestic credit ceiling
neutrality of money
exchange rate overshooting
purchasing power parity (PPP)
self-fulfilling expectations
foreign exchange market intervention
sterilized/nonsterilized intervention
spillover (interdependence) effects
speculative bubble

GRAPH IT 19

In this Graph It, we ask you to find out whether US imports actually rise when the dollar appreciates. We do not, however, ask you to draw a graph. Instead, we ask you to use a computer to examine the relationship between the real value of US imports, real US GDP, and the nominal, multilateral trade–weighted value of the dollar for the years 1967–1979. Gather your data from the Economic Data Tables in the back of this book.

Estimate the following three relations:

   imports = constant + aY
   imports = constant + (b × value of the dollar)
   imports = constant + aY + (b × value of the dollar)

What do you find for a and b? Do your estimates change when you include both income and the exchange rate in your regression?

If you don't have easy access to a computer or haven't taken any econometrics courses yet, go ahead and flip to the answers section.

THE LANGUAGE OF ECONOMICS 19

Sterilization

How exactly does the central bank go about *sterilizing* its intervention in foreign exchange markets—off-setting the effect of this intervention on the domestic money supply? The answer is fairly mundane: it conducts open market purchases or sales of bonds.

If, for example, the monetary authority exchanged foreign for domestic currency in foreign exchange markets, it would have to engage in open market transactions to prevent the money supply from falling. (Think about it.) It could sterilize this intervention by buying bonds.

REVIEW OF TECHNIQUE 19

Units of Measurement

We generally write our equations and variables without reference to the units in which they are measured. Care must be taken, however, to see that these units are consistent throughout an equation.

Consider, for example, the formula used to calculate the real exchange rate:

$$R = \frac{eP_f}{P}$$

we know that e represents the nominal exchange rate, and that P and P_f represent the domestic and foreign price levels, respectively. How do we know what units the nominal exchange rate is measured in? What units the rest exchange rate is measured in?

Let's stop and reason through this: P_f, we know, is measured in units of foreign currency. Marks, perhaps. If we use the a price index to measure it, its units will be marks per German basket of goods. P will be written in unit of foreign currency, say dollars. When it is measured by a price index like the CPI, its units will be dollars per US basket. If the units in which the nominal exchange rate is measured are to be consistent with the units in which the domestic and foreign price levels are measured, e must be written in *units of domestic currency per unit of foreign currency—not* in the conventional way.

Observe how the units of measurement in this equation cancel:

$$\frac{(\text{units domestic currency}/\text{unit foreign currency})(\text{unit foreign currency}/\text{foreign basket of goods \& services})}{(\text{unit domestic currency}/\text{domestic basket of goods \& services})}$$

$$=$$

$$\frac{\text{domestic basket of goods \& services}}{\text{foreign basket of goods \& services}}$$

The real exchange rate isn't measured in terms of any currency at all; it measures the quantity of domestic baskets for which a foreign basket of goods can be exchanges. An increase means that a foreign basket can be traded for more domestic baskets, and represents an improvement in the *terms of trade*. ALWAYS KNOW THE UNITS IN WHICH YOUR VARIABLE IS MEASURED.

The variable whose units are most often confused is the interest rate. We can write an interest rate as 5% or 0.05, or even as 500 "basis points" (a basis point is 1/100 of a percentage point). It is understood in all of these cases that the rate is 5% *per year*. Obviously, our units don't matter so long as we are consistent. The statement "the interest rate rose 10%" can be another source of confusion. It does *not* (or, at least, should not) mean the same thing as the statement "the interest rate rose 10 percentage points" …from 5% to 25% in our example. A 10% rise in the interest rate is much smaller: 1/2 a percentage point, in this case. A 10% increase in the interest rate only raises it from 5% to 5.5%. NEVER CONFUSE PERCENTAGE CHANGES WITH CHANGES IN PERCENTAGE POINTS FOR VARIABLES MEASURED IN "RATES".

CROSSWORD

ACROSS

4 Malaysia's currency

6 India's currency

8 Bhutan's currency

11 Thailand's currency

12 France's currency

13 Britain's currency

15 Italy's currency

16 Ethiopia's currency

17 Argentina's currency

18 China's currency

20 Malawi's currency

22 US's currency

23 Morocco's currency

FILL-IN QUESTIONS

1. Proponents of the monetary approach to the balance of payments argue that _____ is a major cause of chronic balance of payments deficits.

2. A central bank can offset the effect of foreign exchange market intervention on the domestic money supply by _____ it.

3. A(n) _____ exists when a government's goals of internal and external balance are in conflict with one another.

4. _____ can improve the performance of interdependent countries.

5. The _____ shows the response of imports, over time, to a currency devaluation.

6. The _____ is a measure of the trade balance.

7. Economic linkages between different countries can cause _____, or _____ effects.

DOWN

1 Costa Rica's currency
2 Saudi Arabia's currency
3 Kuwait's currency
4 Indonesia's currency
5 Armenia's currency
7 Portugal's currency
9 Currency used in Bangladesh
10 South Africa's currency
12 Hungary's currency
13 Spain's currency
14 Greece's currency
15 Romania's currency
16 Venezuela's currency
18 Japan's currency
19 Germany's currency
20 Currency of Czech Republic
21 Korea's currency

FILL-IN QUESTIONS (CONTINUED)

8. A policy intended to encourage consumption of domestically–produced goods and discourage consumption of goods produced in other countries is called an expenditure _____ policy.

9. A policy intended to decrease overall aggregate demand is called an expenditure _____ policy.

10. Devaluing the nominal exchange rate is only effective if it causes a _____.

TRUE–FALSE QUESTIONS

T F 1. Nominal exchange rates adjust in order to keep the relative price of imports and domestically produced goods from changing.

T F 2. A devaluation of the domestic currency reduces aggregate demand.

T F 3. An increase in foreign prices increases aggregate demand.

T F   4. An increase in world interest rates causes domestic interest rates to rise.

T F   5. With perfect capital mobility, GDP must equal potential GDP.

T F   6. If purchasing power parity holds between two countries, changes in their exchange rates must exactly offset the difference in their rates of inflation.

T F   7. Given enough time, an open economy will reach full–employment and balance of payments equilibrium without any government intervention.

T F   8. Government intervention can, however, achieve the same result more quickly and with less pain.

T F   9. Tariffs and devaluation are both expenditure switching policies.

T F   10. Contractionary monetary or fiscal policies are expenditure reducing policies.

MULTIPLE–CHOICE QUESTIONS

1. Countries can fix their real rather than their nominal exchange rates by using a
   a. monetary approach
   b. crawling peg
   c. clean float
   d. J curve

2. Which of the following suggests that the terms of trade should remain roughly constant in the long run?
   a. monetary approach
   b. crawling peg
   c. PPP
   d. hysteresis

3. Which of the following refers to the possibility that trade patterns could be permanently affected by overvalued currencies?
   a. monetary approach
   b. J curve
   c. PPP
   d. hysteresis

4. Empirical evidence shows that, following a devaluation, the value of imports
   a. rises, then falls
   b. falls, then rises
   c. immediately falls
   d. remains unchanged

5. Capital will flow into a country when its interest rate, adjusted for expected changes in the exchange rate, is _____ foreign interest rates.
   a. the same as
   b. lower than
   c. higher than
   d. no relation to interest rates

CONCEPTUAL PROBLEMS

1. When the real exchange rate, given by the equation

$$R = \frac{eP_f}{P}$$

   rises, is there a real appreciation or a real depreciation of the domestic currency. Should net exports rise or fall?

2. Why might long–term currency overvaluations be able to permanently affect trade patterns?

3. What is the J–curve effect?

TECHNICAL PROBLEMS

1. If the central bank is selling foreign currency in order to prevent the domestic currency from depreciating, what can it to *sterilize* this intervention?

2. Do nominal devaluations usually manage to cause real devaluations? What does the evidence suggest?

3. If interest rates in the US are 3 percentage points higher than interest rates in Germany, what must people expect to happen to the dollar in the near future?

20 ADVANCED TOPICS

FOCUS OF THE CHAPTER

- This chapter presents an overview of four recent ideas and models that have revolutionized modern macroeconomics—rational expectations modeling, the random walk theory of GDP, real business cycle theory, and New Keynesian models of price stickiness. Not all of these ideas fit together—some, in fact, contradict each other.

- Much of the technical material developed in this chapter is optional, or even super–optional— you may or may not be required to work through it. Section 8.1 of the textbook provides a very readable overview of the ideas developed in later, optional sections, however. If you read nothing else, read that.

SECTION SUMMARIES

1. An Overview of the New Macroeconomics

This section provides an informal introduction to four subjects: rational expectations modeling, the random walk theory of GDP, real business cycle theory, and New Keynesian models of price stickiness. We discuss each briefly, noting how each is related to the traditional aggregate supply–aggregate demand model.

The rational expectations model outlined in this chapter (the Lucas model) tries to explain how output can deviate from potential output and unemployment from its natural rate without requiring that prices adjust sluggishly.

We took a preliminary, non–technical look at this model in chapter 6 (section 6–3). You may recall some of the following: In Lucas's model, people cannot directly observe the price level, and must therefore form *expectations* of it. When these expectations are wrong, people's estimates of the real wage are also wrong, which causes them to supply "too much" or "too little" labor—an amount greater or less than they would choose to supply if they knew what their real wage really was. The labor market does clear in this model; the main way in which the aggregate supply assumptions differ from the classical case of the AS–AD model is that the labor supply, in this case, depends on the expected real wage rather than the actual real wage.

The assumption that people's expectations are formed *rationally* (see The Language of Economics 6 for a review of what this means) creates an even greater difference between this model and the standard AS–AD model: only unanticipated AD shifts can affect output and unemployment in the short run. Instead of a price level which is slow to adjust to economic shocks (as is the case with the AS–AD model), we have here an expectation of the price level which sometimes—when events occur without people's knowledge—fails, in the short run, to respond to changes in the economy (eventually, as more information becomes available, such errors correct themselves).

Unanticipated AD shifts do not affect people's expectations of the price level, so that nominal wage increases intended only to compensate workers for a higher price level look, to them, like increases in the in the real wage. This increased real wage they believe they are receiving makes them want to work more hours, raising output above its full–employment level for a time.

Anticipated AD shifts do affect people's expectations of the price level. They correctly guess, as a result, that the higher nominal raise that they are receiving as a result of the AD shift is merely compensating them for a higher price level, and choose to supply the same amount of labor.

Demand–side policies have little place in Lucas's world: unless they come as a surprise to the public, they accomplish nothing. Announcements are the only tool that is needed to stabilize output; all that the government need do to combat a recession is to correct people's expectational errors.

Real Business Cycle (RBC) theory is a natural outgrowth of rational expectations models like this one. Having ruled out aggregate demand shocks as the source of business cycle fluctuations, the proponents of RBC theory turn to *productivity shocks* to explain why output can and does deviate from its full–employment (potential) level. They argue that small changes in productivity, which, because the labor market is assumed to remain in equilibrium, cause small changes in the real wage, can generate large fluctuations employment (and therefore in output) because people are substitute leisure over time—work more hours when their wage temporarily rises, and take time off when their wage temporarily falls.

Both of these theories have a significant drawback: changes in the money supply, both anticipated and unanticipated, *do* appear to affect both output and unemployment in the short run in the real world. By testing the *random walk theory of GDP*—the theory that economic shocks have permanent rather than temporary effects on output—economists have tried to determine whether AS or AD shifts dominate the business cycle. (Recall that only supply shocks have permanent effects on output; AD shocks affect output only in the short run.)

New Keynesian models of price stickiness try to justify, in microeconomic terms, the assumption made in the AS–AD model that prices do not adjust immediately to clear markets.

2. The Rational Expectations Revolution

This section develops a simplified rational expectations model, and compares it to a basic AS–AD model with exogenously specified expectations of the price level. Perfect foresight models—models in which people always correctly guess the price level, so that the difference between it and the expected price level is always zero—are introduced, and shown to be equivalent to rational expectations models when people have all the information they need to correctly ascertain the state of the economy (i.e., output never deviates from potential output in this model, because people's expectations are always exactly correct).

The result that anticipated changes in the money supply cannot effect output in rational expectations models is derived carefully and in great detail, as is the result that unanticipated changes in the money supply can.

The authors note that empirical evidence does not strongly support these results; anticipated changes in the money supply do appear to have real effects in the short run.

3. The Microeconomics of the Imperfect Information Aggregate Supply Curve (optional section)

This section develops Lucas's imperfect information model of the AS curve. While the model itself is interesting and worth working through for its own sake, the real benefit of this section is that it allows you to work with, instead of reading about, rational expectations. If you read nothing else, read Box 8–2, "A Visual Example of Forming an Expectation".

The main result of the Lucas imperfect information model is derived: The amount that unanticipated changes in aggregate demand affect output depends on the relative importance of aggregate shocks (shocks that hit the entire economy) and idiosyncratic shocks (shocks specific to one industry or region).

4. The Random Walk of GDP—Does Aggregate Demand Matter, or is it all Aggregate Supply?

This section introduces *trend and difference stationary* processes. A trend stationary process is one which is dominated by transitory shocks—shocks whose effect eventually dies away. A difference stationary process, on the other hand, is dominated by permanent shocks—shocks whose effects accumulate over time. The *random walk* is the classic example of such a process.

If GDP is trend rather than difference stationary, business cycles must be caused by short–lived aggregate demand shocks, as economists have traditionally believed. If it proves to be difference stationary, on the other hand, supply shocks must be driving output, as Real Business Cycle theorists believe.

Statistically, it does look like output is dominated by permanent shocks—a controversial result, as it makes the sorts of fiscal and monetary policy that we have studied appear relatively unimportant. Luckily, there is a third possibility—one also supported by statistical evidence: GDP may instead be *trend stationary with breaks*, so that, while permanent shocks to productivity occur on rare occasions, aggregate demand shocks drive the business cycle within decades–long subperiods.

Statistical difficulties make it hard to determine with any certainty whether output is best characterized as difference stationary or as trend stationary with breaks. For this reason, the importance of AD shocks in the business cycle is likely to remain controversial for some time.

5. Real Business Cycle Theory

This section develops a simple RBC model, in which temporary fluctuations in the productivity of labor cause people to work more in periods of high productivity, and less in periods of low productivity.

The degree to which people substitute leisure over time determines whether or not small shocks to people's productivity can generate fluctuations in output that are big enough to explain the business cycle. This is shown to depend on two *deep parameters*—parameters which are fundamental determinants of the microeconomic decisions people make (consumption, labor supply, etc.): β and γ. These appear too small to generate enough *intertemporal substitution* to explain the business cycle.

6. A New Keynesian Model of Sticky Nominal Prices

This section highlights several key aspects of New Keynesian models of price stickiness: their reliance on imperfect competition, so that individual firms have enough market power to set prices; the assumption that there is a small cost that firms incur when they choose to change their nominal prices; and the assumption that the private benefits of one firm changing its price are significantly smaller than the social benefits—i.e., there is an *externality* involved.

These elements, together, can be combined in such a way that an individual firm will not find it optimal to raise its price in response to a demand shock, despite the fact that it would be best for society if it (and all other firms) did so.

KEY TERMS

rational expectations equilibrium	imperfect competition
rational expectations	Lucas critique
policy irrelevance	perfect foresight
random walk of GDP	Imperfect-information model
real business cycle (RBC) theory	trend (secular) component of GDP
propagation mechanism	cyclical component of GDP
intertemporal substitution of leisure	trend stationary
productivity shock	difference stationary
New Keynesian economics	trend stationary with breaks
price stickiness	deep parameters
menu cost	New Classical economics

GRAPH IT 20

This Graph It asks you two graph a trend stationary and a difference stationary process that are subjected to the same shocks for six periods. Table 8–1 provides the equations which describe each process, and the shocks to which both processes are subjected. You should graph the trend stationary process on Chart 8–1 and the difference stationary process on Chart 8–2. Compare them. If you saw them in a book somewhere, would you be able to guess which was which?

TABLE 20 – 1

Period (t)	Shock (u_t)	Trend Stationary Process ($y_t = 3t + u_t$)	Difference Stationary Process ($y_t = y_{t-1} + 3 + u_t$)
0	0	0*	0*
1	1	4	4
2	2	8	9
3	1	10	13
4	0	12	16
5	-1	14	18
6	0	18	21

* we assuming, for simplicity, that $y_o = 0$ for both processes.

THE LANGUAGE OF ECONOMICS 20

New Keynesians and New Classicists

Perhaps the biggest division in contemporary macroeconomics is between *New Keynesian* and *New Classical* economists. While both ground their theories in rational, maximizing behavior, they disagree about one fundamental aspect of the economy—whether or not markets clear.

This is, of course, what the original Keynesians and Classicists disagreed about. The main difference today is that, instead of arguing generally about whether shifts in AD affect output, New Keynesians and New Classicists argue about whether *anticipated* changes in AD do so.

The rules of the argument have changed as well; while the original Keynesians were able to support their assumptions by arguing that prices in the real world simply did not appear to adjust quickly enough to keep markets in equilibrium, the New Keynesians face a more formidable task. They must show that these sticky prices can arise in a world full of rational, utility maximizing agents—that they are not inconsistent with fundamental microeconomic principles. Only then can they challenge the New Classicists on their own ground.

228   CHAPTER 20

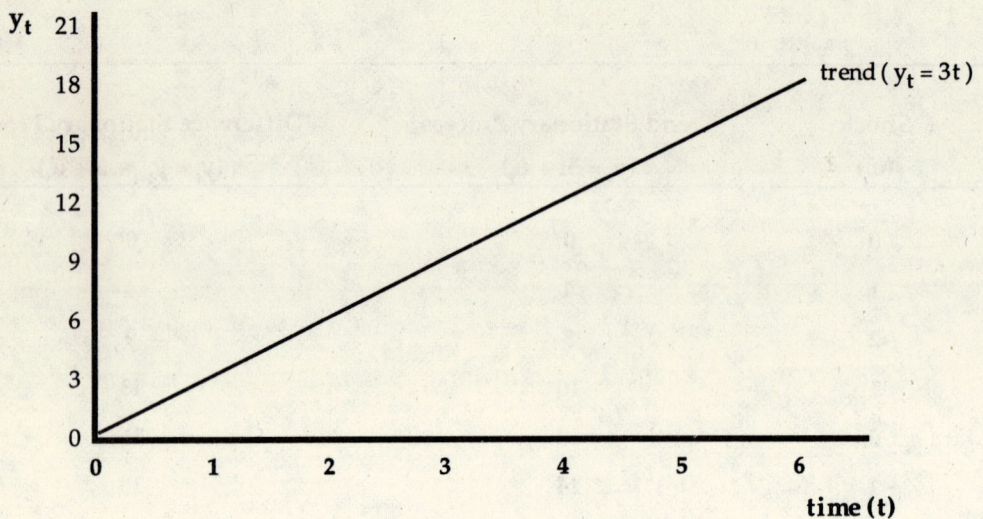

Chart 20 - 1

TREND STATIONARY PROCESS

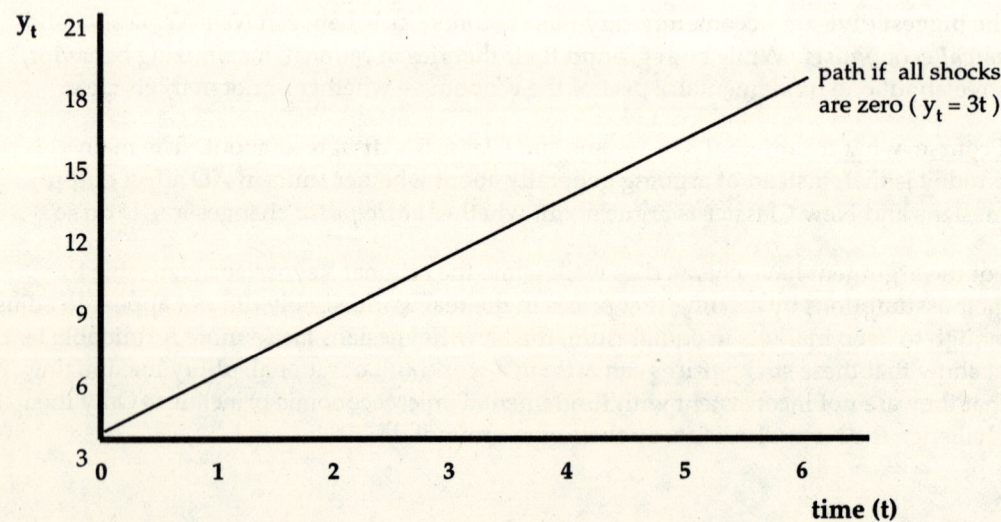

Chart 20 - 2

DIFFERENCE STATIONARY PROCESS (RANDOM WALK)

REVIEW OF TECHNIQUE 20

Taking a Random Walk

A *random walk* is the classic example of a difference stationary process—one whose level is permanently affected by brief, transitory shocks. This Review of Technique tells you how you might take a random walk:

Imagine yourself walking through a city. Every time you hit an intersection, you take the path of least resistance: you move in whatever direction the walk signs suggest. You then continue moving in that direction until you hit another intersection that causes you to turn...

You can imagine that a person following this rule would not be able to predict where he or she would end up on any particular walk (this would be a bad strategy for, say, going to the zoo). Because all changes of direction have a permanent effect, his or her path is, in effect, random.

When a variable follows a random walk, it exhibits no tendency to return to its previous path after something makes it deviate from that path (the walk sign, in our example above). Notice that this is true for y in the equation below:

$$y_t = y_{t-1} + u_t.$$

The level of y does not change here unless y is hit by a shock (i.e., unless u_t is non-zero). When it does change, it changes permanently; it will not, except by coincidence, return to its previous level. This remains true when we add a "drift" term—a term which causes y to increase, or drift upwards, at a constant rate:

$$y_t = y_{t-1} + \beta + u_t.$$

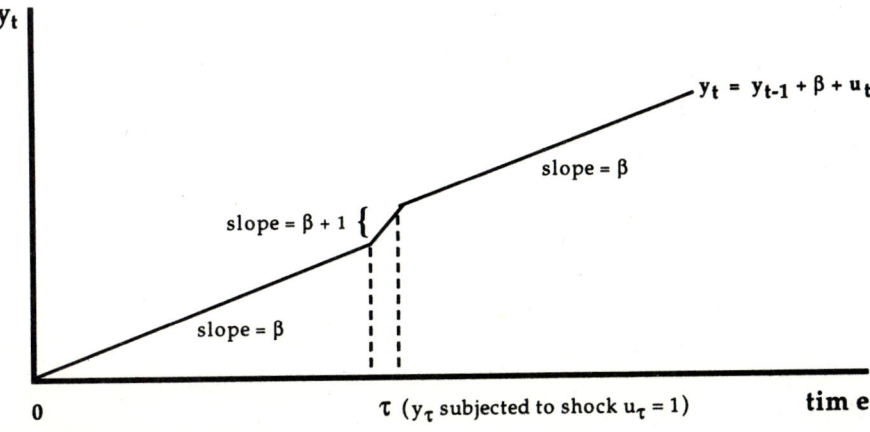

Figure 8 - 1

CROSSWORD

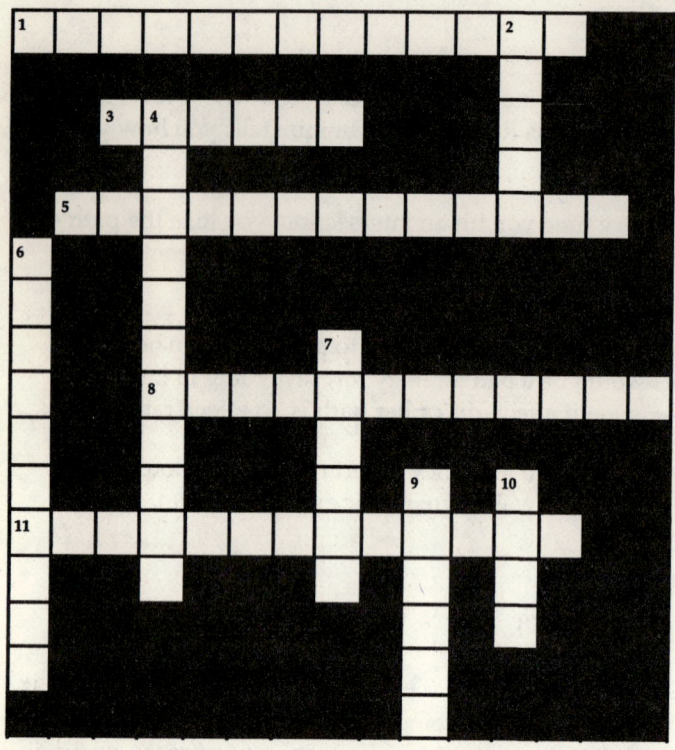

ACROSS

1. errors in rationally formed expectations are
3. ___ walk
5. across time
8. type of shock, drives business cycle in RBC models
11. New Keynesian models of price stickiness depend on these

DOWN

2. people substitute this across time
4. ___ monetary policy has no effect in rational expectations equilibrium models
6. the random walk is an example of a ___ stationary process

DOWN (CONTINUED)

7. the random walk model of GDP suggests that this type of shock drives the business cycle
9. New Keynesian create models with these kinds of prices
10. type of cost, firms incur when changing their prices

As before, shocks have a permanent effect on the level of y in this equation. Figure 8–1, which shows the path of a variable that follows this second process when it is interrupted only once by a shock $u_\tau = 1$, provides an example.

FILL-IN QUESTIONS

1. The _____ theory of output argues that most shifts in output are permanent, rather than transitory.

2. When expectations are formed _____, people use all (relevant) available information to make them.

3. There is no need for accommodating monetary or fiscal policy in a _____ _____. Deviations from full employment, and thus from potential output, result entirely from expectational errors.

4. If most shocks to output have permanent effects, changes in _____ are relatively unimportant.

5. In equilibrium real business cycle (RBC) theory, changes in output are primarily attributed to _____ shocks.

6. In RBC theory, transitory shocks can have permanent effects because people substitute _____ over time.

7. We call this *intertemporal substitution* a _____ mechanism.

8. New Keynesian models of price stickiness, which suggest that firms do not find it optimal to change their prices immediately in response to a shock, require firms to be able to set their prices, and thus assume that markets are _____ competitive.

9. The small cost associated with increasing one's prices is called a _____.

10. In Lucas's rational expectations equilibrium model, _____ changes in monetary policy have no effect on output.

TRUE–FALSE QUESTIONS

T F 1. None of the models or ideas presented in this chapter contradict any of the others.

T F 2. People make systematic errors, even when expectations are formed rationally.

T F 3. Menu costs must be *huge* in order to prevent firms from changing their prices.

T F 4. The random walk model of output is not consistent with the AS–AD model.

T F 5. The random walk model of output suggests that shocks to AD are less important than shocks to AS.

T F 6. RBC theory suggests that business cycles are driven by monetary fluctuations.

T F 7. RBC theory suggests that business cycles are driven by fluctuations in productivity (supply shocks).

T F 8. The assumption that people form expectations *rationally* is not consistent with the AS–AD model.

T F 9. The assumption that markets clear at every instant is not consistent with the AS–AD model.

T F 10. New Keynesians and New Classicists disagree about whether people behave rationally (*weigh the costs and benefits of their actions, and act accordingly*).

MULTIPLE–CHOICE QUESTIONS

1. Which of the following models/ideas does *not* go with the others?
   a. RBC theory
   b. random walk theory of output
   c. rational expectations equilibrium
   d. New Keynesian "sticky price" models

2. If output appears to fluctuate around a trend, changes in output are most likely driven by
   a. supply shocks
   b. demand shocks
   c. both
   d. neither

3. In the random walk model of output, changes in output are driven primarily by
   a. supply shocks
   b. demand shocks
   c. both
   d. neither

4. Supply shocks, in this chapter, are assumed to have _____ on the level of output.
   a. a temporary effect
   b. a permanent effect
   c. an unpredictable effect
   d. no effect

5. Demand shocks have _____ on the level of output.
   a. a temporary effect
   b. a permanent effect
   c. an unpredictable effect
   d. no effect

6. When expectations are formed rationally, expectational errors
   a. never occur
   b. can always be predicted
   c. can sometimes be predicted
   d. can never be predicted

7. In the New Keynesian model of price stickiness covered in this chapter, prices are sticky because
   a. there are long term contracts
   b. there are menu costs
   c. of the insider–outsider problem
   d. expectations are irrational

8. New Keynesians and New Classicists disagree about whether
   a. markets always clear
   b. output can diverge from potential output
   c. unanticipated changes in monetary policy affect output
   d. individuals behave rationally

9. In real business cycle theory, fluctuations in output are assumed to be caused primarily by
   a. supply shocks
   b. demand shocks
   c. both
   d. neither

10. Which of the following is *not* a characteristic of real business cycle theory?
    a. markets always clear
    b. anticipated changes in monetary policy affect output
    c. aggregate demand shocks are not important
    d. individuals behave rationally

CONCEPTUAL PROBLEMS

1. What are the New Keynesians trying to accomplish by building their models of price stickiness?

2. Why should anyone care whether or not prices are sticky?

3. Does the random walk model of GDP suggest that the AS–AD model is theoretically flawed? Explain.

4. What do real business cycle theorists believe causes output fluctuations?

TECHNICAL PROBLEMS

1. Identify the "deep parameters" used in this chapter's RBC model. What values will cause strong intertemporal substitution? Justify your answer, appealing to a relevant equation.

2. Does empirical evidence suggest that the parameter values that you identify in question 1 are realistic? (i.e., Does there appear to be strong intertemporal substitution of leisure in our world?)

3. When, in Lucas's Imperfect Information Model, will unexpected changes in AD have the biggest effect on output? Why?

4. Do AD or AS supply shocks appear to drive the business cycle, according to the empirical evidence presented in section 20–4? Explain.

Answers to Questions and Problems

Chapter 1

Graph It 1 (See next page for Table 1–1)

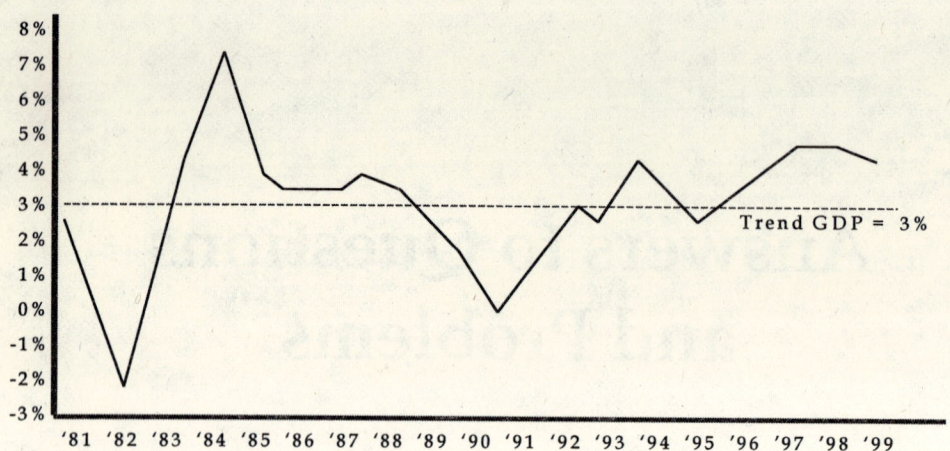

Chart 1 - 1

PERCENTAGE CHANGE IN GDP

Crossword

ACROSS

2. CPI
6. AS
8. growth
9. macroeconomics
11. time

DOWN

1. potential
3. inflation
4. business
5. long
7. models
8. output

Fill-In Questions

1. growth theory
2. aggregate supply/demand
3. aggregate supply
4. aggregate demand
5. aggregate supply
6. zero
7. consumer price index

TABLE 1-1

Year	GDP	Percent change from previous year
1980	4,900.9	—
1981	5,021.0	2.5
1982	4,919.3	−2.0
1983	5,132.3	4.3
1984	5,505.2	7.3
1985	5,717.1	3.8
1986	5,912.4	3.4
1987	6,113.3	3.4
1988	6,368.4	4.2
1989	6,591.8	3.5
1990	6,707.9	1.8
1991	6,676.4	-0.5
1992	6,880.0	3.0
1993	7,062.6	2.7
1994	7,347.7	4.0
1995	7,543.8	2.7
1996	7,813.2	3.6
1997	8,159.5	4.4
1998	8,515.7	4.4
1999	8,875.8	4.2

Source: See Table B, Economic Data Tables

True–False Questions

1. True.
2. False—only when all inputs are assumed to be fully employed is the AS curve vertical.
3. True.
4. False—*nearly everything* you will learn can be fit into this framework!

Chapter 2

Graph It 2

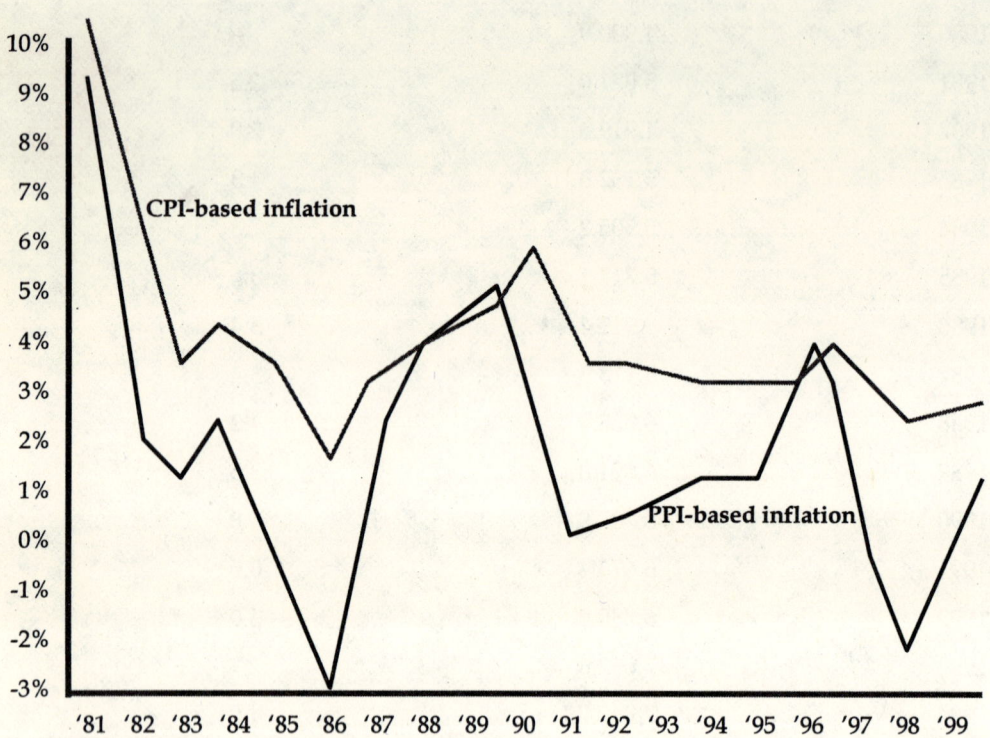

Chart 2 – 1
CPI- AND PPI-BASED INFLATION

Crossword

ACROSS

2. save
6. gross
7. exogenous
9. endogenous
13. CPI
14. durable
15. NDP (or NNP)
17. income

DOWN

1. real
3. adjusted
4. investment
5. consumers
6. GNP
8. accounting
10. deflation
11. exports
12. GDP
16. final

TABLE 2-1

Year	CPI	Percent change from previous year
1980	82.4	--
1981	90.9	10.3
1982	96.5	6.2
1983	99.6	3.2
1984	103.9	4.3
1985	107.6	3.6
1986	109.6	1.9
1987	113.6	3.6
1988	118.3	4.1
1989	124.0	4.8
1990	130.7	5.4
1991	136.2	4.2
1992	140.3	3.0
1993	144.5	3.0
1994	148.2	2.6
1995	152.4	2.8
1996	156.9	3.o

Source: See Tables G & F, Economic Data Tables

Fill-In Questions

1. GDP
2. depreciation
3. factors of production; factor payments
4. transfer payments
5. gross private domestic investment
6. exports; imports
7. government budget deficit
8. value added
9. adjusted GNP
10. GDP deflator

True-False Questions

1. False—roughly 3/4 of all factor payments are paid to *labor*.
2. True.
3. True.
4. True.
5. False.
6. True.
7. False—the text discusses several reasons GDP (& GNP) are imperfect measures of welfare.
8. False—the GDP deflator does not include import prices.
9. True.
10. True.

Multiple-Choice Questions

1. c   2. b   3. b   4. d   5. d   6. d   7. d   8. a   9. d   10. d

Conceptual Problems

1. GDP would increase. This would not necessarily reflect a change in the physical output of the economy.
2. Personal computers are an example.
3. The trade deficit ($-NX$) must equal the budget deficit ($G + TR - T$)
4. The government could decrease its spending, reduce the amount of money it gives out in the form of transfer payments, or increase taxes. An increase in savings without a corresponding increase in investment could also achieve this, as could an increase in exports without a corresponding increase in imports. Keep in mind, however, that it isn't always easy to change just one of these things...

Technical Problems

1. $GDP = C + I + G = \$1,000 + \$100 + \$300 = \$1,400$

    Because the government's budget is balanced and net exports are zero, saving equals investment: $S = I = \$100$.

2. We know that $(S - I) = (G + TR - T) + NX$. If we solve this equation for I, we find that investment is equal to savings minus the budget deficit + the trade deficit, or that investment equals $160: $I = S - (G + TR - T) + (-NX) = \$200 - \$50 + \$10 = \$160$.

3. Disposable Income = Total Income + Transfers - Taxes = Total Output + Transfers - Taxes. Total output (*GDP*) is given to us in the problem; the difference between taxes and transfers ($TR - T$) is not. We do know enough about the government's budget deficit, however, to figure it out: $(G + TR - T) = (\$250 + TR - T) = \$40$, so $TR - T = \$40 - \$250 = -\$210$.

    Disposable Income = $GDP + TR - T = \$1,000 - \$210 = \$790$.

4. We know that GDP = C + I + G + NX. This tells us that NX = GDP − C − I − G. GDP, C, and I are given to us; G is not. Luckily we can figure it out from the information that we have been given about the budget deficit (BD), and about the difference between transfers and taxes: BD = G + TR − T, so G = BD − (TR − T) = \$120 − \$20 = \$100.

NX = GDP − C − I − G = \$500 − \$350 − \$150 − \$100 = − \$100.

5. Inflation (π) is just the *rate of change* of the price level: π = (2 − 1.75)/2 = .125, or 12.5%.

6. With 6% inflation our real interest rate would be 0%: you would have 6% more money, but it would be worth 6% less. With 8% inflation you would actually have a negative return: you would have 6% more money, but it would be worth 8% less, leaving you a real interest rate of approximately 2% (8 − 2).

Chapter 3

Graph It 3

It's difficult to say, based on the graph below, whether the growth rates of Japan and the US are converging. Convergence occurs so slowly that it is difficult to observe in short time samples.

Because Japan's growth rates are not falling in any easily observable way, this graph cannot help us to argue that Japan's high growth rates in the 1950's and 1960's were a transitory phenomenon.

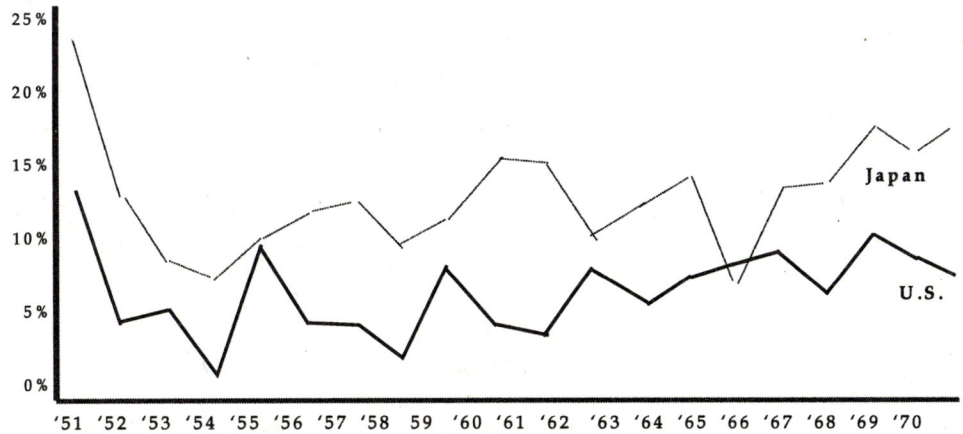

Chart 3 - 1

PERCENTAGE CHANGE IN GDP FOR JAPAN AND THE U.S.

Crossword

ACROSS
1. diminishing
6. exogenous
9. neoclassical
10. zero
11. potential
13. production
14. population

DOWN
2. human
3. constant
4. converge
5. stock
7. saving
8. flow
12. equal

Fill-In Questions

1. Growth accounting
2. production function
3. marginal product of labor; decreases
4. total factor productivity
5. per-capita output
6. physical
7. human
8. steady-state
9. converge
10. level

True-False Questions

1. False — it will change the rate at which *total* potential output grows at the steady-state.
2. True.
3. True.
4. False — the savings rate does not affect the growth rate of output at the steady-state.
5. True.
6. True.
7. True.
8. True.
9. False — they must also have the same savings rate.
10. True.

Multiple-Choice Questions

1. c   2. d   3. d   4. d   5. a   6. d   7. b   8. a   9. c   10. b

Conceptual Problems

1. I'm pretty sure mine does! At some point, human capital probably does have diminishing marginal returns... but don't worry. You're not there yet.

2. Natural resources probably do just the opposite — when left to themselves, over time, they grow. (Coal, oil, wood, clean air, clean water increase when we leave them alone, albeit for a very long time.) They should have diminishing marginal returns just like any other factor of production.

3. All factors of production have diminishing marginal returns; productivity growth (technological improvement) is exogenous.

4. (a) and (b) are stock variables; (c) and (d) are flow variables (depreciation is a flow out of the capital stock; investment in a flow into it).

Technical Problems

1. a) Capital's share of income = 1/4. It is always the power to which K is raised in a constant returns to scale, Cobb–Douglas production function.

    In general, capital's share of income is given by the equation:
    $(i \times K)/Y = (MPK \times K)/Y$.

    b) We know from (a) that $MPK \times K/Y = 1/4$. All we need to do is rearrange this equation: $(Y/K) = MPK/(1/4) = 4 \times MPK$. = *capital's share of income* $\times MPK$.

    c) Labor's share of income = 3/4. It is always the power to which L is raised in a constant returns to scale, Cobb–Douglas production function.

    In general, capital's share of income is given by the equation:
    $(w \times L)/Y = (MPL \times L)/Y$.

    d) We know from (c) that $MPL \times L/Y = 3/4$. Rearrange this equation, we find:
    $(Y/L) = MPL/(3/4) = (4/3) \times MPL$. = *labor's share of income* $\times MPL$.

    e) This function does have constant returns to scale: $(1/4) + (3/4) = 1$. To show this more rigorously, try doubling both the amount of capital and labor used in production. The level of output should double as well: if $Y_0 = K_0^{1/4} L_0^{3/4}$, then $Y_1 = (2K_0)^{1/4}(2L_0)^{3/4}$ can be written as:

    $$Y_1 = (2K_0)^{1/4}(2L_0)^{3/4} = (2)^{1/4}(K_0)^{1/4}(2)^{1/4}(L_0)^{3/4} = (2)^{1/4+3/4} K_0^{1/4} L_0^{3/4}$$

    $$= 2(K_0^{1/4} L_0^{3/4}) = 2Y_0. \text{ Doubling } K \text{ and } L \text{ doubles } Y.$$

    f) $\dfrac{Y}{L} = \dfrac{K^{1/4} L^{3/4}}{L} = \left(\dfrac{K^{1/4}}{L^{1/4}}\right)\left(\dfrac{L^{3/4}}{L^{3/4}}\right) = \left(\dfrac{K}{L}\right)^{1/4}$, or $y = k^{1/4}$.

2. a) It will increase. (Total output increases because the number of worker's increases; the investment function $(sf(k))$ shifts upward. The population, however, has NOT increased; there's more output for everyone to share.

    b) Nothing.

    c) Labor's share of income can't have changed. It's still the power (θ) to which L is raised in the Cobb–Douglas production function.

d) Labor's productivity ($Y/L = (1/\theta) \times MPL$) will fall. The increase in the labor supply will drive down the marginal product of labor.

3. a) Nothing.

   b) Nothing.

   c) Nothing.

   d) This will still fall, for the same reason as before.

4. The investment function ($sf(k)$) will shift upward. Per-capita output will increase, quickly at first, and then more slowly, gradually moving toward its new steady-state level.

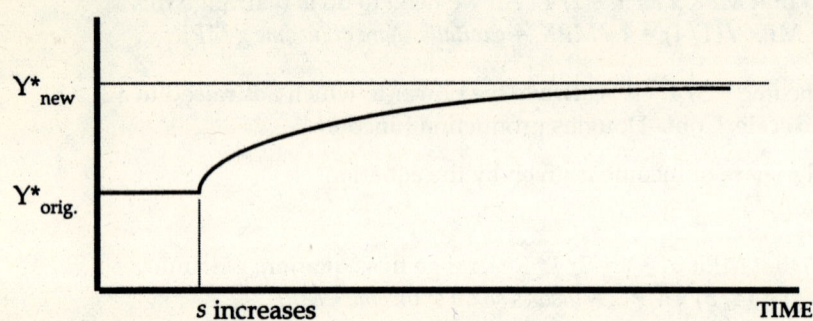

Figure A - 1

5. $\Delta Y/Y = [(1-\theta) \times \Delta N/N] + [\theta \times \Delta K/K] + \Delta A/A = [(1-.25) \times (.5)] + [(1-.75) \times (.5)] + 0 = 0.5$ (or 50%.) The capital-labor ratio will not change, as capital and labor are both increasing by the same amount.

Chapter 4

Graph It 4

Figure 4 - 1

GROWTH RATE OF PER CAPITA GDP, BULGARIA

Bulgaria's revolution occurred in 1989. As was (and is) the case with many transition economies, its output fell for several years following the adoption of basic market reforms.

Crossword

ACROSS
1. capital
3. saving
5. convergence
6. output
9. diminishing
10. exogenously

DOWN
2. absolute
4. increasing
7. transition
8. constant

TABLE 4 – 1

Year	per capita GDP	Percent change from previous year
1980	3139	—
1981	3623	15.4
1982	3888	7.3
1983	4221	8.6
1984	4366	3.4
1985	4773	9.3
1986	6284	31.7
1987	6918	10.1
1988	8030	16.1
1989	8135	1.3
1990	7529	− 7.4
1991	6715	− 10.8
1992	6774	0.9

Source: Penn World Tables

Fill-In Questions

1. diminishing
2. constant
3. returns to scale
4. steady-states
5. technology
6. exogenous
7. saving (or investment)
8. saving
9. absolute; conditional
10. conditionally

True–False Questions

1. False — not as long as there are external benefits associated with private investment (i.e., as long as individual producers are unable to capture all of the benefits associated with their investment).
2. True. (At least no non-zero ones.)

3. False—such growth is driven by technological improvement.
4. True.
5. False.
6. False—changes in the rate of saving do affect the steady-state.
7. False—they must also have the same rate of saving the and same marginal product of capital.
8. True.
9. False—changes in the saving rate permanently raise the growth rate of output in endogenous growth models.
10. False.

Multiple-Choice Questions

1. a   2. a   3. c   4. a   5. c   6. b   7. b   8. a   9. a   10. d

Conceptual Problems

1. Capital has a constant marginal product, where before it had a diminishing marginal product. The production function, as a result, has increasing rather than constant returns to scale.

2. Yes—the exponents add to 1.

    No—the exponents do not add to 1. (Because they add to a number greater than 1, this second production function has increasing returns.)

3. An increase in the rate of savings will increase the growth rate of output in an endogenous growth model.

4. An increase in the rate of savings will have no effect on the growth rate of output in the neoclassical model, as it is assumed not to affect the rate of technological improvement.

5. Endogenous growth theory, insofar as it is able to explain what determines the growth rate of technology, can explain what causes countries on the cutting edge of technology to grow. It *can't* explain differences in growth rates across countries.

Technical Problems

1. a) $\dfrac{Y}{L} = \dfrac{K^{1/2}L^{1/2}}{L} = \dfrac{K^{1/2}}{L^{1/2}} = \left(\dfrac{K}{L}\right)^{1/2} = k^{1/2}$ or $y = \sqrt{k}$

   b) $\dfrac{1}{2\sqrt{k_{gold}}} = n + d = 0.25$

   $\sqrt{k_{gold}} = \dfrac{1}{2 \times 0.25} = \dfrac{1}{0.5} = 2$

   $k_{gold} = (2)^2 = 4$

2. We know that y grows at the rate $sa - (n + d)$, where $a = y/k$. All that we have to do is plug in the values of a $(a = y/k = f(k)/k = k/k = 1)$, n, d, and s given in the problem:
$\Delta y/y = sa - (n + d) = (0.3 \times 1) - (0.05 + 0.20) = 0.3 - 0.25 = 0.05$ or 5%.

3. When we endogenize the rate of population growth, we get two steady-states—one with high per-capita output, one with low per-capita output. We do have to make some assumptions about the relationship between per-capita output and the rate of population growth, however: the rate of population growth must first increase with y, then decrease with it, eventually leveling off near zero.

4. We can generate such a model by allowing society to choose how much to invest in two different types of capital—the sort of capital that creates external benefits (i.e., research and development), and the sort that doesn't (i.e., potato chips).

Chapter 5

Graph It 5

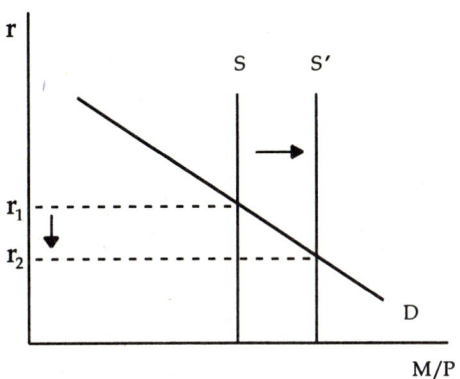

Chart 5-1

AN INCREASE IN THE MONEY SUPPLY LOWERS THE REAL INTEREST RATE

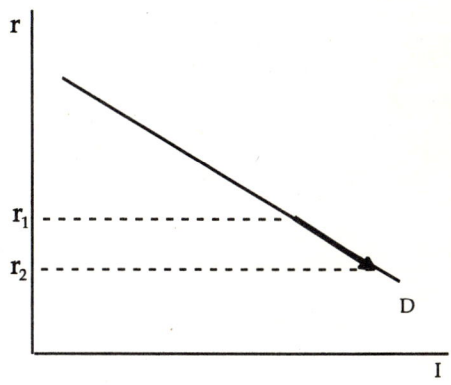

Chart 5-2

THIS DECREASE IN THE REAL INTEREST RATE INCREASES THE QUANTITY OF INVESTMENT DEMANDED

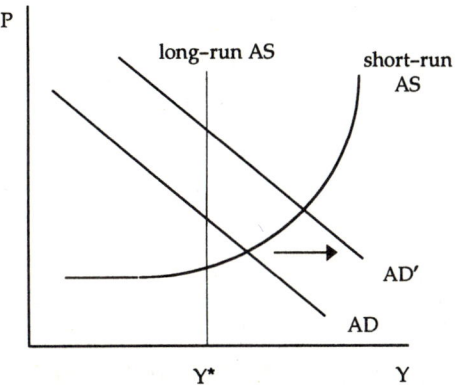

Chart 5-3

THE INCRASE IN INVESTMENT CAUSES THE AD CURVE TO SHIFT OUTWARD

In the short run, this increase in AD raises both output and the price level.

In the long run, output falls back to its long run value (potential output), and only the price level is affected.

Crossword

ACROSS
1. real
3. demand
6. potential
8. natural
9. contractionary
10. Keynesian

DOWN
2. expansionary
4. nominal
5. classical
7. quantity

Fill-In Questions

1. endogenous
2. exogenous/policy
3. aggregate supply
4. aggregate demand
5. vertical; potential output
6. horizontal
7. frictional; natural rate
8. classical
9. aggregate demand
10. aggregate supply

True–False Questions

1. False — Classical assumptions are most appropriate in the long run.
2. True.
3. True.
4. True.
5. False.
6. False — it shows how *actual output* changes.
7. True.
8. False.
9. True.
10. False.

Multiple-Choice Questions

1. b 2. b 3. d 4. a 5. c 6. a 7. a 8. a 9. b 10. c

Conceptual Problems

1. The aggregate demand curve slopes downward because as the price level falls, real money balances increase and cause the real interest rate to fall. This decrease in the real interest rate raises investment demand, which, in turn, increases aggregate demand.

2. It seems senseless to assume that we can increase output an infinite amount; there has to be some limit.

3. They raise the productivity of one or more factors of production (labor, capital, etc.).

4. a, b, d, and f are expansionary; c, e, and g are contractionary. If g seemed challenging, don't worry... we'll talk a lot more about money and the quantity theory in later chapters.

Technical Problems

1. Taxes, government transfers, government spending, and the money supply are all held constant along the AD curve.

2. a) output will increase; the price level may also increase.

   b) in the long run, output will return to potential output (i.e., will fall if it exceeds potential output in the short run, and will rise if it is below potential output). The price level will adjust in whatever way makes this happen (i.e., will rise if output exceeds potential output in the short run, and will fall if output is below potential output in the short run.)

   c) In order to answer parts (a) and (b), we must first assume a starting point for AD... do we begin with output below potential output, equal to potential output, or above potential output? ...If we begin at a point where output lies below potential output, me must make an assumption about the AD shift: at the new short-run equilibrium, does output equal potential output, exceed potential output, or still lie below it? These assumptions will change the way we think output will behave in the transition from the short to the long run.

3. a) A reduction in the money supply raises real interest rates.

   b) This increase in real interest rates makes investment more costly (imagine that the firm has to borrow the money to invest). Investment demand falls and, as a result, so does aggregate demand.

Chapter 6

Graph It 6

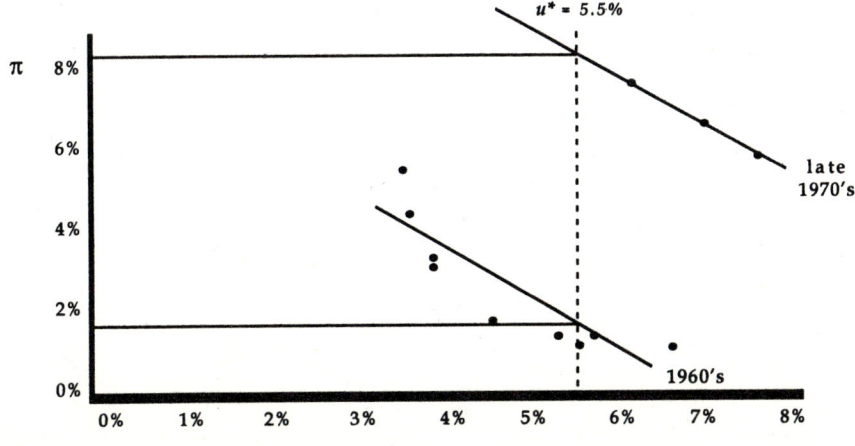

TABLE 6-1

Year	CPI	Rate of Inflation	Civilian Rate of Unemployment
1960	29.6	—	
1961	29.9	1.0%	6.7%
1962	30.2	1.0%	5.5%
1963	30.6	1.3%	5.7%
1964	31.0	1.3%	5.2%
1965	31.5	1.6%	4.5%
1966	32.4	2.9%	3.8%
1967	33.4	3.1%	3.8%
1968	34.8	4.2%	3.6%
1969	36.7	5.5%	3.5%
1976	56.9	5.8	7.7%
1977	60.6	6.5	7.1%
1978	65.2	7.6	6.1%

Source: See Tables C & F, Economic Data Tables

People seem to have expected roughly 1.5% inflation in the 1960's and 8.2% in the late 1970's (These are the points on the Phillips curves we've sketched at which unemployment is at its natural rate and therefore the points at which inflation equals expected inflation.).

Crossword

ACROSS
1. unemployment
4. Phillips
5. sticky
7. supply
8. accommodation
9. efficiency
10. insiders
11. information

DOWN
2. expectations
3. staggered
6. rational
7. stagflation

Fill-In Questions

1. rise
2. fall
3. sticky
4. labor; unemployment
5. rise
6. Phillips
7. aggregate supply
8. efficiency wage theory
9. insider/outsider
10. supply shock

True-False Questions

1. False—the economy is only at full employment when output equals potential output.
2. False—the economy returns to full employment in the long run.
3. True.
4. False—in the long run, unemployment is at its natural rate, and inflation equals expected inflation.
5. False—changes in policy can affect people's inflationary expectations, shifting the Phillips curve and making this inflation/unemployment tradeoff much more difficult to exploit.
6. True.
7. True.
8. True.
9. False.
10. False—it causes <u>higher</u> prices and lower output.

Multiple-Choice Questions

1. b   2. a   3. a   4. c   5. a   6. d   7. a   8. a   9. a   10. a

Conceptual Problems

1. Output and unemployment are connected through the production function; when unemployment rises, firms use less labor and, therefore, produce less output.

2. It tells you how quickly prices adjust; higher values of λ mean that prices will adjust more quickly to return the economy to its long-run equilibrium. Both our recessions and our booms would become shorter if λ increased, making it less important for the government to intervene in order to stabilize output.

3. No. First, these policies can cause substantial inflation. Second, if the supply shock has permanent effects (reduces potential output/causes the long-run aggregate supply curve to shift inward), we <u>should</u> let output fall.

Technical Problems

1. a) In the short run, output will increase, unemployment will fall.

b) In the long run, when output must equal potential output and unemployment must be at its natural rate, both will revert back to their original values. (Output will fall; unemployment will rise.)

c) The short-run AS curve shifts gradually upward. *See figure at right.*

Note: You can, if you prefer, picture the AS curve rotating inward, growing steeper over time. Each AS curve will then represent a different time horizon... the steeper the curve, the longer the horizon.

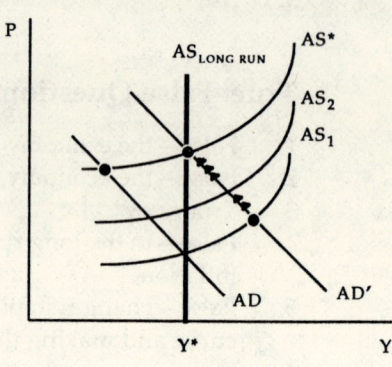

2. a) Output will fall; the price level will rise.

b) It depends on whether the supply sock has permanent effects. If it does not, output will rise and the price level will fall. (If it *does*, nothing at all should happen.)

c) If the supply shock did not affect long run AS (i.e., had no effect on potential output), the government could use expansionary monetary or fiscal policy to return output to its long run level.

See figure at right.

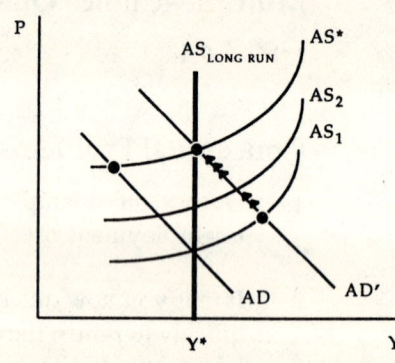

Chapter 7

Graph It 7

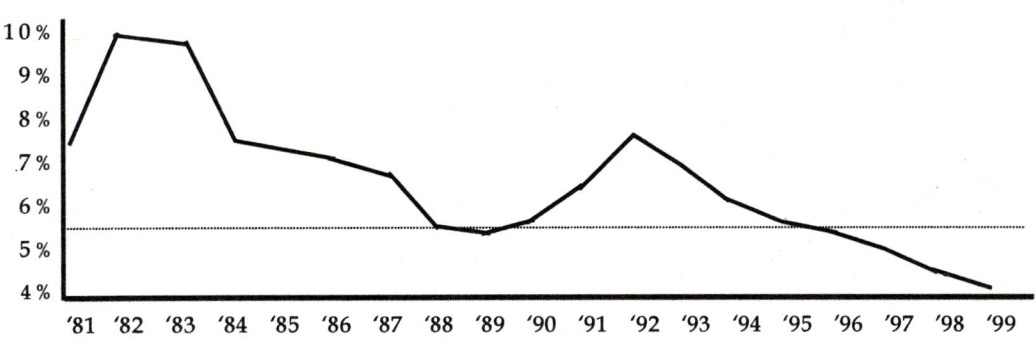

Chart 7 - 1

UNEMPLOYMENT IN THE US: 1981-1999

We would hope to find that unemployment is below its natural rate when output growth is above its trend. Unfortunately, we don't. Perhaps the trend assumed in Chart 1-1 is incorrect, or has "breaks" — points at which the trend changes. (See Chapter 8 for a more discussion of trends and difficulties involved with estimating them.)

Crossword

ACROSS
4. Okun
7. replacement
8. lenders
9. two
11. hysteresis
12. discouraged
13. layoff

DOWN
1. natural
2. borrowers
3. indexation
5. weighting
6. teenagers
10. misery

Fill-In Questions

1. creditors; debtors
2. cash
3. sacrifice ratio
4. Okun's Law
5. labor force
6. raise
7. frequency
8. duration
9. natural rate
10. hysteresis

True–False Questions

1. False—although we call it a "rate," it is actually a stock variable.
2. False—a person must also be actively seeking work.
3. True.
4. False.
5. True.
6. True.
7. True.
8. False—there would be no frictional employment.
9. True.
10. False—unemployment benefits can change it.

Multiple-Choice Questions

1. b   2. a   3. b   4. d   5. b   6. b   7. a   8. a   9. c   10. c

Conceptual Problems

1. A person may enter the labor force and begin seeking a job, or may quit their job, be laid off, or be fired.

2. A person may leave the unemployment pool by finding a new job, being recalled to his/her old job, or may stop looking for work and, by definition, leave the labor force.

3. Lost output for society, lost income & lower standard of living for unemployed.

4. If the longer period of job search helps individuals to find jobs at which they are happier and more productive, this effect of unemployment insurance may be entirely a good thing. If it simply allows people to stay home and watch more television, it may not.

5. It is hard to imagine a society with no frictional unemployment, where nobody ever spends time between jobs. We could, of course, pass a law that prevents people from quitting their job unless they have another one lined up, but would that really be a good thing?

6. Section 7–6 suggests that small amounts of inflation may actually be good for the economy, although it also mentions that this idea is a controversial one. We know that there are extremely small costs associated with low (i.e., single digit) levels of inflation, especially when this inflation is perfectly anticipated. We also will find, later in the text, that it can be quite costly, in the short run, to reduce inflation. These two ideas suggest that it may not be worthwhile for us to completely eliminate inflation—the costs may well outweigh the benefits.

Technical Problems

1. When teenagers make up 40% of the labor force, the aggregate rate of unemployment is
$[(.4) \times (.10)] + [(.6) \times (.05)] = .075$ or 7.5%

When teenagers make up 60% of the labor force, the aggregate rate of unemployment is
$[(.6) \times (.10)] + [(.4) \times (.05)] = .080$ or 8.0%

2. In any given month, there will be two people who are unemployed just for that month, three people who are at different points in their three-month spells of unemployment, and 12 people who are each at a different point in their 12-month spell of unemployment. Adding these together, we find that 17 out of every 100 people are in the unemployment pool in the typical month, or that the rate of unemployment in this typical month is $17/100 = .17$ or 17%.

The average duration of unemployment is $(1+1+3+12)/4 = 17/4 = 4.25$ months.

Chapter 8

Graph It 8

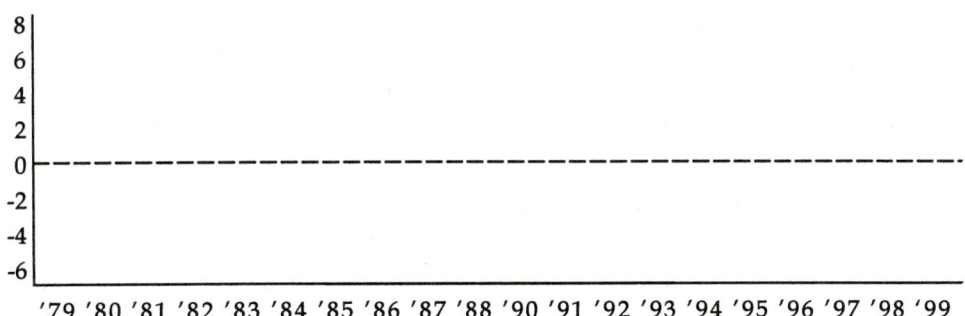

Crossword

ACROSS
1. lags
3. indicators
6. targets
8. credibility
9. Lucas
11. distributed
12. outside
13. recognition

DOWN
2. action
4. inside
7. instruments
10. decision

Fill-In Questions

1. inside
2. outside
3. lags, expectations, uncertainty
4. decision
5. automatic stabilizers
6. inside
7. outside
8. Lucas critique
9. bull, bears
10. bulls, bears

True–False Questions

1. F
2. T
3. F
4. F
5. T
6. F
7. T (at least never at the same time)
8. T
9. F
10. T

Multiple-Choice Questions

1. b   2. a   3. a   4. d   5. b   6. b   7. d   8. b   9. c   10. d

Conceptual Problems

1. This is an introspective question. You must find your own answer.

2. This is another one of those introspective questions. Many people worry about the effect of policy lags on such fine-tuning; there is some question whether the timing of policy effects can be predicted accurately enough to allow successful fine-tuning. Of course, even those people acknowledge that Alan Greenspan does quite a fine job of it...

Chapter 9

Graph It 9

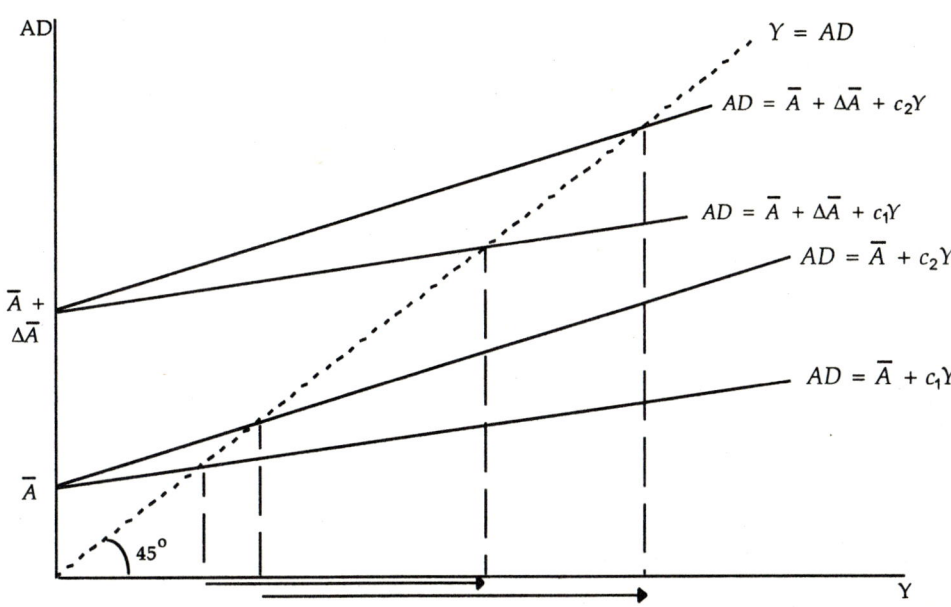

Crossword

ACROSS
1. disposable
2. inventories
5. fiscal
6. multiplier
7. income
8. output

DOWN
1. deficit
3. one
4. exogenous
6. mpc

Fill-In Questions

1. equilibrium
2. endogenous
3. marginal propensity to consume
4. disposable income
5. multiplier
6. marginal propensity to save
7. budget deficit
8. automatic stabilizer
9. full–employment budget surplus
10. one

True-False Questions

1. False.
2. False.
3. True.
4. False.
5. False.
6. True.
7. False.
8. False.
9. False.
10. True.

Multiple-Choice Questions

1. a   2. b   3. a   4. b   5. b   6. a   7. c   8. a   9. b   10. b

Conceptual Problems

1. $1 million increase in government spending; the multiplier for government spending is greater than the multiplier for government transfers.

2. a, b, c, and d are endogenous; e and f are exogenous.

3. Tax revenues change with the business cycle. As a result, so does the budget deficit.

4. The effect of business cycle fluctuations on the budget deficit is eliminated.

Technical Problems

1. $S = Y - C = Y - \overline{C} - cY = -\overline{C} + (1-c)Y$

2. a) $\alpha_G = 1/(1-0.9) = 1/0.1 = 10$

   b) $100 \times \alpha_G = 100 \times 10 = 100$

   c) $100 \times (\alpha_G \times mpc) = 100 \times 10 \times 0.9 = 90$

3. a) $\alpha_G = 1/(1-0.9(2/3)) = 1/(1-0.6) = 1/0.4 = 2.5$

   b) $100 \times \alpha_G = 100 \times 2.5 = 25$

   c) The increase in government spending will increase the deficit by $100; tax revenues, however will also rise... in this case, by $250 \times 1/3 \cong \$83.33$. The budget deficit, as a result, will rise (or the surplus fall) by $100 - \$83.33 = \$16.67$.

d) The balanced budget surplus will not be affected by the upswing in the business cycle — the increase in tax revenues resulting from higher output. It, therefore, will fall (the balanced budget deficit will rise) by the full increase in government spending: $10 .

Chapter 10

Graph It 10

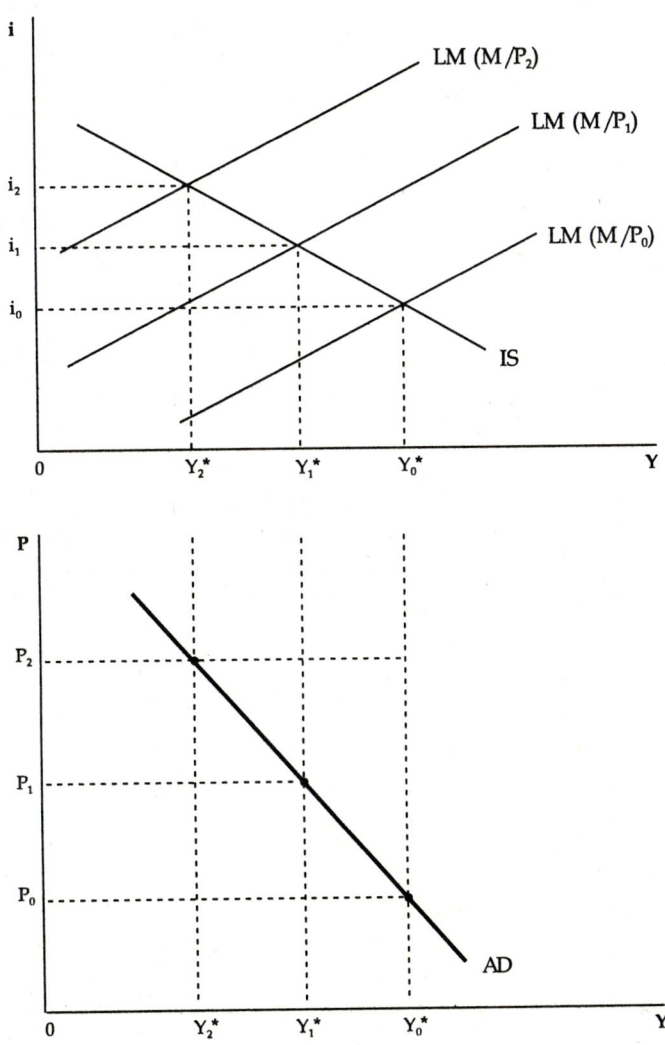

Chart 10 - 2

DERIVING THE AD CURVE

Crossword

ACROSS
3. five
4. monetary
8. fiscal
11. endogenous

DOWN
1. central
2. goods
5. exogenous
6. AD
7. price
9. income
10. money

Fill-In Questions

1. goods
2. investment
3. flatter
4. money
5. cash
6. steep
7. flat
8. fiscal; monetary
9. equilibrium conditions
10. AD

True–False Questions

1. False.
2. True.
3. True.
4. True.
5. False — decreasing the money supply raises interest rates, which lowers investment.
6. True — there will different equilibria for different combinations of taxes, transfers, and government spending.
7. True — there will be different equilibria when real money balances differ.
8. True.
9. False — it depends on the tax rate.
10. False — the increase in government purchases shifts it further.

Multiple-Choice Questions

1. b 2. c 3. b 4. b 5. d 6. b 7. b 8. b 9. c 10. b

Conceptual Problems

1. output, income, disposable income, the price level, the real interest rate, investment, and consumption.

2. Changes in the IS–LM equilibrium represent shifts in/movements along the aggregate demand curve.

3. The marginal propensity to consume, the tax rate (when proportional income taxes are used), and the sensitivity of investment demand to changes in the interest rate.

4. The sensitivity of money demand to changes in income and the interest rate.

Technical Problems

1. a) The equation for the IS curve can be found as follows:

    $Y = C + I + G = (100 + .8(Y - 500)) + (200 - 1000i) + 550$

    $(1 - .8)Y = 450 - 1000i$

    $Y = \frac{1}{0.2}(450 - 1000i)$, or $Y = 2250 - 5000i$

    b) The equation for the LM curve can be found by setting the supply of real money balances equal to the demand for them:

    $900 = \frac{1}{2}Y - 7000i$, or $Y = 1800 + 14000i$

    c) We find the equilibrium real interest rate by locating for the intersection of these two curves (i.e., setting output along the IS curve equal to output along the LM curve and solving for i):

    $2250 - 5000i = 1800 + 14000i$

    $19000i = 450$

    $i = 450/19000 \cong 0.024$, or 2.4%

    We then plug the equilibrium value of i back into the equation for either the IS or the LM curve (we choose the IS curve here):

    $Y = 2250 - (5000 \times (450/19000)) \cong \$2131.58$

    Having found Y, we can now find $(Y - \overline{T})$ and solve for C:

    $C = 100 + .8(Y - \overline{T}) \cong 100 + .8(2131.58 - 500) = \$1405.26$

    And, knowing i, we can solve for I:

    $I = 200 - 1000i = 200 - (1000 \times (450/19000)) \cong 176.32$

2. a) The equation for the IS curve can be found in the following way:

    $Y = C + I + G = (100 + .8(1 - t)Y) + (200 - 1000i) + 700$

    $(1 - (0.8 \times 0.66))Y = 1000 - 1000i$

    $(1 - 0.528Y) = 1000 - 1000i$

    $Y = \frac{1}{0.472}(1000 - 1000i)$, or $Y \cong 2118.64 - 2118.64i$

b) The equation for the LM curve can be found by setting the supply of real money balances equal to the demand for them:

$$900 = \tfrac{1}{2} Y - 7000i, \quad \text{or} \quad Y = 1800 + 14000i$$

c) In order to answer this question, we must first find the equilibrium value of Y—the level of output for which both goods and money markets are in equilibrium. We could solve for i first, as we did in the last problem. We could also, however, write the equations for the IS and LM curves as functions of i rather than Y:

IS: $1000i = 1000 - 0.472Y$, or $i = (1000 - 0.472Y)/1000$

LM: $14000i = Y - 1800$, or $i = (Y - 1800)/14000$

and set the real interest rates along each curve equal to each other:

$$\frac{1000 - .472Y}{1000} = \frac{Y - 1800}{14000}$$

$(1000 - 0.472Y) \times 14000 = (Y - 1800) \times 1000$
$7650Y = 15800000$, or $Y \cong \$2065.36$

We can now find the initial value of the budget deficit $(\overline{G} - tY)$:

$$\overline{G} - tY \cong 700 - (0.33 \times 2065.36) = \$18.43$$

d) First, let's figure out how much income needs to be increased, if tax revenues are to exactly offset government spending $(\overline{G} = tY)$:

$$Y = \overline{G}/t = 700/0.33 \cong \$2121.21$$

Having found this, we can easily find the level of real money balances required to generate it. As before, we set real interest rates along the IS and LM curves equal to each other. Now, however, we plug in the value of Y that we need and solve for the real money balances (M/P):

IS: $1000i = 1000 - 0.472Y$, or $i = (1000 - 0.472Y)/1000$

LM: $14000i = Y - 1800 = Y - 2(\overline{M}/P)$ or $i = (Y - 2(\overline{M}/P))/14000$

$$\frac{1000 - (.472 \times (700/0.33))}{1000} = \frac{(700/0.33) - 2(\overline{M}/P)}{14000}$$

$(1000 - (0.472 \times (700/0.33))) \times (14000/1000) = ((700/0.33) - 2(\overline{M}/P))$
$2(\overline{M}/P) = (700/0.33) + (0.472 \times (700/0.33) \times 14) - 14000 \cong \$2138.18$
$\overline{M}/P \cong \$2138.18/2 \cong \$1069.09$

Real money balances must be increased by $1069.09 − $900 = $169.09 in order to balance the budget.

d) We know that in the long run, increasing the money supply will only cause inflation.

Chapter 11

Graph It 11

TABLE 11 – 1

Year	Unemployment	M1	CPI	Real Money Balances
1986	7.0	724.4	109.6	6.61
1987	6.2	749.8	113.6	6.60
1988	5.5	786.9	118.3	6.65
1989	5.3	794.2	124.0	6.41
1990	5.6	825.8	130.7	6.32
1991	6.8	897.2	136.2	6.59
1992	7.5	1,024.4	140.3	7.30
1993	6.9	1,128.6	144.5	7.81
1994	6.1	1,148.7	148.2	7.75
1995	5.6	1,124.9	152.4	7.38
1996	5.4	1,076.9	156.9	6.86
1997	4.9	1,075.2	160.5	6.70
1998	4.5	1,093.7	163.0	6.71
1999	4.2	1,125.4	166.6	6.76

Source: Economic Data Tables

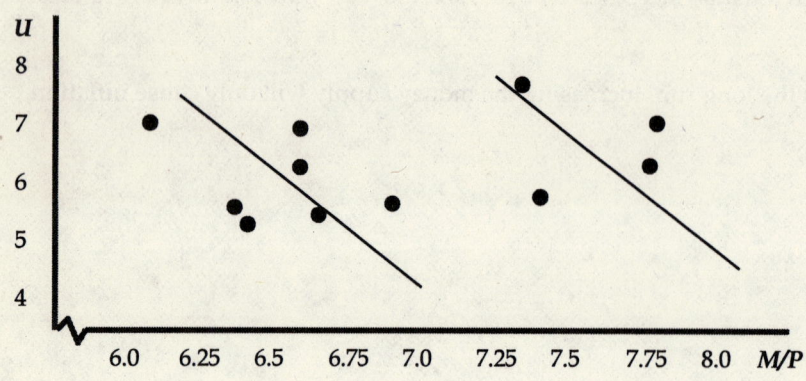

Chart 11 - 1

We can't draw one downward–sloping line through these points, but we could draw two. Perhaps some factor for which we have not accounted caused this relationship to change, or the initial curve (the one at the left of the graph) to shift outwards, in the early 1990's.

I myself would be reluctant to draw any conclusions whatsoever from this graph; it's dangerous to look at something this casually and think you know what's going on. Be warned.

Crossword

ACROSS
2. multipliers
4. accommodating
7. monetary
10. investment
11. vertical

DOWN
1. increase
3. liquidity
5. monetizing
6. flatter
8. steeper
9. real

Fill-In Questions

1. liquidity trap
2. classical case
3. relatively steep
4. relatively flat
5. crowding out
6. accommodating
7. nominal interest rate; rate of inflation
8. level
9. decreases
10. open market operations

True–False Questions

1. True.
2. True.
3. False.
4. False — it also depends on the slope of the IS curve.

5. False.
6. True.
7. True.
8. False.
9. False.
10. True.

Multiple-Choice Questions

1. b   2. a   3. c   4. b   5. b   6. a   7. d   8. a   9. c   10. a

Conceptual Problems

1. When proportional income taxes are present, the multiplier α_G becomes smaller. This makes the IS curve steeper, reducing the effectiveness of monetary policy. (Section 10-5 demonstrates this quite rigorously.)

2. The smaller multiplier associated with proportional income taxes makes fiscal policy less effective as well.

Technical Problems

1. The IS curve will shift outward by an amount $100 \times \alpha_G$.

2. The AD curve will shift outward, but, if the LM curve is upward sloping, by an amount that is smaller than that of the IS shift. (Optional section 10-5 explains how to calculate more precisely the distance of this shift.)

3. Holding i constant, we see that Y increases (the LM curve shifts outward) by an amount $\$100/k$.

   Recall that k tells us how sensitive people's demand for money is to changes in their income. A large k means that their money demand is relatively sensitive to changes in their income; a small k means that it is relatively insensitive to such changes.

4. The AD curve will shift outward, but (with a downward-sloping IS curve) by an amount that is smaller than that of the LM shift. (Optional section 10-5 explains how to calculate more precisely the distance of this shift.)

5. When the AS curve is flat—the price level is fixed.

6. When the AS curve is vertical—the level of output is fixed.

*7. To answer this, we must see how the equation for the IS curve is affected. Let's begin by simply writing the equation for the goods market equilibrium: $Y = C + I + G$.

$$Y = \overline{C} + c(1-t)Y + \overline{I} - bi + \overline{G} + d(Y_P - Y)$$

Having done this, we must solve for i (write i as a function of Y):

$$i = -\tfrac{1}{b}\left[(1 - c(1 - t) + d)Y - \overline{C} - \overline{I} - \overline{G} - dY_P\right]$$
$$= -\tfrac{1}{b}\left[\left(\tfrac{1}{\alpha_G} + d\right)Y - \overline{C} - \overline{I} - \overline{G} - dY_P\right]$$

The slope of this alternatively-specified IS curve is: $-\tfrac{1}{b}\left(\tfrac{1}{\alpha_G} + d\right)$.

It is steeper (more negative) than the slope of our regular IS curve: $-\tfrac{1}{b}\left(\tfrac{1}{\alpha_G}\right)$.

Monetary policy less effective than it would otherwise be, as any expansions that it generates will be automatically offset by fiscal contractions (decreases in government spending), and any contractions it causes will be offset by fiscal expansions (increases in government spending).

Chapter 12

Graph It 12

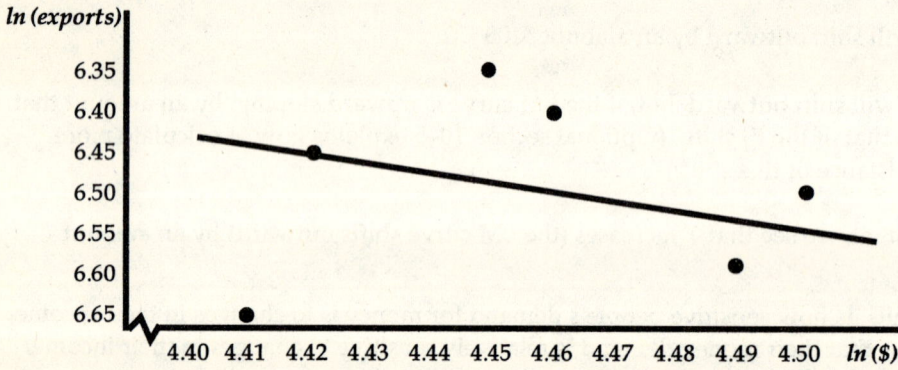

Chart 12 - 1

Exports seem to fall by roughly 10 or 11 percent when the real exchange rate rises one percent. We should be careful drawing conclusions from this graph, however: our estimate is, first, based on too few data points (six is never enough), second, leaves out other variables which may also affect exports (for example, foreign income), and, finally, is no more than a very loose visual approximation.

TABLE 12-1

Year	Real Exports	Natural Log of Real Exports	Real Value of the dollar*	Natural Log of the Dollar
1990	564.4	6.34	86.0	4.45
1991	599.9	6.40	86.5	4.46
1992	639.4	6.46	83.4	4.42
1993	658.2	6.49	90.0	4.50
1994	712.0	6.57	88.7	4.49
1995	775.4	6.65	82.5	4.41

*March 1973 = 100.

Source: Economic Data Tables

Crossword

ACROSS
3. dirty
5. LM
6. external
7. IS
8. current
9. appreciation
10. clean

DOWN
1. revaluation
2. devaluation
3. depreciation
4. open
7. internal

Fill-In Questions

1. fixed
2. flexible (floating)
3. falls; rises
4. rises; falls
5. appreciation; revaluation
6. depreciation; devaluation
7. beggar-thy-neighbor policy
8. into; increasing; rise
9. external balance
10. fall; rise

True–False Questions

1. True.
2. True.
3. True.

4. False—A fiscal expansion can increase both foreign and domestic income when exchange rates are fixed.
5. False—Any policy that causes a real depreciation of the domestic currency adversely affects other countries' trade balances and, as a result, can reduce their incomes.
6. False.
7. True.
8. False.
9. False.
10. True.

Multiple-Choice Questions

1. a 2. a 3. c 4. b 5. c 6. b 7. a 8. a 9. a 10. c

Conceptual Problems

1. Fiscal policy; the central bank is committed to maintaining the value of the currency.

2. If exchange rates were flexible, monetary policy would be more effective. The central bank can put upward or downward pressure on domestic interest rates; the exchange rate will adjust to keep domestic interest rates in line with foreign interest rates.

3. Fixed exchange rates reduce the risk of buying from/selling to people in other countries. They also prevent the central bank from being able to use monetary policy to stabilize output—arguably a bad thing.

4. See Data Table I.

Technical Problems

1. (a), (g) will increase the current account surplus, and hence improve the balance of payments

   (b), (e), (f) will decrease the current account surplus, and hence reduce the balance of payments

   (c), (d) will increase the capital account surplus, and hence improve the balance of payments

2. Go back to the national income accounting equation: $Y = C + I + G + (X - Q)$. Plug in the equation for Q. You will find that the coefficient on Y is (0.9 − 0.1), or 0.8... making the multiplier for government spending

$$\alpha_G = \frac{1}{1 - 0.8} = 5$$

3. If a 25% income tax were imposed, the coefficient on Y would be $0.8 \times (1 - .25)$, or 0.6. The multiplier would then be

$$\alpha_G = \frac{1}{1 - 0.8(1 - .25)} = \frac{1}{1 - 0.6} = 2.5$$

*4. The important thing to remember is that Country A's imports are Country B's exports, and vice versa. This enables us to write out the national income accounting equation ($Y = C + I + G + (X - Q)$) in gory detail:

$$Y_A = \bar{C} + 0.9Y_A + \bar{I} + \bar{G} + Q_B - Q_A$$

$$Y_A = \bar{C} + 0.9Y_A + \bar{I} + \bar{G} + \bar{Q}_B + 0.1(Y_B - \bar{T}_B) - \bar{Q}_A - 0.1(Y_A - \bar{T}_A)$$

$$Y_A = \bar{A}_A + 0.9Y_A + 0.1Y_B - 0.1Y_A = \bar{A}_A + 0.8Y_A + 0.1Y_B,$$

(collapsing all of the autonomous terms into $\bar{A}_A$)

Rewriting this last equation—bringing all of the Y_A's to one side—we find that

$$Y_A = \frac{1}{0.2}(\bar{A}_A + 0.1Y_B) = 5\bar{A}_A + 0.5Y_B$$

Running through this same process for Country B, we see that its national income accounting equation reduces to

$$Y_B = \frac{1}{0.3}(\bar{A}_B + 0.1Y_A) \cong 3.33\bar{A}_B + 0.333Y_A$$

Putting these together (substituting Y_B into Y_A), we get

$$Y_A = 6\bar{A}_A + 2\bar{A}_B$$

$$Y_B = 4\bar{A}_B + 2\bar{A}_A$$

An increase in domestic spending in Country A will increase Y_A by 6. An increase in domestic spending in Country A will increase Y_B by 4. The multipliers for an increase in government spending in Country A on Country A's output and for an increase in government spending in Country B on Country B's output are 6 and 4, respectively.

Note that we could also find the multipliers for an increase in government spending in Country A on Country B's output, and vice versa. Both are equal to 2.

Chapter 13

Graph It 13

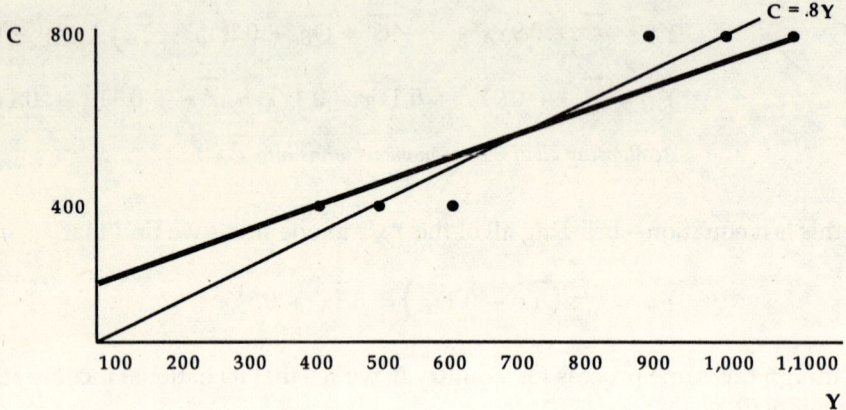

Chart 13 – 1

People having bad years look like they're consuming too much; people having good look like they're consuming too much. The mpc appears to be smaller than 0.8 and the consumption function looks like it has a positive intercept. We'd really like to graph consumption against permanent income.

TABLE 13 – 1

Permanent Income (YP)	Total Income (Y)	Consumption* (C = cYP)
$500	$400	$400
$500	$500	$400
$500	$600	$400
$1,000	$900	$800
$1,000	$1,000	$800
$1,000	$1,100	$800

* We assume that c, the marginal propensity to consume, is 0.8

Crossword

ACROSS

1. hypothesis
5. random
7. unanticipated
8. transitory
10. mpc
12. Modigliani
13. Friedman

DOWN

2. precautionary
3. permanent
4. liquidity
6. anticipated
9. retained
11. firms

Fill-In Questions

1. life-cycle/permanent income
2. save
3. greater
4. greater
5. random walk
6. working; in retirement
7. life-cycle
8. durable goods
9. booms; recessions
10. borrow

True-False Questions

1. True.
2. False—they draw very similar conclusions.
3. True.
4. True.
5. False—it changes too little.
6. False—they should see savings fall.
7. True.
8. True.
9. False.
10. False—most is done by firms.

Multiple-Choice Questions

1. c   2. b   3. c   4. a   5. c   6. a   7. a   8. c   9. a   10. d

Conceptual Problems

1. People use all available information to estimate their permanent income; only *new information* (inherently unpredictable) will cause them to change those estimates. Because people try to consume roughly the same amount of goods and services each period, only a change in those estimates will cause them to consume a different amount one period than another.

2. If people live longer and continue to retire at the same age, the fraction of their lives spent working will fall. They will have to save more during their working years to provide for their longer retirements.

3. An increase in the interest rate should reduce the present value of people's future income; permanent income should fall.

4. This question requires a bit of introspection. If you are young and short on collateral, however, you probably are at least somewhat liquidity constrained.

Technical Problems

1. We want to spread the financial gain that we get from this tax cut evenly over the rest of our lives.

    A permanent tax cut will raise our lifetime income by 30 x $100, or $3,000 — our labor income by $100 each year. We want to spread that gain over the next 40 years. This means that we can increase our consumption by $3,000/40, or $75 each year. A temporary tax cut will raise our permanent income by much less; a tax cut that lasted only 1 year, once we spread its benefit over our lifetimes, would allow us each to increase consumption by only $100/40, or $2.50 each year.

2. Expansionary fiscal policy will be more effective when people are liquidity constrained. They will spend more of the money they receive (their marginal propensities to consume are higher). The multiplier will be larger.

Chapter 14

Graph It 14

TABLE 14-1

Year	Real GDP	Investment	Annual Change in Real GDP	Annual Change in Investment
1985	5,717.1	863.4		
1986	5,912.4	857.7	3.42	-15.4
1987	6,113.3	879.3		
1988	6,368.4	902.8		
1989	6,591.8	936.5		
1990	6,707.9	907.3		
1991	6,676.4	829.5		
1992	6,880.0	899.8		
1993	7,062.6	977.9		
1994	7,347.7	1,107.0		
1995	7,543.8	1,140.6		
1996	7,813.2	1,242.7		
1997	8,159.5	1,393.3		
1998	8,515.7	1,566.8		
1999	8,875.8	1,669.7		

Source: See Economic Data Table B

Crossword

ACROSS
4. inventories
5. depreciation
6. rental
8. assets
9. stock

DOWN
1. flexible
2. residential
3. investment
7. falls

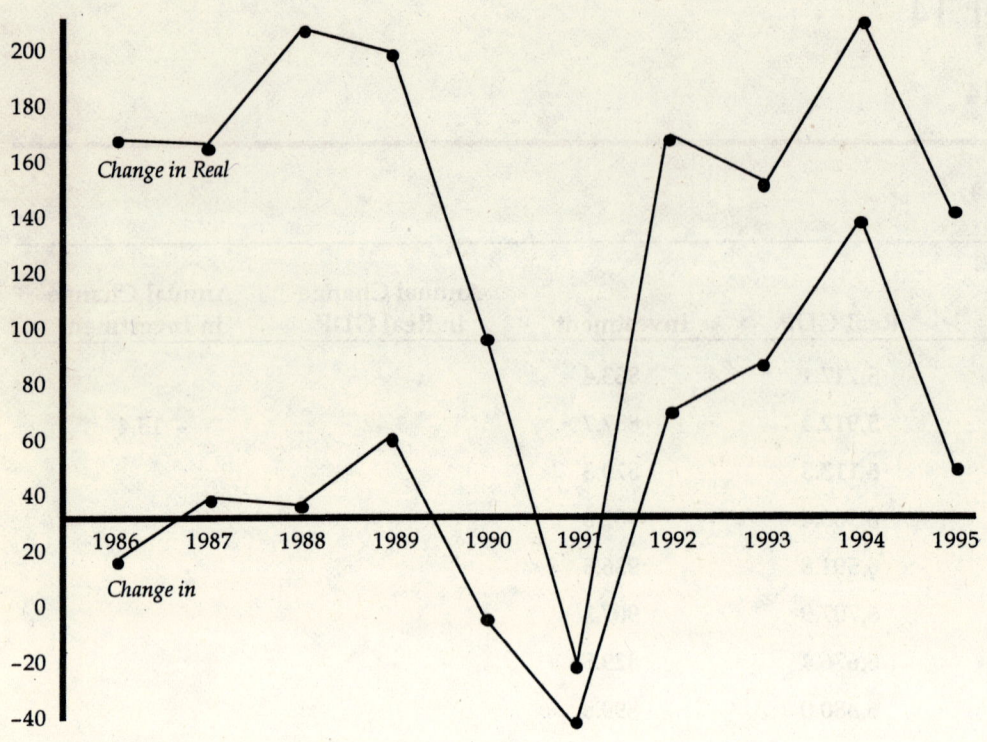

Chart 14 - 1

Fill-In Questions

1. business fixed investment; residential investment; inventory investment
2. business fixed investment
3. depreciation
4. user
5. flexible accelerator
6. just-in-time
7. investment tax credits
8. q
9. inventories
10. potential output

True–False Questions

1. True.
2. False — rising interest rates decrease investment.
3. True.
4. False — investment is a flow variable.
5. True.
6. True.
7. True.
8. True.
9. True.
10. True.

Multiple-Choice Questions

1. b 2. a 3. d 4. a 5. b 6. a 7. b 8. a 9. a 10. a

Conceptual Problems

1. An increase in the real interest rate raises the rental costs of capital; the marginal benefit of using capital to produce goods and services is unaffected. As a result, the capital stock at which the marginal benefit and the marginal cost of acquiring another unit of capital are equal (the desired capital stock) falls.

2. An increase in the rate of depreciation also raises the rental cost of capital. The argument made in question 1 applies here as well. Intuitively, the increase in the rate of depreciation makes any given capital stock more costly to maintain.

3. The price of whatever product the firm is making will rise with the price level; the firm's profits will therefore also rise (in nominal terms) with the price level. The firm will be able to costlessly repay the component of the nominal interest rate that reflects that increasing price level out of its higher nominal profits.

Technical Problems

1. Next period's investment will be $\frac{1}{2}(20000 - 12000) = \frac{1}{2}(8000) = 4000$.

   Next period's capital stock will therefore be $12000 + 4000 = 16000$, making the subsequent period's investment equal to $\frac{1}{2}(20000 - 16000) = \frac{1}{2}(4000) = 2000$.

2. a) $K^* = (0.25 \times 16000)/((0.12 - 0.06) + 0.10) = 4000/0.16 = 25000$
   b) $K^* = (0.25 \times 32000)/((0.12 - 0.06) + 0.10) = 8000/0.16 = 50000$
   c) $K^* = 4000/(2 \times 0.16) = 12500$

3. In the first instance, $q = \frac{35m}{50m} < 1$. This tells us *not* to accumulate any more capital.

   In the second instance, $q = \frac{80m}{50m} > 1$. We should invest.

Chapter 15

Graph It 15

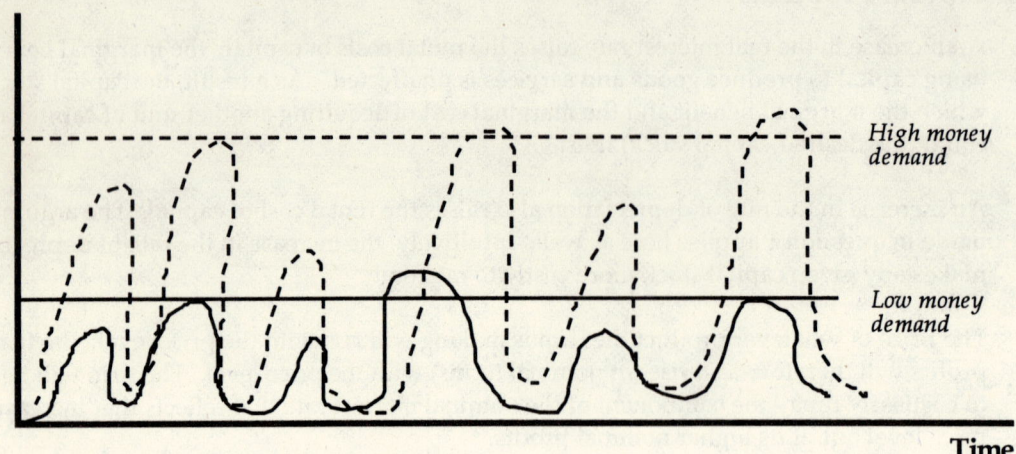

Chart 15 - 2

Crossword

ACROSS
2. transactions
5. exchange
7. precautionary
9. savings

DOWN
1. currency
3. speculative
4. velocity
6. account
8. value

Fill-In Questions

1. more
2. more
3. speculative
4. precautionary
5. transactions
6. store of value
7. medium of exchange
8. flight out of money
9. quantity
10. velocity

True–False Questions

1. True.
2. False.
3. True.
4. False.
5. True.
6. True.
7. False.
8. False.
9. True.
10. True.

Multiple-Choice Questions

1. d 2. c 3. a 4. d 5. b 6. d 7. a 8. c 9. c 10. d

Conceptual Problems

1. I hold money only to pay bills and buy coffee in the morning.

2. The ones that immediately spring to mind are gold, silver, gems, beads, and giant stone slabs — the last on the Isle of Yap in the Pacific.

Technical Problems

1. $V = \dfrac{1000000}{500000} = 2$

2. The classical quantity theory of money tells us that $\%\Delta M + \%\Delta V = \%\Delta P + \%\Delta Y$: Assuming that velocity is constant (we've already seen that that isn't such a bad assumption in the long run), this implies that the rate of inflation ($\%\Delta P$) is equal to $\%\Delta M + \%\Delta V - \%\Delta Y$, or $8\% + 0\% - 3\% = 5\%$.

3. The Baumol–Tobin equation says that the amount of money you will wish to hold is given by the equation

$$M^* = \sqrt{\dfrac{tcY}{2i}}$$

Plugging in the values for tc, Y and i that are given in the problem, we find that

$$M^* = \sqrt{\dfrac{\$1.50 \times 100000}{2 \times 0.06}} = \sqrt{1250000} \cong \$1118.03.$$

Chapter 16

Graph It 16

TABLE 16 – 1
First Balance Sheet

FRED				BANK			
ASSETS		*LIABILITIES*		*ASSETS*			*LIABILITIES*
Deposit	$200	None		Reserves	$200	$200	Deposit
				(Required	*$20)*		
				(Excess	*$20)*		
		$200	Net Worth				
	$200	$200			$200	$200	

TABLE 16 – 2
Second Balance Sheet

FRED				BANK			
ASSETS		*LIABILITIES*		*ASSETS*			*LIABILITIES*
Deposit	$ 380	$180	Loan	Reserves	$200	$ 380	Deposit
				(Required	*$ 38)*		
				(Excess	*$ 162)*		
		$ 200	Net Worth	Loan	$180		
	$ 380	$ 380			$ 380	$ 380	

TABLE 16 – 3
Third Balance Sheet

FRED				BANK			
ASSETS		*LIABILITIES*		*ASSETS*		*LIABILITIES*	
Deposit	$ 542	$ 342	Loan	Reserves	$ 200	$ 542	Deposit
				(Required	*$ 54.20)*		
				(Excess	*$145.80)*		
		$ 200	Net Worth	Loans	$342		
	$ 542	$ 542			$ 542	$ 542	

TABLE 16 – 4
Final Balance Sheet

FRED				BANK			
ASSETS		*LIABILITIES*		*ASSETS*		*LIABILITIES*	
Deposit	$ 2,000	$ 1,800	Loan	Reserves	$ 200	$ 2,000	Deposit
				(Required	*$ 200)*		
				(Excess	*$0)*		
		$ 200	Net Worth				
	$ 2,000	$ 2,000			$ 2,000	$ 2,000	

Crossword

ACROSS
2. instruments
4. FDIC
6. base
7. intermediate
9. FOMC
11. Greenspan

DOWN
1. ultimate
3. reserve
5. credit
8. discount
10. Fed

Fill-In Questions

1. required; excess
2. discount rate
3. fed funds rate
4. money multiplier
5. high-powered money
6. currency-deposit ratio
7. reserve ratio
8. FDIC
9. open market transactions
10. fractional-reserve

True–False Questions

1. True.
2. False—it reduces the money supply.
3. False—it reduces the money supply.
4. False—it reduces the money supply.
5. False.
6. False—it reduces the money supply.
7. True.
8. True.
9. False.
10. False.

Multiple-Choice Questions

1. c   2. c   3. c   4. d   5. b   6. a   7. c   8. a   9. b   10. c

Conceptual Problems

1. To meet withdrawal needs of depositors; to make sure they have enough reserves left at the end of each day to meet the Fed's reserve requirements.

2. It can buy bonds, lower the discount rate, or lower the required reserve ratio.

3. Over time, it is the increase in the money base that causes inflation. Targeting the interest rate could cause the Fed to increase the money supply too much.

4. This is an introspective question. There is no right answer… only a careful argument.

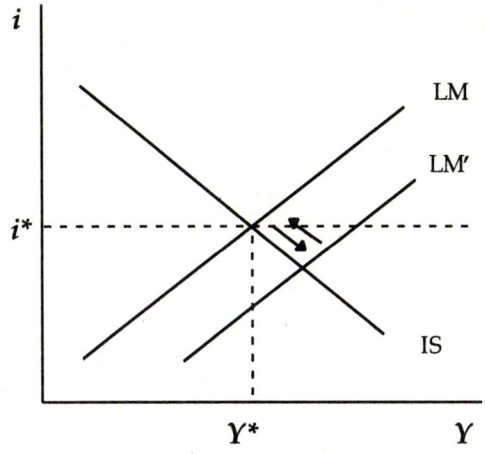 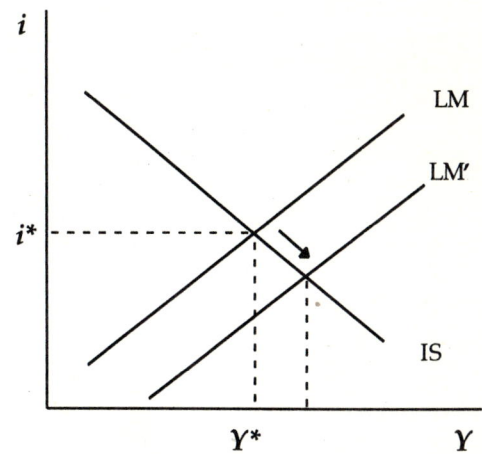

Figure 16 - 1A

INTEREST RATE TARGETING (THE PANEL ON THE LEFT) WORKS BETTER THAN MONEY BASE TARGETING (THE PANEL ON THE RIGHT) WHEN MOST SHOCKS HIT THE MONEY MARKET. WHEN THE FED USES TARGETS THE MONEY BASE, IT DOES NOT RESPOND AT ALL TO SHOCKS WHICH HIT OTHER PARTS OF THE FINANCIAL COMMUNITY. WHEN THERE ARE NO SHOCKS TO THE IS CURVE, INTEREST RATE TARGETING STABILIZES OUTPUT PERFECTLY.

5. Consider this a research question. What can you find out?

Technical Problems

1. The money base will fall, driving up the interest rate and, in the short run, reducing output.

2. The money base. See figure 16–1A.

3. $mm \equiv \dfrac{1 + cu}{re + cu} = \dfrac{1.2}{0.3} = 4$

Chapter 17

Graph It 17

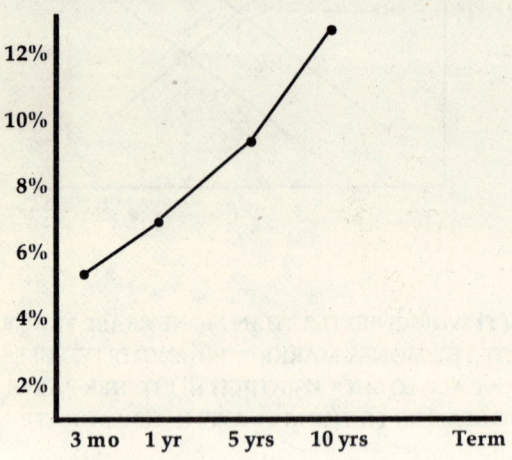

Chart 17 – 3

People must expect interest rates to rise.

Crossword

ACROSS
2. yield
4. perpetuity
7. fall
9. substitutes
10. random

DOWN
1. lowers
3. efficient
5. maturity
6. coupon
8. term

Fill-In Questions

1. term structure of interest
2. riskier
3. yield
4. coupon
5. face value
6. unpredictable
7. uncovered interest parity
8. depreciate
9. maturity
10. arbitrage

True–False Questions

1. True.
2. True.
3. False—when interest rates rise, bond prices fall.

4. False.
5. False—they are the vehicle through which monetary policy affects the economy.
6. False—they affect home mortgages and people's pensions, for example.
7. False—they should be *unpredictable*.
8. True.
9. True.
10. True.

Multiple-Choice Questions

1. d   2. d   3. b   4. a   5. b   6. a   7. b   8. a   9. c   10. d

Conceptual Problems

1. It may signal tight monetary policy.

2. Interest rates rise for all sorts of other reasons. Rising interest rates could be the result of expansionary fiscal policy.

3. It all goes back to the *rational expectations hypothesis*. Because people use all of the information to which they have access to form expectations of asset returns, any changes in the price of an asset must occur because new information has become available. We can't predict the content of this new information; hence, we should not be able to predict the changes in asset prices that result from it.

4. An increase in nominal interest rates would raise the return on bonds, making them more attractive to hold. Some investors will sell stocks and buy bonds, depressing stock prices.

Technical Problems

1. It should be the average of the short-term rates for that year:
   $(0.06 + 0.065 + 0.07 + 0.075)/4$, or 6.75%

2. 8% − 6% = 2%

3. US interest rates should be roughly 2 percentage points higher than Japanese interest rates.

Chapter 18

Graph It 18

TABLE 18 – 1

Year	GDP	Percent change from previous year
1929	790.9	—
1930	719.7	− 9.0
1931	674.0	− 6.3
1932	584.3	− 13.3
1933	577.3	− 1.2
1934	641.1	11.1
1935	698.4	8.9
1936	790.0	13.1
1937	831.5	5.3
1938	801.2	− 3.6
1939	866.5	8.2
1940	941.2	8.6
1941	1,101.8	17.1
1942	1,308.9	18.8

Source: Bureau of Economic Analysis, National Income and Product Accounts

Fill-In Questions

1. wars
2. incomes policies
3. seigniorage
4. inflation tax
5. monetize
6. primary (or non-interest)
7. heterodox
8. sells bonds; expand money base
9. bull; bears
10. budget deficits

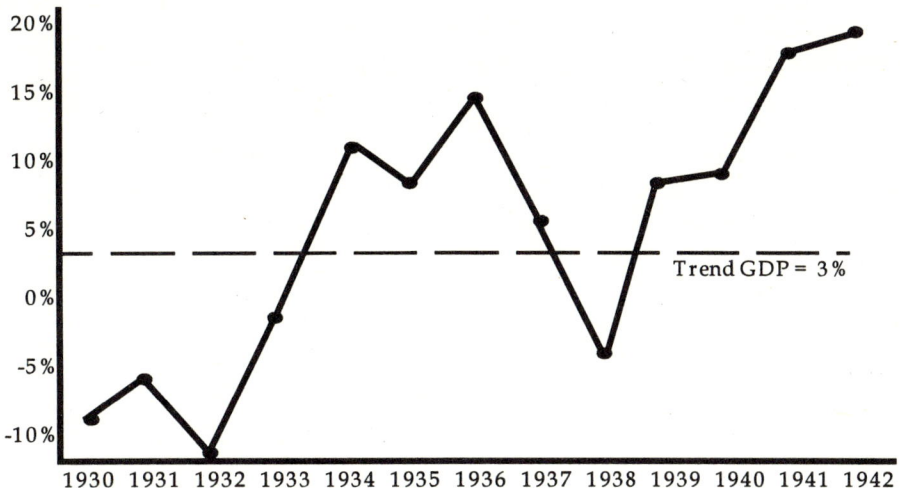

Chart 18 - 2

True-False Questions

1. False
2. True
3. False
4. False
5. False
6. False
7. False – at least not by themselves
8. True
9. False
10. False

Multiple-Choice Questions

1. d 2. d 3. a 4. c 5. c 6. a 7. a 8. c 9. a 10. d

Conceptual Problems

1. The expansionary monetary run by the Fed directly after the 1989 crash and the greater stability of the US banking system may have helped a great deal.

2. a) Printing money can provide the short-term revenues necessary to meet the debt obligation. Ultimately, however, this creates inflation. This happened in several Latin American countries in the 1980s. Debt forgiveness ultimately helped to eliminate the budget deficits driving the inflation.

288 ANSWERS TO QUESTIONS AND PROBLEMS

b) This is much the same. If a country is unable to pay its war reparations with existing revenues, printing money may enable them to meet these obligations. Post W.W.I Germany is a classic example.

c) When the government is unable to collect a formal tax, it can expand the money base and use the inflation tax as a substitute. Some economists attribute the high levels of inflation that followed liberalization in Russia to its inability to collect taxes.

3. The government can spend all of the money it prints. Imagine having a printing press in your home and being able to use it when you're low on cash…

3. This is an introspective question. What do you think?

Chapter 19

Graph It 19

The regression of imports on GDP looks pretty reasonable. The coefficient a is estimated to be 0.13; a $i billion increase in GDP should raise exports by about $130 million. The regression of imports on the value of the dollar estimates b to be –3.4. Oops! We know that the relation should be positive. This proves that you can't always look at just one factor in a complex relationship and expect to get a sensible result. The last regression estimates a to be 0.16 and b to be 0.91. An increase in GDP should actually raise imports even more than the first regression suggested! A $1 billion increase in GDP should raise imports, here, by roughly $160 million; a 1% increase in the value of the dollar should increase imports by about $910 million.

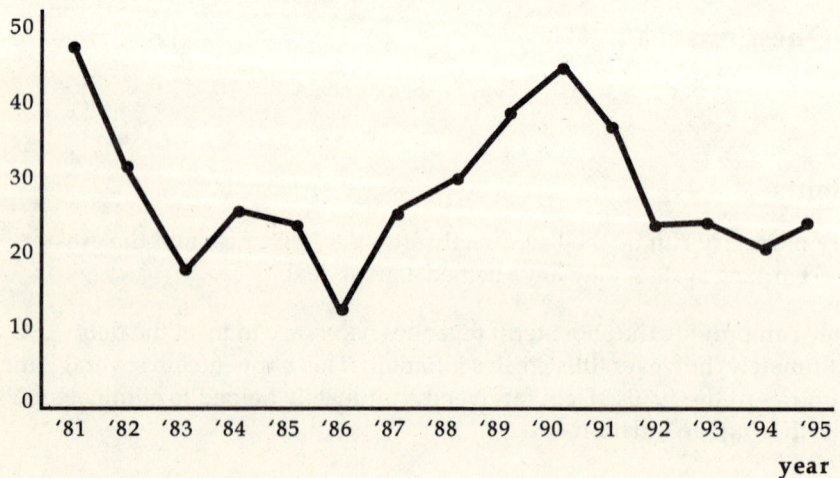

Chart 19 - 1

Crossword

ACROSS
4. ringgit
6. rupee
8. ngultrum
11. baht
12. franc
13. pound
15. lira
16. birr
17. peso
18. yuan
20. kwacha
22. dollar
23. dirham

DOWN
1. colon
2. riyal
3. dinar
4. rupiah
5. dram
7. escudo
9. taka
10. rand
12. forint
13. peseta
14. drachma
15. leu
16. bolivar
18. yen
19. mark
20. koruna
21. won

Fill-In Questions

1. excessive money growth
2. sterilizing
3. policy dilemma
4. policy synchronization
5. J curve
6. real exchange rate
7. spillover; interdependence
8. switching
9. reducing
10. real devaluation

True–False Questions

1. False — terms of trade have actually fluctuated quite a bit under the current flexible exchange rate regime.
2. False — because it will increase net exports, it will actually increase aggregate demand.
3. True.
4. True.
5. False.
6. True.
7. True.
8. True.
9. True.
10. True.

Multiple-Choice Questions

1. b   2. c   3. d   4. a   5. a   6. c

Conceptual Problems

1. There is a real depreciation (remember that we're using the unconventional units of measurement of *e* in this formula). Net exports should rise.

2. Firms might gain market share and customer loyalty or even open factories in other countries which will later be hard to disassemble.

3. The J curve effect is the tendency of imports to rise immediately following a real devaluation, and then, only later, to depreciate.

Technical Problems

1. When the central bank sells its foreign currency reserves, it is reducing the monetary base. To compensate for this, it must do something to increase it—buy bonds, perhaps, or lower the discount rate.

2. Nominal devaluations only seem to cause real devaluations when the monetary authority does not run expansionary policy alongside them.

3. People must expect the dollar to depreciate roughly 3%.

Chapter 20

Graph It 20

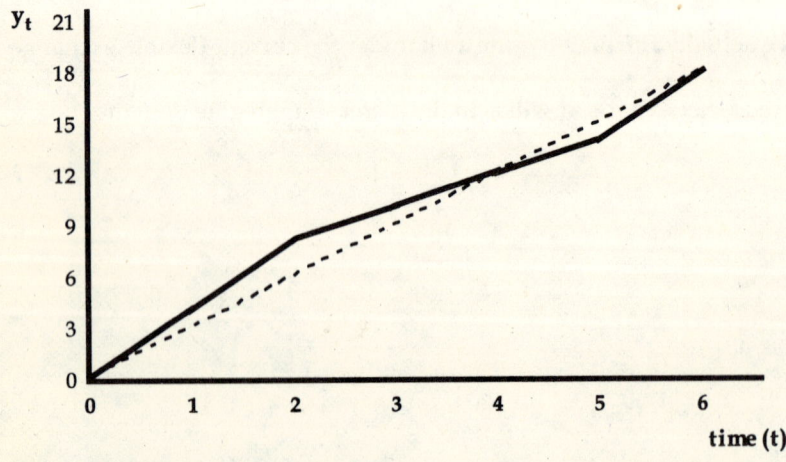

TREND STATIONARY PROCESS

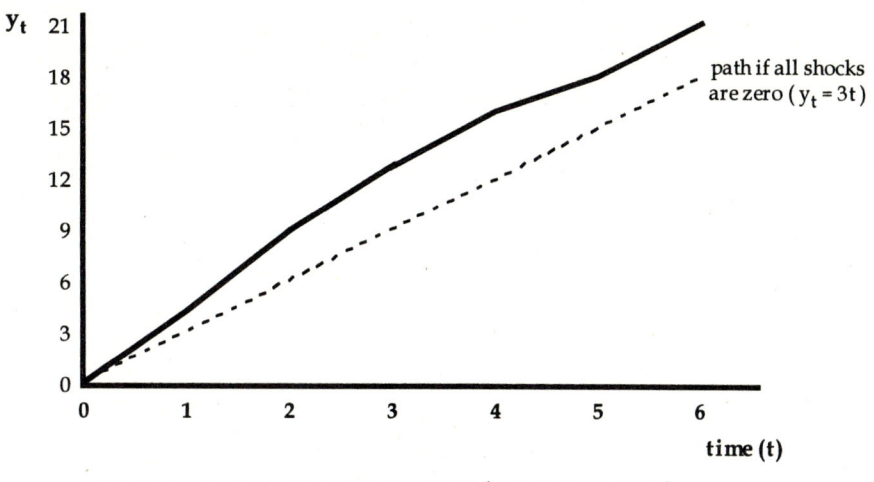

DIFFERENCE STATIONARY PROCESS (RANDOM WALK)

<u>Note</u>: *It's not always so easy to tell the difference between these processes... especially when the trend (or "drift" in the case of the difference stationary process) and shocks are not known.*

Crossword

ACROSS

1. unpredictable
3. random
5. intertemporal
8. productivity
11. externalities

DOWN

2. labor
4. anticipated
6. difference
7. supply
9. sticky
10. menu

Fill-In Questions

1. random walk
2. rationally
3. rational expectations equilibrium model
4. aggregate demand
5. productivity (or supply, technology)
6. labor (or leisure)
7. transmission
8. imperfectly
9. menu cost
10. anticipated (or expected)

True–False Questions

1. False.
2. False.
3. False.
4. False—it merely suggests that supply rather than demand shocks drive the business cycle.

5. True.
6. False.
7. True.
8. False.
9. True.
10. False.

Multiple-Choice Questions

1. d   2. b   3. a   4. b   5. a   6. d   7. b   8. a   9. a   10. b

Conceptual Problems

1. New Keynesian models of price stickiness try to justify, on microeconomic foundations, the assumption that prices do not adjust quickly enough in the short run to clear markets, so that output need not equal potential output. In doing this, they build an environment in which anticipated changes in fiscal and monetary policy can affect output.

2. If prices are not sticky (i.e., if they are able adjust to keep markets in equilibrium), fiscal and monetary policy have little, if any role in stabilizing output. Anticipated changes in AD will not affect output.

3. No. The random walk model of GDP merely suggests that supply shocks are more prevalent than demand shocks.

4. Real business cycle theorists argue that changes in the productivity of labor (we could call these supply or technology shocks) drive output fluctuations (the business cycle).

Technical Problems

*1. β and γ. Equation 35 in Chapter 8 suggests that there will be strong intertemporal substitution of leisure when $\beta + \gamma$ is close to 1:

$$\%\Delta L = 3 \times \left[\frac{(1-\gamma)}{(1-\gamma-\beta)}\right] \times \%\Delta a$$

*2. No. There seems to be very little intertemporal substitution of labor.

*3. Unexpected changes in AD will have the greatest effect on output when they occur very rarely (i.e., when most changes in the price of a firm's good turn out to be changes in its relative price). "You can't fool all of the people all of the time."

*4. The jury's still out on this one. We cannot reject the hypothesis that supply shocks have played an important role in driving output fluctuations. We are not sure, however, how often they occur; if they occur very rarely, demand shocks may play an important role in the business cycle.

GLOSSARY

absolute convergence   Tendency of both the levels and growth rates of output in different countries to approach each other over time, and for their steady-state values to be the same.

accelerator model   Asserts that investment spending is proportional to the change in output, and is not affected by the cost of capital; describes the behavior of inventory investment surprisingly well.

accommodation   Use of policy to offset a shock. For example, increase in money supply to prevent increase in interest rate resulting from outward shift in IS curve. See also *accommodation of supply shocks*.

accommodation of supply shocks   Use of demand-side policies to prevent GDP from falling in response to a temporary drop in aggregate supply.

action lag   Period between the time a policy is decided upon and the time it is implemented.

activist policies   Policies that responds to the current state of the economy, try to stabilize output.

activist rules   Rules that have countercyclical features.

adjusted GNP   Series which tries to correct for the inclusion of welfare-reducing "goods" in GNP, and for its inability to capture quality improvements; a measure of welfare.

adverse supply shock   Inward shift in the aggregate supply curve; the increase in the price of oil that resulted from the OPEC oil embargo of the early 1970's is a classic example.

aggregate demand   Sum of the values of all of the final goods purchased in an economy.

aggregate demand (AD) curve   Relationship between the amount of goods and services people wish to purchase and the price level.

aggregate demand schedule   Synonym, aggregate demand curve.

aggregate supply (AS) curve   Relationship between the amount of final goods and services produced in an economy and the price level.

aggregate supply-demand model   Uniquely determines price level and level of output for which both goods and money market are in equilibrium.

anticipated inflation   Inflation that people expect.

anticipatory monetary policy   Monetary policy adopted in response to problems (i.e., inflationary pressure) which are expected to arise in the future.

appreciation   Increase in the value of the domestic currency relative the currencies of other countries. Used when exchange rates are flexible.

arbitrage   Buying/selling assets to take advantage of differences in returns.

augmented Phillips curve   Phillips curve that includes inflationary expectations as a determinant of the inflation rate.

automatic adjustment mechanisms   Mechanisms which automatically act to eliminate balance of payments problems.

automatic stabilizer   Policy that reduces the impact of an economic shock without requiring case-by-case intervention; proportional income taxes and unemployment insurance are examples.

balance of payments   Measures the net flow of currency into the country from abroad.

balance-of-payments deficit   Occurs when more money is leaving the country than is entering it.
balance-of-payments surplus   Occurs when more money is entering the country than is leaving it.
balanced budget multiplier   Increase in output that results from equal increases in taxes and government purchases.
bank run   A rapid withdrawal of deposits from a bank. This can result in the forced sale of a bank's illiquid assets at fire-sale prices, causing the bank, even if healthy, to fail.
beggar-thy-neighbor policy   Attempt to increase domestic output at the expense of the output of other countries.
Board of Governors of the Federal Reserve   A government agency; oversees regional Federal Reserve Banks, has sole authority over changes in reserve requirements, and forms a part of the Federal Open Market Committee (FOMC). Its chairman has traditionally had the power to determine US monetary policy.
bubble   See *speculative bubble*.
budget constraint   Limit to the amount of money an individual, firm or the government can spend. An individuals purchases might be constrained by their income (or wealth).
budget deficit   The difference between the amount of money the government spends and the revenue that it taxes in.
budget surplus   Opposite of *budget deficit*.
buffer-stock saving   Excess consumer savings used to maintain consumption when income is lower than usual (saving for a rainy day).
Bundesbank   Germany's central bank.
burden of the debt   Each individual's share of the national debt.
business cycle   Pattern of expansion and contraction of the economy.
business fixed investment   Annual increase in machinery, equipment, and structures used in production.
business saving   Saving by firms; profits not paid out to owners/stockholders.
capital account   Net flow of dollars into the country resulting from the acquisition of domestic assets by foreigners.
capital stock   The amount of capital available for use in the economy.
capital-labor ratio   The amount of capital available for use by each worker; the capital stock divided by the labor supply.
central bank   Bank which has control over the money supply. In the US, the Federal Reserve. In Germany, the Bundesbank.
classical adjustment process   Process by which the economy automatically moves toward internal and external balance.
classical aggregate supply curve   Vertical AS curve; output equals potential output.
classical case   Vertical LM curve; case in which money demand is completely insensitive to changes in the real interest rate.
classical quantity theory   See quantity theory of money.
clean floating   Flexible exchange rate system in which the central bank does not intervene in foreign exchange markets. Contrast *dirty floating*.
Cobb-Douglas production function   Production function with constant returns to scale, constant elasticity of output, and unit elasticity of substitution between input factors.
COLA   See *cost of living adjustment*.
cold-turkey strategy   Strategy of moving immediately to the desired target rather than trying to spread the cost of adjustment out over time.
competitive depreciation   Occurs when one country allows its currency to depreciate in order to improve its trade balance, hurting another country. A series of retaliatory depreciations.
composition of output   Relative amounts of consumption, investment, and government purchases that make up GDP.

conditional convergence   Tendency of growth rates of output in different countries to approach each other over time, and for their steady-state values to be the same.
consol (or perpetuity)   An asset which pays a fixed amount (coupon) each period forever.
consumer durables   Consumer goods that yield services over a period of time; washing machines are an example.
consumer price index (CPI)   Fixed weight price index that measures the cost of the goods purchased by the typical urban family.
consumer spending   Spending by consumers.
consumption function   Equation relating consumption to *disposable income*.
convergence   See *conditional* and *absolute convergence*.
cost-of-living adjustment   Indexes wages to the inflation rate.
coupon   Periodic payment made to the holders of a bond.
crawling peg   Exchange rate policy; exchange rate is devalued at a rate roughly equal to the inflation differential between a country and its trading partners.
credibility   The degree to which the public that the government will implement its announced policies.
credible policy   Policy which people believe their government will follow.
credit rationing   Limiting the amount of money that individuals can borrow at the prevailing interest rate.
credit targeting   Using monetary policy to achieve a particular level of debt.
crowding out   Reduction in some component of aggregate demand — usually investment — that results from an increase ion government spending.
currency-deposit ratio   Ratio of the currency to bank deposits. A primary determinant of the money multiplier.
current account   Net flow of dollars into the country resulting from the sale of domestic goods and services, and from net transfers from abroad.
cyclical component of GDP   Fluctuations of output around its trend; the output gap.
cyclical deficit   Portion of the budget deficit which results from business cycle fluctuations. Contrast *structural deficit*.
cyclical unemployment   Unemployment resulting from business cycle fluctuations.
debt-income ratio   Ratio of national debt to GDP.
decision lag   Period of time required to decide on the proper response to a macroeconomic shock.
deep parameters   Parameters which describe the preferences of individuals and the production of firms, and which can be identified from microeconomic studies.
deflation   Rate at which the price level falls, in percentage terms. Opposite of *inflation*.
demand for real balances   Quantity of real money balances people wish to hold.
demand shock   A shock which causes the AD curve to shift.
demand-side policy   Policy which causes the aggregate demand curve to shift.
depreciation   Decrease in the value of the domestic currency relative the currencies of other countries. Used when exchange rates are flexible.
depreciation   Rate at which the capital stock wears out.
desired capital stock   Capital stock that maximizes profits.
devaluation   Decrease in the value of the domestic currency relative the currencies of other countries. Used when exchange rates are fixed.
difference stationary   Temporary shocks to a variable permanently affect its level. A random walk is an example of a difference stationary process.
dirty floating   Flexible exchange rate system in which the central bank intervenes in foreign exchange markets in order to affect the (short-run) value of its currency. Contrast *clean floating*.
discount rate   Interest rate charged by the Fed to banks that borrow money from it.
discounted cash flow analysis   Method of determining the present value of cash to be received in the future.

discrete lag   Time that passes before an effect is felt. Contrast *distributed lag*.
discretionary outlays   Portion of the federal budget under immediate annual congressional control. Contrast *entitlement spending*.
disintermediation   Withdrawal of deposits from financial intermediaries when interest rates rise above the regulated ceiling rates on time deposits.
disposable income   Income available for a household to spend; total income less taxes plus transfers.
dissaving   Negative saving; borrowing/spending out of accumulated wealth.
distributed lag   Time that passes while an effect gradually accumulates. Contrast *discrete lag*.
diversification of policy instruments   Simultaneous use of different policy instruments.
durable goods   Goods that yield services over a period of time. See *consumer durables*.
dynamic inconsistency   Tendency of optimal policy to be different, at different points in time.
dynamic programming   A way of solving a problem by working backwards through time; choices made at one point in time anticipate choices that will need to be made later.
econometric model   Model used to make quantitative economic predictions.
efficiency wage theory   Theory suggesting that wages might be set above the market clearing rate in order to motivate workers. A possible explanation for wage rigidity, labor market disequilibrium.
employment stability   Low rate of job layoff, turnover.
endogenous growth   Steady-state output growth determined by endogenous variables, for example the savings rate.
endogenous variable   Variable that is determined within a particular model (whose value is affected by the values of other variables).
entitlement programs   Programs which transfer money from the government to individuals; Social Security, unemployment insurance, and Aid to Families with Dependent Children (AFDC) are examples.
equilibrium level of output   Level of output at which aggregate supply equals aggregate demand.
equity   Share of ownership in a company; claim to a fraction of its profits.
European Exchange Rate Mechanism (ERM)   Agreement between a number of European countries to loosely fix their exchange rates, allowing them to fluctuate only in a narrow band.
European Monetary Union (EMU)   Will exist when and if the countries which have signed the Maastricht Treaty adopt a common currency. Box 12–1 in your textbook reviews the status of this union.
excess reserves   Reserves held by banks over and above the level required by the Federal Reserve.
excess sensitivity   When one variable's response to changes in another is larger than theory predicts. Consumption, for example, is said to exhibit excess sensitivity; it changes more in response to predictable income changes than the life-cycle/permenant-income theory suggests
excess smoothness   When one variable's response to changes in another is smaller than theory predicts. Consumption, for example, exhibits excess smoothness; it changes by a smaller amount than the life-cycle/permenant-income theory suggests in response to unexpected changes in income.
exchange rate   Price of foreign currency per unit of domestic currency.
exchange rate overshooting   Movement of the exchange rate past its target. Adjustment of exchange rates toward long run equilibrium is frequently accompanied by a move, in the medium run, of the exchange rate past its final position.
exogenous variable   Variable that is determined outside of a particular model (whose value is independent of the values of a model's other variables).
expansion   See *recovery*.
expectations theory of the term structure   States that long-term interest rates are equal to the average of current and expected future short-term interest rates, plus a term premium.
expectations–augmented Phillips curve   See *Augmented Phillips curve*.
expenditure-reducing (increasing) policies   Policies aimed at offsetting the effects of expenditure switching policy.

expenditure-switching policies Policies aimed at increasing purchases of domestic goods and decreasing purchases of imported goods.

experience rating The unemployment insurance tax is higher for firms whose employees have high unemployment rates.

external balance Occurs when output the balance of payments is neither in surplus nor in deficit; when the current account and the capital account exactly offset each other.

external balance Occurs when the balance of payments surplus is equal to zero.

external deficit Balance of payments deficit.

face value The amount which a bond pays its holder upon expiration. The market value of a bond will equal its face value when the market interest rate is equal to the rate of return on the bond.

factor payments Payments made to factors of production; wages paid to labor are an example.

factor shares Portion of national income paid to each productive input.

factors of production Inputs to the production; capital, labor, and natural resources are examples.

Fed Short for Federal Reserve.

Federal Deposit Insurance Corporation (FDIC) Government agency that insures deposits of most commercial banks and mutual savings banks to a maximum of $100,000.

federal funds rate The cost to a bank of borrowing from other banks.

Federal Open Market Committee (FOMC) Oversees open market operations, sets monetary targets. Made up of the Board of Governors of the Federal Reserve System, the President of the New York Federal Reserve Bank, and the presidents of 4 other regional banks on a rotating basis.

Federal Reserve United States' central bank. See *Federal Reserve System*.

Federal Reserve System Consists of twelve Federal Reserve Banks, each representing its own district, all overseen by the Board of Governors of the Federal Reserve System.

final goods Goods which are sold to firms, the public, or the government for any purpose other than use as an input to production; all goods excluding intermediate ones.

finance The sale/purchase of assets.

fine tuning Continuous attempts to stabilize the economy in the face of small disturbances.

fiscal accommodation Fiscal response to a supply shock; prevents it from affecting output.

fiscal policy Government policy with respect to government purchases, transfer payments, and the tax structure.

fiscal policy multiplier Increase in aggregate demand for a $1 increase in government purchases (or other changes in autonomous demand).

Fisher effect Tendency of inflation and nominal interest rates to move together.

Fisher equation $r^e = i - \pi^e$

fixed exchange rate system A system in which exchange rates are determined by governments and central banks rather than the free market, and maintained through *foreign exchange market intervention*.

flexible (floating) exchange rate system A system in which exchange rates are allowed to fluctuate with the forces of supply and demand. See also *clean floating* and *dirty floating*.

flexible accelerator model Asserts that firms plan their investment to close a fraction of the gap between their actual capital stock and their desired capital stock; a result is that more firms with a larger gap between their actual and desired capital stocks accumulate capital more quickly than other firms.

flight out of money Tendency of people to hold goods rather than assets during periods of high inflation.

flow variable A variable that is measured in rates of change rather than levels. Contrast *stock variable*.

foreign exchange market intervention The sale/purchase of currency in foreign exchange markets for the express purpose of increasing or decreasing the value of the domestic currency. Carried out by a country's central bank.

fractional reserve banking Banks are only required to keep a fraction of their deposits in the form of cash, or cash equivalents.

frequency of unemployment The average number of times, per period, that workers become unemployed.

frictional unemployment Unemployment associated with the movement of workers in and out of jobs in "normal" times.

full crowding out Total displacement of private spending by increasing government spending. See *classical aggregate supply curve* and *classical case*.

full-employment budget surplus What the budget surplus would be (hypothetically) with existing fiscal policy if the economy were at full employment.

full-employment output See *potential output*.

GDP deflator Measure of the price level obtained by dividing nominal GDP by real GDP.

GDP gap Difference between potential GDP and actual GDP. See *output gap*.

GDP per capita GDP per person.

globalization Notion that the world is moving toward a single global economy.

golden-rule capital stock The steady state level of capital that provides the most consumption each period. When the capital stock is at the golden rule level, the marginal product of capital is equal to the rate of depreciation plus the rate of population growth (and, when there is growth in technology, the rate of technological progress).

goods market equilibrium schedule See IS curve.

government budget constraint The government can finance its deficits only by selling bonds (accumulating debt) or by increasing the monetary base.

government budget deficit Excess of government expenditure over government revenue.

government expenditure Total government spending; includes both government purchases and transfers.

government purchases Government spending on goods and services. Contrast *government expenditure*.

government saving Saving by the government; the difference between the revenues taken in (i.e., from taxes) and the money used/given away (i.e., transfer payments, interest payments on the national debt).

gradualism Policy strategy of moving toward a desired target slowly.

Great Depression A historical period during of very low output and very high unemployment that occurred during the years 1929–1941 in the United States. A number of other countries also experienced severe depressions during this period.

gross domestic product (GDP) Measure of all goods and services produced within the country in one year. Real GDP measured in units of constant value. Nominal GDP measured in dollars.

gross investment Total investment; flow into the capital stock.

gross national product (GNP) Measure of the value of all final goods and services produced by domestically owned factors of production.

growth accounting The theory of measurement of the sources of economic growth.

growth rate Rate at which a variable increases in value; percentage change in the level of a variable.

growth theory Tries to explain why output grows over time, and to identify the factors that affect it growth rate.

heterodox approach to stabilization Coordinated use of monetary, fiscal, and exchange rate policies accompanied by wage and price controls.

high-powered money See monetary base.

human capital Education and training of individuals to increase productivity.

hyperinflation Very rapid price increase, usually defined as over 100 percent per month.

hysteresis Occurs when temporary fluctuations in one variable have permanent effects on another. See also *unemployment hysteresis*.

imperfect competition Firms have market power — can chose, to some extent, the price at which they will sell the goods they produce.
imperfect information Forecasts based on imperfect information will be less than fully accurate, though not necessarily biased.
income elasticity of money Amount that demand for real money balances changes, in percentage terms, when income increases by 1%.
income velocity Ratio of income to the money stock.
incomes policies Attempts to reduce inflation by wage or price controls.
increasing returns to scale A production function has increasing returns to scale when doubling all of the inputs to the production process more than doubles output.
indexation Automatic adjustment of prices and wages according to inflation rate.
inflation Percentage rate of increase in the general price level.
inflation differential Difference between domestic and foreign rates of inflation.
inflation targeting Using monetary policy to achieve a particular inflation rate.
inflation tax Revenue gained by the government because of inflation's devaluation of money holdings.
inflation-adjusted deficit Measure of the budget deficit that adjusts for effects of inflation; specifically, the correction reduces the measured budget deficit by the capital gain on nominal bonds.
inside lag Period between the time a disturbance occurs and the time action is taken.
insider-outsider theory Theory which argues that wages remain above the market clearing level because those who are unemployed do not sit at the bargaining table.
instruments "Tools" that the central bank can use to affect the domestic money supply.
interest differential Difference between rates of interest paid in different countries for the same asset, or in the same country for different assets.
interest elasticity of money Percentage change in the demand for real money balances resulting from a 1% increase in the interest rate.
intergenerational accounting Evaluates the costs and benefits of taxes and spending for various age groups in society.
intermediate goods Goods which are used to produce other goods or services; flour purchased by bakers is an example.
intermediate target Policy targets used for control rather than because of their inherent interest. For example, the money supply might be an intermediate target in the attempt to ultimately control inflation. Contrast *ultimate targets*.
internal balance Occurs when output equals potential output.
International Monetary Fund (IMF) International Organization created to promote international monetary cooperation; makes its resources temporarily available, under stringent conditions, to member countries experiencing balance of payments problems.
international trade The exchange of goods and services between countries.
intertemporal substitution of leisure The extent to which temporarily high real wages cause workers to work harder today and enjoy more leisure tomorrow.
intervention Sales or purchases of foreign exchange by the central bank in order to stabilize exchange rates.
inventory cycle Response of inventory investment to changes in sales that causes further changes in aggregate demand.
inventory investment Increase in the stock of goods on hands.
investment Purchase of new capital, principally by the business sector.
investment subsidy Government payment of part of the cost of private investment.
investment tax credit Tax credit given to firms when they reinvest their earnings.
***IS* curve** Shows all of the combinations of the real interest rate and the level of output for which the goods market is in equilibrium ($Y = C + I + G + NX$).

IS-LM model   Interaction of IS and LM curves determines the real interest rate and the level of income for a given price level, for which both goods and money markets are in equilibrium.
J-curve effect   Observation that when a currency depreciates, the value of net exports rises temporarily, and then falls.
just-in-time inventory management   Inventory management strategy; firms holds inventories for as short a time as possible by sending goods out as soon as they are produced, and ordering parts only as they are needed.
Keynesian aggregate supply curve   Horizontal aggregate supply curve.
labor force   Consists of people who are working and people who are actively looking for work
life-cycle hypothesis   Consumption theory emphasizing that consumers consume and save out of total life income and plan to provide for retirement.
lifetime budget constraint   Limits amount of money we can spend over our lifetimes; the total amount of money that we earn/inherit/find on the street over our lifetimes.
lifetime utility   The total benefit we derive from consumption (and whatever other activities we value) over our lifetimes.
liquidity   A measure of the ability to make funds available on short notice.
liquidity constraint   Limitations on ability to borrow in order to finance consumption plans.
liquidity trap   Horizontal LM curve; due to extreme interest sensitivity of money demand.
***LM* curve**   Shows all of the combinations of the real interest rate and the level of output for which the demand for real money balances equals the supply of real money balances. Drawn for a given price level.
long run   A period of time long enough for prices to clear all markets so that output is equal to potential output, but short enough for potential output to be fixed. Represented in AS-AD model by a vertical AS curve.
Lucas (econometric policy evaluation) critique   Points out that many macroeconomic models assume that expectations are given by a particular function, when that function can change.
M1   Currency plus checkable deposits.
M2   M1 plus small time and savings deposits, overnight repurchase agreements (RP's) and Eurodollars, and money market funds.
M3   M2 plus other liquid assets.
Maastricht Treaty   Would create a common European currency and central bank.
managed (dirty) floating   Flexible exchange rate system in which central banks intervene in exchange markets to moderate short-run fluctuations in exchange rates.
mandatory outlays   Spending made under *entitlement programs*.
marginal product of capital (*MPK*)   Increment to output obtained by adding one unit of capital, with other factor inputs held constant.
marginal product of labor (*MPL*)   Increment to output obtained by adding one unit of labor, with other factor inputs held constant.
marginal propensity to consume   Increase in consumption for each $1 increase in disposable income.
marginal propensity to import   The increase in the demand for imports that results from a 1 unit increase in domestic income.
marginal propensity to save   Increase in savings for each $1 increase in disposable income. Equals 1 minus the marginal propensity to consume.
marginal utility of consumption   The increase in utility from consuming an additional unit of some good.
market share   The fraction of a market's sales made by a firm, or by firms from a particular country.
maturity (or term) of bond   Length of time until a bond expires.
medium of exchange   One of the roles of money; asset used to make payments.
menu cost   Small cost incurred when the nominal price of a good is changed; for example, the cost for a restaurant of reprinting its menus when it raises/lowers its prices.

misery index   Index used by political analysts to measure people's unhappiness with the dual problems of inflation and unemployment; the sum of inflation and unemployment.

monetary accommodation   Use of monetary policy to stabilize interest rates during active fiscal policy operations; also the use of monetary policy to prevent a supply shock from affecting output.

monetary approach to the balance of payments   Emphasizes monetary causes of balance of payments problems.

monetary base   See *high powered money*.

monetary policy multiplier   Increase in aggregate demand for $1 increase in the money supply.

monetary-base targeting   Using monetary policy to keep the monetary base at a particular level.

monetizing budget deficits   Purchase of government debt by the Federal Reserve, thus indirectly funding the deficit by printing money.

money (money stock)   Assets that can be used for making immediate payment.

money illusion   Belief that the numbers used to express prices have significanceÑthat changes in the nominal price of a good are meaningful in and of themselves.

money market equilibrium schedule   See *LM curve*.

money multiplier   Ratio of money stock to the monetary base.

multiplier   Increase in endogenous variable for each $1 increase in exogenous variable. Particularly, increase in GDP for each $1 increase in government purchases.

multiplier uncertainty   Uncertainty about effects of policy changes due to uncertainty about value of fiscal policy multiplier, monetary policy multiplier, etc.

Mundell-Fleming model   Model first proposed by Robert Mundell and Marcus Fleming that explores economy with flexible exchange rates and perfect capital mobility.

myopia   Shortsightedness by households regarding future income streams.

national income   Total payments to factors of production. Net national product minus indirect taxes.

national income accounting identity $Y = C + I + G + NX$.

natural rate of unemployment   Rate of unemployment at which the flows into and out of the unemployment pool balance; also the point on the augmented Phillips curve at which expected inflation equals actual inflation.

neoclassical growth theory   Theory which asserts that the growth rate of output is determined by exogenous technological growth.

net domestic product (NDP)   GDP minus allowance for depreciation of capital.

net exports   Exports minus imports.

net investment   Total (or gross) investment less depreciation; increase in capital stock.

net investment   Total investment less depreciation; measures the increase in the capital stock each period.

net investment income   The interest and profits that result from foreign assets held by domestic residents less the income foreigners earn on the domestic assets *they* own.

net present value   Same as *present value*. Amount today that is equivalent to a future payment—the amount of money that, invested at the market interest rate, would generate that amount of money.

neutrality of money   Proposition that equiproportional changes in the money stock and prices leave the economy unaffected.

New Classical economics   Belief that the private economy is inherently efficient and that the government ought not to attempt to stabilize output and unemployment.

New Deal   Slogan for Franklin D. Roosevelt's economic policy reforms.

New Economics   Economic policy of the Kennedy-Johnson years, emphasizing the use of Keynesian theory to maintain full employment.

New Keynesian economics   Models whose basis is rational behavior and conclude that the economy is not inherently efficient and that, at times, the government ought to stabilize output and unemployment.

nominal GDP Value of all final goods and services produced in the economy; not adjusted for inflation.

nominal GDP targeting Using monetary policy to achieve a certain level of GDP, or to achieve a particular rate of growth of GDP.

nominal money supply Nominal value of bills and coins in circulation; says nothing about the amount that these bills and coins can purchase.

Okun's law Empirical "law" relating GDP growth to changes in unemployment; named for its discoverer, the late Arthur Okun.

OPEC Organization of Petroleum Exporting Countries; an international oil cartel.

open economy An economy which trades goods, services, and assets with other countries.

open market operation Federal Reserve purchase or sale of Treasury bills in exchange for money.

operational bequest motive A reason for saving; desire to leave some of one's money behind for descendants/friends/charity.

optimal Best.

output gap Difference between potential GDP and actual GDP.

outside lag Time required for a policy change to take effect.

parameter Type of exogenous variable; gives a function its specific form. The parameter θ in the function $K^\theta L^{1-\theta}$ is an example.

pay-as-you-go social security system Social security system in which payments to retirees are made with funds provided, not by their social security taxes, but by the social security taxes of the working populace.

perfect capital mobility Capital is perfectly mobile when it has the ability to move instantly, and with a minimum of transactions costs, across national borders in search of the highest return.

perfect foresight Assumption that people know the future value of all relevant variables, or that their expectations are always correct.

permanent-income theory Says that people form expectations of their future income and choose how much to consume based on those as well as their current income.

personal saving Saving by individuals and families.

Phillips curve Relation between inflation and unemployment; in a sense, a dynamic version of the aggregate supply curve.

policy irrelevance Refers to the inability of monetary or fiscal policy to affect output in rational expectations equilibrium models.

policy mix Combination of fiscal and monetary policy to achieve both *internal* and *external* balance.

policy variable An exogenous variable whose value is determined by government policy.

political business cycle theory Theory that politicians deliberately manipulate the economy to produce an economic boom at election time.

portfolio The mix of assets someone owns.

portfolio disequilibrium Occurs when people are holding more of some asset (i.e., money) at the prevailing interest rate than they wish to.

potential output Output that is produced when all factors are fully employed.

precautionary motive A reason people hold money; they do not know how much they'll need to spend.

primary (or noninterest) deficit The budget deficit except for interest payments.

private saving Saving by individuals, by families, and by firms; saving by everyone other than the government.

producer price index (PPI) Price index based on a market basket of goods used in production. The PPI replaced the wholesale price index (WPI).

production function Technological relation showing how much output can be produced for a given combination of inputs.

productivity shock Change in technology that affects workers' productivity. See also *supply shock*.

propagation mechanism Mechanism by which current economic shocks cause fluctuations into the future, for example, intertemporal substitution of leisure.

purchasing power parity (PPP) Theory of exchange rate determination arguing that the exchange rate adjusts to maintain equal purchasing power of foreign and domestic currency.

q theory of investment Investment theory emphasizing that investment will be high when assets are valuable relative to their reproduction cost. The ratio of asset value to cost if called q.

quantity equation Price times quantity equals money times velocity.

quantity theory of money Theory of money demand emphasizing the relation of nominal income to nominal money. Sometimes used to mean a vertical *LM* curve.

random walk A difference stationary process.

random walk of GDP Theory that suggests most shocks to output have permanent effects—that supply shocks play a more important role in explaining business cycle fluctuations than demand shocks.

random-walk model of consumption Model that suggests consumption should follow a random walk. Because consumption is supposedly based on expected future income as well as current income, changes in consumption should not be predictable.

rational expectations Theory of expectations formation in which expectations are based on all available information about the underlying economic variable. Frequently associated with new classical macroeconomics.

rational expectations equilibrium model A model in which expectations are formed rationally, and markets are always in equilibrium.

real balances Real value of the money stock (number of dollars divided by the price level).

real business cycle (RBC) theory Theory that recessions and booms are due primarily to shocks in real activity, such as supply shocks, rather than to changes in monetary factors.

real devaluation A decline in the purchasing power of the dollar relative to other currencies.

real exchange rate Purchasing power of foreign currency relative to the U.S. dollar.

real GDP A measure of output, adjusts value of final goods and services to reflect changes in the price level.

real interest rate Return on an investment measured in dollars of constant value; roughly equal to the difference between the nominal interest rate and the rate of inflation.

real money supply Real value of the bills and coins in circulation; equal to the nominal money supply divided by the price level.

recognition lag Period between the time a disturbance occurs and the time policy makers discover the disturbance.

Rental (user) cost of capital Cost of using a dollar's worth of capital for a given unit of time, usually a year.

repercussion effects Feedback of domestic economic changes through foreign economies and back into the domestic economy.

replacement ratio The ratio of after-tax income while unemployed to after-tax income while employed.

reporting effects These are present when a change in the number of people who claim to be in a certain group affects the measurement of some variable; unemployment can appear to rise, for example, when more people register for unemployment benefits.

required-reserve ratio Fraction of a bank's deposits that it is required to keep on reserve.

reservation wage The lowest wage an individual is willing to accept; if you were offered a job that paid a wage lower than your reservation wage, you would turn it down.

reserve ratio Ratio of bank reserves to bank deposits; a primary determinant of the money multiplier.

reserves Part of a bank's deposit kept at the Fed, or in its vaults; money that a bank keeps on hand instead of lending out.

residential investment Investment in housing.

revaluation Increase in the value of the domestic currency relative the currencies of other countries. Used when exchange rates are fixed.

Ricardian (or Barro-Ricardo) equivalence   Under Barro–Ricardo equivalence, there is no difference between taxes and the accumulation of debt; debt is thought to be the same as future taxes.
risky asset   Asset whose future payoff is uncertain.
sacrifice ratio   During a period of anti-inflation policy, the ratio of cumulative GDP lost to reduction in the inflation rate.
saving   Money that is not spent is saved.
scatterplot   A graph made up of a number of unconnected points.
search unemployment   Unemployment that exists because people have quit one job to search for another.
seigniorage   Revenue derived from the government's ability to print money.
self-fulfilling expectations   Expectations which cause a variable to change in the expected manner; if enough people expect a currency to depreciate, capital flows generated by their expectations will cause it to do so.
short run   A period of time short enough that markets are unable to clear, so that output can deviate from potential output.
Solow residual   A measure of total factor productivity; change in level of production that cannot be accounted for by changes in factor inputs.
speculative bubble   Occurs when the value of a variable departs from the level that the factors that determine its value suggest; when people argue that a stock is over- or under-valued, they are suggesting that such a bubble exists.
speculative motive   A reason people hold money; although the return on holding money is small, people hold it because it reduces the risk associated with their portfolio of assets.
speed of price adjustment   Amount of time that it takes prices to fully adjust so that all markets are in equilibrium and output equals potential output.
spell of unemployment   The amount of time that the average person spends in the unemployment pool.
spillover (interdependence) effects   Occur when policy changes or supply/demand shocks in one country affect output in another.
stable equilibrium   An equilibrium which draws nearby variables into itself; if a variable is moved slightly away from a stable equilibrium, it will return.
stagflation   Simultaneous inflation and recession.
staggered price adjustment   Occurs when firms set their prices/negotiate their contracts at different times.
standard of deferred payment   Asset normally used for making payments due at a later date.
steady-state equilibrium   State in which real (per capita) economic variables are constant.
sterilization   Open market purchase or sale by the Fed in order to offset effects of foreign exchange market intervention on the monetary base.
sterilized intervention   Occurs when the central bank uses monetary policy to offset the effect of foreign exchange market intervention on the domestic money supply.
sticky prices   Prices which are unable to adjust quickly enough to keep markets in equilibrium.
sticky wages   Wages which are unable to adjust quickly enough to clear the labor market.
stock variable   A variable that is measured in levels rather than rates of change. Contrast *flow variable*.
store of value   Asset that maintains its value over time.
structural deficit   Deficit that would exist with current fiscal policy if the economy were at full employment. Formerly called "high-employment" or "full-employment" deficit. Contrast *cyclical deficit*.
supply shock   An economic disturbance whose first impact is a shift in the aggregate supply curve.
supply-side policy   Policy which causes the aggregate supply curve to shift.
target zone   In a target-zone agreement, central banks limit exchange rate fluctuations to a specified range.
tariff   A tax imposed on imported goods.

term premium Compensate holders of bonds for the risk associated with a particular maturity.
term structure of interest The relationship between interest rates on bonds of different maturities.
total factor productivity Rate at which productivity of inputs increases; measure of technological progress. See also *Solow residual*.
trade See *international trade*.
trade balance The net flow of dollars into the country due to sales of goods abroad.
transactions motive A reason people hold money; we use it to purchase goods and services.
transfer payments Money given by the government to individuals, not in exchange for goods or services; welfare payments are an example. See also *entitlement programs*.
transmission mechanism Process by which monetary policy affects aggregate demand.
trend (secular) component of GDP Potential output.
trend path of output The path followed by potential output over time.
trend stationary A variable is trend stationary when temporary shocks do not permanently affect its level. Changes in AD, for example, can only temporarily affect output. If changes in output were driven primarily by demand shocks, output would be trend stationary.
trend stationary with breaks Trend stationary, but with a trend that sometimes changes.
ultimate target Policy targets of inherent interest. For example, the inflation rate might be an ultimate target. Contrast *intermediate targets*.
uncovered interest parity Relationship between interest differentials and expected currency appreciation.
unemployed person A person who does not have a job and is actively seeking one.
unemployment hysteresis Theory, argues recessions may permanently affect the natural rate of unemployment.
unemployment pool Group of individuals in transition between jobs.
unit of account Asset in which prices are denoted.
unstable equilibrium An equilibrium which pushes nearby variables away from itself; if a variable is moved slightly away from an unstable equilibrium, forces will push it even further away.
value added Increase in value of output at a given stage of production. Equivalently, value of output minus cost of inputs.
velocity of money The number of times the typical dollar changes hands during the year.
very long run A period of decades or more, over which potential output is expected to grow. The domain of growth theory.
wage-price spiral A process in which changes in prices feed back into wages, and from there again into prices.
World Trade Organization (WTO) International organization that works out rules of trade between its member nations; created January 1, 1995 as a result of the Uruguay Round of the General Agreement on Tariffs and trade (GATT).
yield curve Shows how interest rates change as bond maturities increase.

Data Tables

TABLE A
U.S. GROSS DOMESTIC PRODUCT (billions of dollars)

| Year | GDP | PERSONAL CONSUMPTION EXPENDITURES | | | | Gross private domestic invest. | FIXED INVESTMENT | | | | |
| | | Total | Durable goods | Non-durable goods | Services | | Total | NONRESIDENTIAL | | | Residential |
								Total	Structures	Producers durable eqipment	
1965	720.1	444.3	63.3	191.6	189.5	118.2	109	74.8	28.3	46.5	34.2
1966	789.3	481.8	68.3	208.8	204.7	131.3	117.7	85.4	31.3	54	32.3
1967	834.1	508.7	70.4	217.1	221.2	128.6	118.7	86.4	31.5	54.9	32.4
1968	911.5	558.7	80.8	235.7	242.3	141.2	132.1	93.4	33.6	59.9	38.7
1969	985.3	605.5	85.9	253.2	266.4	156.4	147.3	104.7	37.7	67	42.6
1970	1039.7	648.9	85	272	292	152.4	150.4	109	40.3	68.7	41.4
1971	1128.6	702.4	96.9	285.5	320	178.2	169.9	114.1	42.7	71.5	55.8
1972	1240.4	770.7	110.4	308	352.3	207.6	198.5	128.8	47.2	81.7	69.7
1973	1385.5	852.5	123.5	343.1	385.9	244.5	228.6	153.3	55	98.3	75.3
1974	1501	932.4	122.3	384.5	425.5	249.4	235.4	169.5	61.2	108.2	66
1975	1635.2	1030.3	133.5	420.7	476.1	230.2	236.5	173.7	61.4	112.4	62.7
1976	1823.9	1149.8	158.9	458.3	532.6	292	274.8	192.4	65.9	126.4	82.5
1977	2031.4	1278.4	181.2	497.2	600	361.3	339	228.7	74.6	154.1	110.3
1978	2295.9	1430.4	201.7	550.2	678.4	436	410.2	278.6	91.4	187.2	131.6
1979	2566.4	1596.3	214.4	624.4	757.4	490.6	472.7	331.6	114.9	216.7	141
1980	2795.6	1762.9	214.2	696.1	852.7	477.9	484.2	360.9	133.9	227	123.2
1981	3131.3	1944.2	231.3	758.9	954	570.8	541	418.4	164.6	253.8	122.6
1982	3259.2	2079.3	240.2	787.6	1051.5	516.1	531	425.3	175	250.3	105.7
1983	3534.9	2286.4	281.2	831.2	1174	564.2	570	417.4	152.7	264.7	152.5
1984	3932.7	2498.4	326.9	884.7	1286.9	735.5	670.1	490.3	176	314.3	179.8
1985	4213	2712.6	363.3	928.8	1420.6	736.3	714.5	527.6	193.3	334.3	186.9
1986	4452.9	2895.2	401.3	958.5	1535.4	747.2	740.7	522.5	175.8	346.8	218.1
1987	4742.5	3105.3	419.7	1015.3	1670.3	781.5	754.3	526.7	172.1	354.7	227.6
1988	5108.3	3356.6	450.2	1082.9	1823.5	821.1	802.7	568.4	181.6	386.8	234.2
1989	5489.1	3596.7	467.8	1165.4	1963.5	872.9	845.2	613.4	193.4	420	231.8
1990	5803.2	3831.5	467.6	1246.1	2117.8	861.7	847.2	630.3	202.5	427.8	216.8
1991	5986.2	3971.2	443	1278.8	2249.4	800.2	800.4	608.9	183.4	425.4	191.5
1992	6318.9	4209.7	470.8	1322.9	2415.9	866.6	851.6	626.1	172.2	453.9	225.5
1993	6642.3	4454.7	513.4	1375.2	2566.1	955.1	934	682.2	179.4	502.8	251.8
1994	7054.3	4716.4	560.8	1438	2717.6	1097.1	1034.6	748.6	187.5	561.1	286
1995	7400.5	4969	589.7	1497.3	2882	1143.8	1110.7	825.1	204.6	620.5	285.6
1996	7813.2	5237.5	616.5	1574.1	3047	1242.7	1212.7	899.4	225	674.4	313.3
1997	8318.4	5529.3	642.5	1641.6	3245.2	1390.5	1327.7	999.4	255.8	743.6	328.2
1998	8790.2	5850.9	693.9	1707.6	3449.3	1549.9	1472.9	1107.5	283.2	824.3	365.4
1999	9299.2	6268.7	761.3	1845.5	3661.9	1650.1	1606.8	1203.1	285.6	917.4	403.8

SOURCE: Bureau of Economic Analysis (http://www.bea.doc.gov)

	Net Exports of Goods and Services			Government Purchases of Goods and Services					
						Federal			
Year	Net Exports	Exports	Imports	Total	Total	National Defense	Non Defense	State and Local	Percentage Change in GDP from preceding year
1965	3.9	35.4	31.5	153.7	82.1	–	–	71.6	
1966	1.9	38.9	37.1	174.3	94.4	–	–	79.9	9.6%
1967	1.4	41.4	39.9	195.3	106.8	–	–	88.6	5.7%
1968	-1.3	45.3	46.6	212.8	114	–	–	98.8	9.3%
1969	-1.2	49.3	50.5	224.6	116.1	–	–	108.5	8.1%
1970	1.2	57	55.8	237.1	116.4	–	–	120.7	5.5%
1971	-3	59.3	62.3	251	117.6	–	–	133.5	8.6%
1972	-8	66.2	74.2	270.1	125.6	–	–	144.4	9.9%
1973	0.6	91.8	91.2	287.9	127.8	–	–	160.1	11.7%
1974	-3.1	124.3	127.5	322.4	138.2	–	–	184.2	8.3%
1975	13.6	136.3	122.7	361.1	152.1	–	–	209	8.9%
1976	-2.3	148.9	151.1	384.5	160.6	–	–	223.9	11.5%
1977	-23.7	158.8	182.4	415.3	176	–	–	239.3	11.4%
1978	-26.1	186.1	212.3	455.6	191.9	–	–	263.8	13.0%
1979	-24	228.7	252.7	503.5	211.6	–	–	291.8	11.8%
1980	-14.9	278.9	293.8	569.7	245.3	–	–	324.4	8.9%
1981	-15	302.8	317.8	631.4	281.8	–	–	349.6	12.0%
1982	-20.5	282.6	303.2	684.4	312.8	–	–	371.6	4.1%
1983	-51.7	277	328.6	735.9	344.4	–	–	391.5	8.5%
1984	-102	303.1	405.1	800.8	376.4	–	–	424.4	11.3%
1985	-114.2	303	417.2	878.3	413.4	–	–	464.9	7.1%
1986	-131.9	320.3	452.2	942.3	438.7	–	–	503.6	5.7%
1987	-142.3	365.6	507.9	997.9	460.4	–	–	537.5	6.5%
1988	-106.3	446.9	553.2	1036.9	462.6	–	–	574.3	7.7%
1989	-80.7	509	589.7	1100.2	482.6	–	–	617.7	7.5%
1990	-71.4	557.2	628.6	1181.4	508.4	–	–	673	5.7%
1991	-20.7	601.6	622.3	1235.5	527.4	–	–	708.1	3.2%
1992	-27.9	636.8	664.6	1270.5	534.5	–	–	736	5.6%
1993	-60.5	658	718.5	1293	527.3	–	–	765.7	5.1%
1994	-87.1	725.1	812.1	1327.9	521.1	–	–	806.8	6.2%
1995	-84.3	818.6	902.8	1372	521.5	–	–	850.5	4.9%
1996	-89	874.2	963.1	1421.9	531.6	–	–	890.4	5.6%
1997	-89.3	966.4	1055.8	1487.9	538.2	–	–	949.7	6.5%
1998	-151.5	966	1117.5	1540.9	540.6	–	–	1000.3	5.7%
1999	-254	990.2	1244.2	1634.4	568.6	–	–	1065.8	5.8%

TABLE B
U.S. REAL GROSS DOMESTIC PRODUCT (billions of chained 1996 dollars)

Year	GDP	personal consumption expenditures	Gross private domestic invest.	Exports	Imports	Government purchases of goods and services	Percentage Change in GDP from previous year
1965	3028.5	1897.6	402	116.5	142.9	791.1	6.4
1966	3227.5	2006.1	437.3	124.3	164.2	862.1	6.6
1967	3308.3	2066.2	417.2	127	176.2	927.1	2.5
1968	3466.1	2184.2	441.3	136.3	202.4	956.6	4.8
1969	3571.4	2264.8	466.9	143.7	213.9	952.5	3
1970	3578	2317.5	436.2	159.3	223.1	931.1	0.2
1971	3697.7	2405.2	485.8	160.4	235	913.8	3.3
1972	3898.4	2550.5	543	173.5	261.3	914.9	5.4
1973	4123.4	2675.9	606.5	211.4	273.4	908.3	5.8
1974	4099	2653.7	561.7	231.6	267.2	924.8	-0.6
1975	4084.4	2710.9	462.2	230	237.5	942.5	-0.4
1976	4311.7	2868.9	555.5	243.6	284	943.3	5.6
1977	4511.8	2992.1	639.4	249.7	315	952.7	4.6
1978	4760.6	3124.7	713	275.9	342.3	982.2	5.5
1979	4912.1	3203.2	735.4	302.4	347.9	1001.1	3.2
1980	4900.9	3193	655.3	334.8	324.8	1020.9	-0.2
1981	5021	3236	715.6	338.6	333.4	1030	2.5
1982	4919.3	3275.5	615.2	314.6	329.2	1046	-2
1983	5132.3	3454.3	673.7	306.9	370.7	1081	4.3
1984	5505.2	3640.6	871.5	332.6	461	1118.4	7.3
1985	5717.1	3820.9	863.4	341.6	490.7	1190.5	3.8
1986	5912.4	3981.2	857.7	366.8	531.9	1255.2	3.4
1987	6113.3	4113.4	879.3	408	564.2	1292.5	3.4
1988	6368.4	4279.5	902.8	473.5	585.6	1307.5	4.2
1989	6591.8	4393.7	936.5	529.4	608.8	1343.5	3.5
1990	6707.9	4474.5	907.3	575.7	632.2	1387.3	1.8
1991	6676.4	4466.6	829.5	613.2	629	1403.4	-0.5
1992	6880	4594.5	899.8	651	670.8	1410	3
1993	7062.6	4748.9	977.9	672.7	731.8	1398.8	2.7
1994	7347.7	4928.1	1107	732.8	819.4	1400.1	4
1995	7543.8	5075.6	1140.6	808.2	886.6	1406.4	2.7
1996	7813.2	5237.5	1242.7	874.2	963.1	1421.9	3.6
1997	8159.5	5423.9	1393.3	981.5	1094.8	1455.4	4.4
1998	8515.7	5678.7	1566.8	1003.6	1224.6	1486.4	4.4
1999	8875.8	5978.8	1669.7	1033	1355.3	1536.1	4.2

SOURCE: Bureau of Economic Analysis (http://www.bea.doc.gov)

TABLE C
U.S. CIVILIAN UNEMPLOYMENT RATE BY DEMOGRAPHIC CHARACTERISTICS

		WHITE						
			MALES			FEMALES		
Year	All Civilian Workers	Total	Total	16–19 years	20+ years	Total	16–19 years	20+ years
1965	4.5	4.1	3.6	12.9	2.9	5.0	14.0	4.0
1966	3.8	3.4	2.8	10.5	2.2	4.3	12.1	3.3
1967	3.8	3.4	2.7	10.7	2.1	4.6	11.5	3.8
1968	3.6	3.2	2.6	10.1	2.0	4.3	12.1	3.4
1969	3.5	3.1	2.5	10.0	1.9	4.2	11.5	3.4
1970	4.9	4.5	4.0	13.7	3.2	5.4	13.4	4.4
1971	5.9	5.4	4.9	15.1	4.0	6.3	15.1	5.3
1972	5.6	5.1	4.5	14.2	3.6	5.9	14.2	4.9
1973	4.9	4.3	3.8	12.3	3.0	5.3	13.0	4.3
1974	5.6	5.0	4.4	13.5	3.5	6.1	14.5	5.1
1975	8.5	7.8	7.2	18.3	6.2	8.6	17.4	7.5
1976	7.7	7.0	6.4	17.3	5.4	7.9	16.4	6.8
1977	7.1	6.2	5.5	15.0	4.7	7.3	15.9	6.2
1978	6.1	5.2	4.6	13.5	3.7	6.2	14.4	5.2
1979	5.8	5.1	4.5	13.9	3.6	5.9	14.0	5.0
1980	7.1	6.3	6.1	16.2	5.3	6.5	14.8	5.6
1981	7.6	6.7	6.5	17.9	5.6	6.9	16.6	5.9
1982	9.7	8.6	8.8	21.7	7.8	8.3	19.0	7.3
1983	9.6	8.4	8.8	20.2	7.9	7.9	18.3	6.9
1984	7.5	6.5	6.4	16.8	5.7	6.5	15.2	5.8
1985	7.2	6.2	6.1	16.5	5.4	6.4	14.8	5.7
1986	7.0	6.0	6.0	16.3	5.3	6.1	14.9	5.4
1987	6.2	5.3	5.4	15.5	4.8	5.2	13.4	4.6
1988	5.5	4.7	4.7	13.9	4.1	4.7	12.3	4.1
1989	5.3	4.5	4.5	13.7	3.9	4.5	11.5	4.0
1990	5.6	4.8	4.9	14.3	4.3	4.7	12.6	4.1
1991	6.8	6.1	6.5	17.6	5.8	5.6	15.2	5.0
1992	7.5	6.6	7.0	18.5	6.4	6.1	15.8	5.5
1993	6.9	6.1	6.3	17.7	5.7	5.7	14.7	5.2
1994	6.1	5.3	5.4	16.3	4.8	5.2	13.8	4.6
1995	5.6	4.9	4.9	15.6	4.3	4.8	13.4	4.3
1996	5.4	4.7	4.7	15.5	4.1	4.7	12.9	4.1
1997	4.9	4.2	4.2	14.3	3.6	4.2	12.8	3.7
1998	4.5	3.9	3.9	14.1	3.2	3.9	10.9	3.4
1999	4.2	3.7	3.6	12.6	3.0	3.8	11.3	3.3

TABLE C (continued)
U.S. CIVILIAN UNEMPLOYMENT RATE BY DEMOGRAPHIC CHARACTERISTICS

	BLACK (includes category "and other" through 1972)						
		MALES			FEMALES		
Year	Total	Total	16–19 years	20 + years			
1965	8.1	7.4	23.3	6.0	9.2	31.7	7.5
1966	7.3	6.3	21.3	4.9	8.7	31.3	6.6
1967	7.4	6.0	23.9	4.3	9.1	29.6	7.1
1968	6.7	5.6	22.1	3.9	8.3	28.7	6.3
1969	6.4	5.3	21.4	3.7	7.8	27.6	5.8
1970	8.2	7.3	25.0	5.6	9.3	34.5	6.9
1971	9.9	9.1	28.8	7.3	10.9	35.4	8.7
1972	10.0	8.9	29.7	6.9	11.4	38.4	8.8
1973	9.4	8.0	27.8	6.0	11.1	36.1	8.6
1974	10.5	9.8	33.1	7.4	11.3	37.4	8.8
1975	14.8	14.8	38.1	12.5	14.8	41.0	12.2
1976	14.0	13.7	37.5	11.4	14.3	41.6	11.7
1977	14.0	13.3	39.2	10.7	14.9	43.4	12.3
1978	12.8	11.8	36.7	9.3	13.8	40.8	11.2
1979	12.3	11.4	34.2	9.3	13.3	39.1	10.9
1980	14.3	14.5	37.5	12.4	14.0	39.8	11.9
1981	15.6	15.7	40.7	13.5	15.6	42.2	13.4
1982	18.9	20.1	48.9	17.8	17.6	47.1	15.4
1983	19.5	20.3	48.8	18.1	18.6	48.2	16.5
1984	15.9	16.4	42.7	14.3	15.4	42.6	13.5
1985	15.1	15.3	41.0	13.2	14.9	39.2	13.1
1986	14.5	14.8	39.3	12.9	14.2	39.2	12.4
1987	13.0	12.7	34.4	11.1	13.2	34.9	11.6
1988	11.7	11.7	32.7	10.1	11.7	32.0	10.4
1989	11.4	11.5	31.9	10.0	11.4	33.0	9.8
1990	11.4	11.9	31.9	10.4	10.9	29.9	9.7
1991	12.5	13.0	36.3	11.5	12.0	36.0	10.6
1992	14.2	15.2	42.0	13.5	13.2	37.2	11.8
1993	13.0	13.8	40.1	12.1	12.1	37.4	10.7
1994	11.5	12.0	37.6	10.3	11.0	32.6	9.8
1995	10.4	10.6	37.1	8.8	10.2	34.3	8.6
1996	10.5	11.1	36.9	9.4	10.0	30.3	8.7
1997	10.0	10.2	36.5	8.5	9.9	28.7	8.8
1998	8.9	8.9	30.1	7.4	9.0	25.3	7.9
1999	8.0	8.2	30.9	6.7	7.8	25.1	6.8

SOURCE: Bureau of Labor Statistics (http://www.bls.gov)

TABLE D
U.S. GOVERNMENT RECEIPTS AND EXPENDITURES (billions of dollars, seasonally adjusted)

Year	TOTAL GOVERNMENT			FEDERAL GOVERNMENT			STATE AND LOCAL GOVERNMENT		
	Receipts	Expenditures	Surplus or Deficit	Receipts	Expenditures	Surplus or Deficit	Receipts	Expenditures	Surplus or Deficit
1965	175.4	165.7	9.7	119.3	116.1	3.2	63.3	56.8	6.5
1966	197.8	187.3	10.5	136.3	133.6	2.7	71.5	63.8	7.7
1967	212.1	213.4	-1.4	144.9	153.2	-8.3	78.9	71.9	7.0
1968	245.3	239.2	6.2	168.5	169.8	-1.3	89.5	82.1	7.5
1969	276.3	258.7	17.6	190.1	180.5	9.6	100.7	92.8	8.0
1970	279.6	286.9	-7.3	184.3	198.6	-14.4	114.6	107.5	7.1
1971	295.9	316.3	-20.4	189.8	216.6	-26.8	129.3	122.9	6.4
1972	338.1	345.0	-6.9	217.5	240.0	-22.5	152.3	136.7	15.6
1973	380.3	375.8	4.5	248.5	259.7	-11.2	166.6	150.9	15.7
1974	419.6	424.2	-4.6	277.3	291.2	-13.9	178.5	169.2	9.3
1975	430.5	497.4	-66.9	276.1	345.4	-69.3	199.6	197.2	2.4
1976	492.6	538.3	-45.7	318.9	371.9	-53.0	224.5	217.2	7.3
1977	552.8	584.8	-32.0	359.9	405.0	-45.2	249.5	236.4	13.1
1978	626.0	634.3	-8.2	417.3	444.2	-26.9	274.3	255.6	18.7
1979	702.7	701.1	1.7	478.3	489.6	-11.4	290.8	277.8	13.0
1980	767.1	812.0	-44.9	522.8	576.6	-53.8	316.6	307.8	8.8
1981	877.6	923.7	-46.2	605.6	659.3	-53.7	344.4	336.9	7.5
1982	890.3	1,025.1	-134.8	599.5	732.1	-132.6	360.3	362.5	-2.3
1983	944.5	1,113.5	-169.1	623.9	797.8	-173.9	392.1	387.3	4.8
1984	1,047.8	1,192.1	-144.2	688.1	856.1	-168.1	436.4	412.6	23.8
1985	1,135.8	1,290.7	-154.9	747.4	924.6	-177.1	469.2	447.0	22.3
1986	1,206.7	1,378.1	-171.4	786.4	978.5	-192.1	507.9	487.2	20.8
1987	1,322.5	1,458.2	-135.7	870.5	1,018.4	-147.9	536.0	523.8	12.2
1988	1,410.9	1,532.7	-121.8	928.9	1,066.2	-137.4	573.7	558.1	15.6
1989	1,530.9	1,641.6	-110.7	1,010.3	1,140.3	-130.0	618.9	599.6	19.3
1990	1,607.7	1,778.0	-170.3	1,055.7	1,228.7	-173.0	663.4	660.8	2.6
1991	1,656.6	1,879.7	-223.1	1,072.3	1,287.6	-215.3	716.0	723.8	-7.8
1992	1,744.4	2,046.9	-302.5	1,121.3	1,418.9	-297.5	777.2	777.2	-4.9
1993	1,857.9	2,130.5	-272.7	1,197.3	1,471.5	-274.1	823.2	821.7	1.5
1994	1,993.0	2,196.7	-203.7	1,293.7	1,506.0	-212.3	873.8	865.2	8.6
1995	2,117.1	2,293.7	-176.7	1,383.7	1,575.7	-192.0	917.9	902.5	15.3
1996	2,269.1	2,384.5	-115.4	1,499.1	1,635.9	-136.8	960.4	939.0	21.4
1997	2,440.5	2,461.8	-21.3	1,627.2	1,676.0	-48.8	1,009.0	981.5	27.5
1998	2,611.8	2,523.1	88.7	1,750.7	1,703.8	46.9	1,070.4	1,028.7	41.7
1999		2,619.7			1,754.9			1,089.0	

SOURCE: *Economic Report of the President*

TABLE E
U.S. MONEY STOCK AND OTHER LIQUID ASSETS (billions of dollars)

Year *	M1	M2	M3	Debt, monthly average
1965	167.8	459.2	482.1	1,004.1
1966	172.0	480.2	505.4	1,071.3
1967	183.3	524.8	557.9	1,145.7
1968	197.4	566.8	607.2	1,237.3
1969	203.9	587.9	615.9	1,327.4
1970	214.4	626.5	677.1	1,416.8
1971	228.3	710.3	776.0	1,550.5
1972	249.2	802.3	885.9	1,706.8
1973	262.9	855.5	985.0	1,892.0
1974	274.2	902.4	1,070.2	2,065.0
1975	287.1	1,016.6	1,171.9	2,252.4
1976	306.2	1,152.6	1,312.3	2,497.2
1977	330.9	1,271.1	1,472.7	2,814.1
1978	357.3	1,366.9	1,646.5	3,202.8
1979	381.8	1,474.7	1,810.1	3,591.9
1980	408.1	1,600.4	1,996.3	3,934.2
1981	436.2	1,756.1	2,254.9	4,345.9
1982	474.3	1,911.2	2,460.9	4,782.2
1983	520.8	2,127.8	2,699.2	5,351.8
1984	551.2	2,311.7	2,992.8	6,148.8
1985	619.4	2,497.4	3,209.8	7,068.7
1986	724.3	2,734.0	3,501.2	7,933.3
1987	749.7	2,832.8	3,692.0	8,673.9
1988	786.3	2,995.8	3,935.2	9,464.0
1989	792.6	3,159.9	4,091.0	10,156.3
1990	824.6	3,279.1	4,155.6	10,818.1
1991	896.7	3,379.8	4,208.6	11,292.8
1992	1,024.5	3,434.1	4,220.0	11,816.8
1993	1,129.4	3,487.5	4,279.9	12,403.5
1994	1,149.9	3,502.2	4,353.9	12,999.6
1995	1,126.9	3,649.3	4,618.6	13,716.6
1996	1,081.6	3,824.2	4,955.8	14,463.6
1997	1,075.2	4,046.7	5,403.4	15,227.9
1998	1,093.7	4,401.4	5,995.7	16,250.4
1999	1,125.4	4,662.7	6,484.9	...

*Averages of daily figures for month of December (not annual averages).

SOURCE: *Economic Report of the President*

TABLE F
U.S. PRICE INDICES

Year *	Consumer Price Index	Producer Price Index	GDP deflator	Chain-type price index (GDP)
1965	31.5	32.3	23.78	23.77
1966	32.4	33.3	24.46	24.45
1967	33.4	33.4	25.21	25.21
1968	34.8	34.2	26.3	26.29
1969	36.7	35.6	27.59	27.59
1970	38.8	36.9	29.06	29.05
1971	40.5	38.1	30.52	30.52
1972	41.8	39.8	31.82	31.81
1973	44.4	45.0	33.6	33.6
1974	49.3	53.5	36.62	36.6
1975	53.8	58.4	40.03	40.03
1976	56.9	61.1	42.3	42.29
1977	60.6	64.9	45.02	45.02
1978	65.2	69.9	48.23	48.22
1979	72.6	78.7	52.25	52.24
1980	82.4	89.8	57.04	57.05
1981	90.9	98.0	62.37	62.37
1982	96.5	100.0	66.25	66.26
1983	99.6	101.3	68.88	68.87
1984	103.9	103.7	71.44	71.44
1985	107.6	103.2	73.69	73.69
1986	109.6	100.2	75.31	75.32
1987	113.6	102.8	77.58	77.58
1988	118.3	106.9	80.21	80.22
1989	124.0	112.2	83.27	83.27
1990	130.7	116.3	86.51	86.53
1991	136.2	116.5	89.66	89.66
1992	140.3	117.2	91.84	91.85
1993	144.5	118.9	94.05	94.05
1994	148.2	120.4	96.01	96.01
1995	152.4	124.7	98.1	98.1
1996	156.9	127.7	100	100
1997	160.5	127.6	101.95	101.95
1998	163.0	124.4	103.22	103.23
1999	166.6	125.5	104.77	104.77

SOURCE: Bureau of Economic Analysis (http://www.bea.doc.gov)

TABLE G
BOND YIELDS AND INTEREST RATES (percent per annum)

Year	U.S. Treasury 3-month bills (new issues)	Corporate bonds (Moody's AAA)	Prime rate charged by banks	Discount Rate Federal Reserve Bank of New York
1965	3.954	4.49	4.54	4.04
1966	4.881	5.13	5.63	4.50
1967	4.321	5.51	5.61	4.19
1968	5.339	6.18	6.30	5.16
1969	6.677	7.03	7.96	5.87
1970	6.458	8.04	7.91	5.95
1971	4.348	7.39	5.72	4.88
1972	4.071	7.21	5.25	4.50
1973	7.041	7.44	8.03	6.44
1974	7.886	8.57	10.81	7.83
1975	5.838	8.83	7.86	6.25
1976	4.989	8.43	6.84	5.50
1977	5.265	8.02	6.83	5.46
1978	7.221	8.73	9.06	7.46
1979	10.041	9.63	12.67	10.28
1980	11.506	11.94	15.27	11.77
1981	14.029	14.17	18.87	13.42
1982	10.686	13.79	14.86	11.02
1983	8.63	12.04	10.79	8.50
1984	9.58	12.71	12.04	8.80
1985	7.48	11.37	9.93	7.69
1986	5.98	9.02	8.33	6.33
1987	5.82	9.38	8.21	5.66
1988	6.69	9.71	9.32	6.20
1989	8.12	9.26	10.87	6.93
1990	7.51	9.32	10.01	6.98
1991	5.42	8.77	8.46	5.45
1992	3.45	8.14	6.25	3.23
1993	3.02	7.22	6.00	3.00
1994	4.29	7.97	7.15	3.60
1995	5.51	7.59	8.83	5.21
1996	5.02	7.37	8.27	5.02

SOURCE:

TABLE H
SELECTED EXCHANGE RATES

Year	Canadian dollar (CN$/US$)	German mark* (DM/US$)	Japanese yen (¥/US$)	U.K. pound (US$/£)	Multilateral trade-weighted value of the US dollar** (index, March 1973 = 100)	
					nominal	real
March 1973	0.9967	2.8132	261.9	2.4724	100.0	100.0
1970	1.0444	3.6465	358.16	2.3959		
1971	1.0099	3.4830	347.79	2.4442		
1972	0.9907	3.1886	303.13	2.5034		
1973	1.0002	2.6715	271.31	2.4525		
1974	0.9780	2.5868	291.84	2.3403		
1975	1.0175	2.4614	296.78	2.2217		
1976	0.9863	2.5185	296.45	1.8048		
1977	1.0633	2.3236	268.62	1.7449		
1978	1.1405	2.0097	210.39	1.9184		
1979	1.1713	1.8343	219.02	2.1224	94.9	88.0
1980	1.1693	1.8175	226.63	2.3246	94.8	90.9
1981	1.199	2.2632	220.63	2.0243	103.6	100
1982	1.2344	2.4281	249.06	1.748	114.2	108.4
1983	1.2325	2.5539	237.55	1.5159	118.1	109.9
1984	1.2952	2.8455	237.46	1.3368	125.8	117.2
1985	1.3659	2.942	238.47	1.2974	130.5	121.1
1986	1.3896	2.1705	168.35	1.4677	107.2	98.8
1987	1.3259	1.7981	144.6	1.6398	94.8	88.4
1988	1.2306	1.757	128.17	1.7813	88.2	83.3
1989	1.1842	1.8808	138.07	1.6382	91.9	87.4
1990	1.1668	1.6166	145	1.7841	87.9	84.3
1991	1.1460	1.661	134.59	1.7674	86.4	82.6
1992	1.2085	1.5618	126.78	1.7663	84.9	81.5
1993	1.2902	1.6545	111.08	1.5016	87.1	84.2
1994	1.3664	1.6216	102.18	1.5319	85.6	83.8
1995	1.3725	1.4321	93.96	1.5785	80.8	79.9
1996	1.3638	1.5049	108.78	1.5607	84.6	85
1997	1.3849	1.7348	121.06	1.6376	91.2	92.3
1998	1.4836	1.7597	130.99	1.6573	95.8	97.3
1999	1.4858	1.0653 US$/€	113.73	1.6172	94.1	96.7

* changed to the euro(€) in 1999
** a weighted average of the foreign exchange value of the dollar against a broad group of U.S. trading partners

SOURCE: *Economic Report of the President*

TABLE I
CURRENCIES OF THE WORLD

Country	Currency	Symbol	Units
Afghanistan	afghani	Af	100 puls
Albania	lek	L	100 qindarka (qintars)
Algeria	dinar	DA	100 centimes
Angola	new kwanza	Kz	100 lwei
Anguilla	dollar	EC$	100 cents
Antarctica	each Antarctic base uses the currency of its home country		
Antigua and Barbuda	dollar	EC$	100 cents
Argentina	peso	$	100 centavos
Armenia	dram		100 luma
Aruba	guilder (*florin, gulden*)	Af.	100 cents
Australia	dollar	A$	100 cents
Australia	dollar	A$	100 cents
Austria	schilling	S	100 groschen
Azerbaijan	manat		100 gopik
Bahamas	dollar	B$	100 cents
Bahrain	dinar	BD	1,000 fils
Bangladesh	taka	Tk	100 paisa (*poisha*)
Barbados	dollar	Bds$	100 cents
Belarus	ruble	BR	
Belgium	franc	BF	100 centimes
Belize	dollar	BZ$	100 cents
Benin	franc	CFAF	100 centimes
Bermuda	dollar	Bd$	100 cents
Bhutan	ngultrum	Nu	100 chetrum
Bolivia	boliviano	Bs	100 centavos
Bosnia-Herzegovina	convertible mark	KM	100 fennig
Botswana	pula	P	100 thebe
Brazil	real	R$	100 centavos
Brunei	ringgit	B$	100 sen (*cents*)
Bulgaria	leva	Lv	100 stotinki
Burkina Faso	franc	CFAF	100 centimes
Burundi	franc	FBu	100 centimes
Cambodia	new riel	CR	100 sen
Cameroon	franc	CFAF	100 centimes
Canada	dollar	Can$	100 cents
Cape Verde Island	escudo	C.V.Esc.	100 centavos
Cayman Islands	dollar	CI$	100 cents
Central African Republic	franc	CFAF	100 centimes

SOURCE: Werner Antweiler., Policy Analysis Computing and Information Facility in Commerce at the University of British Columbia. (*http://pacific.commerce.ubc.ca/xr/currency_table.html*)

TABLE I (continued)
CURRENCIES OF THE WORLD

Country	Currency	Symbol	Units
Chad	franc	CFAF	100 centimes
Chile	peso	Ch$	100 centavos
China	yuan renminbi	Y	10 jiao = 100 fen
Colombia	peso	Col$	100 centavos
Comoros	franc	CF	
Congo	franc	CFAF	100 centimes
Costa Rica	colon	*slashed C*	100 centimos
Côte d'Ivoire	franc	CFAF	100 centimes
Croatia	kuna	HRK	100 lipas
Cuba	peso	Cu$	100 centavos
Cyprus	pound	£C	100 cents
Czech Republic	koruna	Kc	100 haleru
Denmark	krone (pl. kroner)	Dkr	100 øre
Djibouti	franc	DF	100 centimes
Dominica	dollar	EC$	100 cents
Dominican Rep.	peso	RD$	100 centavos
Ecuador	sucre	S/	100 centavos
Egypt	pound	£E	100 piasters
El Salvador	colon	¢	100 centavos
Equatorial Guinea	franc	CFAF	100 centimos
Eritrea	nakfa	Nfa	100 cents
Estonia	kroon (pl. krooni)	KR	100 senti
Ethiopia	birr	Br	100 cents
European Union	Euro	€	100 euro-cents
Falkland Islands	pound	£F	100 pence
Fiji	dollar	F$	100 cents
Finland	markka (pl. markkaa)	mk	100 penniä (sg. penni)
France	franc	F	100 centimes
French Polynesia	franc	CFPF	100 centimes
Gabon	franc	CFPF	100 centimes
Gambia	dalasi	D	100 butut
Georgia	lari		100 tetri
Germany	deutsche mark	DM	100 pfennig
Ghana	new cedi¢		100 psewas
Gibraltar	pound	£G	100 pence
Greece	drachma	Dr	100 lepta (sg. lepton)
Grenada	dollar	EC$	100 cents

TABLE I (continued)
CURRENCIES OF THE WORLD

Country	Currency	Symbol	Units
Guatemala	quetzal	Q	100 centavos
Guinea-Bissau	franc	CFAF	100 centimes
Guinea	syli (*franc*)	FG	
Guyana	dollar	G$	100 cents
Haiti	gourde	G	100 centimes
Honduras	lempira	L	100 centavos
Hong Kong	dollar	HK$	100 cents
Hungary	forint	Ft	
Iceland	króna	IKr	100 aurar (sg. aur)
India	rupee	Rs	100 paise
Indonesia	rupiah	Rp	
International Monetary Fund	*Special Drawing Right*	SDR	
Iran	rial	Rls	10 rials = 1 toman
Iraq	dinar	ID	1,000 fils
Ireland	pound (punt)	IR£	100 pingin or pence
Israel	new shekel	NIS	100 new agorot
Italy Lit	lira	Lit	
Jamaica J$	dollar	J$	100 cents
Japan	yen	¥	
Jordan	dinar	JD	1,000 fils
Kazakhstan	tenge		100 tiyn
Kenya	shilling	K Sh	100 cents
Korea, North	won	Wn	100 chon
Korea, South	won	W	100 chon
Kuwait	dinar	KD	1,000 fils
Kyrgyzstan	som		100 tyyn
Laos	new kip		100 at
Latvia	lat	Ls	100 santims
Lebanon	pound (livre)	£L	100 piastres
Liberia	dollar	$	100 cents
Libya	dinar	LD	1,000 dirhams
Luxembourg	franc	LuxF	100 centimes
Macao (Macau)	pataca	P	100 avos
Macedonia	denar	MKD	100 deni
Madagascar	ariayry = 5 francs	FMG	1 franc = 100 centimes
Malawi	kwacha	MK	100 tambala
Malaysia	ringgit	RM	100 sen

TABLE I (continued)
CURRENCIES OF THE WORLD

Country	Currency	Symbol	Units
Maldives	rufiyaa	Rf	100 lari
Mali	franc	CFAF	100 centimes
Malta	lira	Lm	100 cents
Mauritania	ouguiya	UM	5 khoums
Mauritius	rupee	Mau Rs	100 cents
Mexico	peso	Mex$	100 centavos
Mongolia	tugrik (*tughrik*)	Tug	100 mongos
Montserrat	dollar	EC$	100 cents
Morocco	dirham	DH	100 centimes
Mozambique	metical	Mt	100 centavos
Myanmar	kyat	K	100 pyas
Namibia	dollar	N$	100 cents
Nepal	rupee	NRs	100 paise
Netherlands Antilles	guilder (*florin, gulden*)	NAf.	100 cents
New Caledonia	franc	CFPF	100 centimes
New Zealand	dollar	NZ$	100 cents
Nicaragua	gold cordoba	C$	100 centavos
Niger	franc	CFAF	100 centimes
Nigeria	*naira*	*double-dashed N*	100 kobo
Norway	krone	NKr	100 øre
Oman	rial	RO	1,000 baizas
Pakistan	rupee	Rs	100 paisa
Panama	balboa	B	100 centesimos
Papua New Guinea	kina	K	100 toeas
Paraguay	guarani	*slashed G*	100 centimos
Peru	new sol	S/	100 centimos
Philippines	peso	*dashed P*	100 centavos
Poland	zloty	*dashed Z*	100 groszy
Portugal	escudo	Esc	100 centavos
Qatar	riyal	QR	100 dirhams
Romania	leu	L	100 bani
Russia	new ruble	R	100 new kopecks
Rwanda	franc	RF	100 centimes
Sao Tome & Principe	dobra	Db	100 centimos
Saudi Arabia	riyal	SRls	100 halalat
Senegal	franc	CFAF	100 centimes
Seychelles	rupee	SR	100 cents

TABLE I (continued)
CURRENCIES OF THE WORLD

Country	Currency	Symbol	Units
Sierra Leone	leone	Le	100 cents
Singapore	dollar	S$	100 cents
Slovakia	koruna	Sk	100 halierov
Slovenia	tolar	SIT	100 stotinov
Solomon Island	dollar	SI$	100 cents
Somalia	shilling	So. Sh.	100 centesimi
South Africa	rand	R	100 cents
Spain	peseta	Ptas	100 centimos
Sri Lanka	rupee	SLRs	100 cents
St. Helena	pound	£S	100 new pence
Sudan	dinar		100 piastres
Suriname	guilder (*florin, gulden*)	Sur.f., Sf	100 cents
Swaziland	lilangeni	L	100 cents
Sweden	krona	Sk	100 öre
Switzerland	franc	SwF	100 rappen/centimes
Syria	pound	£S	100 piasters
Taiwan	new dollar	NT$	100 cents
Tajikistan	ruble		
Tanzania	shilling	TSh	100 cents
Thailand	baht	Bht, Bt	100 stang
Togo	franc	CFAF	100 centimes
Tonga	pa'anga	PT, T$	100 seniti
Trinidad and Tobago	dollar	TT$	100 cents
Tunisia	dinar	TD	1,000 millimes
Turkey	lira	TL	100 kurus
Turkmenistan	manat		100 tenga
Uganda	shilling	USh	100 cents
Ukraine	Hryvnia		100 kopiykas
United Arab Emirates	dirham	Dh	100 fils
United Kingdom 100 pence	pound	£	100 pence
United States of America	dollar	$	100 cents
Uruguay	peso	$U	100 centésimos
Uzbekistan	som		100 tiyin
Vanuatu	vatu	VT	100 centimes
Venezuela	bolivar	Bs	100 centimos
Viet Nam	new dong	D	10 hao, 100 xu
Wallis and Futuna Islands	franc	CFPF	100 centimes